ArtScroll® Series

Rabbi Nosson Scherman / Rabbi Gedaliah Zlotowitz
General Editors
Rabbi Meir Zlotowitz ז״ל, *Founder and President*

Living

Published by

ArtScroll®
Mesorah Publications, ltd

THE MILLER FAMILY EDITION

Emunah
FOR TEENS

Achieving a life of serenity through faith

Rabbi David Ashear
Adapted by Chana Nestlebaum

FIRST EDITION
First Impression ... November 2017
Second Impression ... October 2018
Third Impression ... September 2019
Fourth Impression ... February 2020
Fifth Impression ... May 2020

Published and Distributed by
MESORAH PUBLICATIONS, LTD.
313 Regina Avenue / Rahway, N.J. 07065

Distributed in Europe by
LEHMANNS
Unit E, Viking Business Park
Rolling Mill Road
Jarow, Tyne & Wear, NE32 3DP
England

Distributed in Australia and New Zealand
by **GOLDS WORLDS OF JUDAICA**
3-13 William Street
Balaclava, Melbourne 3183
Victoria, Australia

Distributed in Israel by
SIFRIATI / A. GITLER — BOOKS
POB 2351
Bnei Brak 51122

Distributed in South Africa by
KOLLEL BOOKSHOP
Northfield Centre, 17 Northfield Avenue
Glenhazel 2192, Johannesburg, South Africa

ARTSCROLL® SERIES
LIVING EMUNAH FOR TEENS
© Copyright 2017, by MESORAH PUBLICATIONS, Ltd.
313 Regina Avenue / Rahway, N.J. 07065 / (718) 921-9000 / www.artscroll.com

ALL RIGHTS RESERVED
The text, prefatory and associated textual contents and introductions
— including the typographic layout, cover artwork and ornamental graphics —
have been designed, edited and revised as to content, form and style.

No part of this book may be reproduced
IN ANY FORM, PHOTOCOPYING, DIGITAL, OR COMPUTER RETRIEVAL SYSTEMS
— even for personal use without written permission from
the copyright holder, Mesorah Publications Ltd.
except by a reviewer who wishes to quote brief passages
in connection with a review written for inclusion in magazines or newspapers.

THE RIGHTS OF THE COPYRIGHT HOLDER WILL BE STRICTLY ENFORCED.

ISBN 10: 1-4226-1952-4 / ISBN 13: 978-1-4226-1952-0

Typography by CompuScribe at ArtScroll Studios, Ltd.
Printed in the United States of America by Noble Book Press Corp.
Bound by Sefercraft, Quality Bookbinders, Ltd., Rahway, N.J. 07065

We are proud to dedicate this sefer in memory
of our beloved grandparents

הרב אביגדור בן ר׳ ישראל הכהן זצ״ל
חנה עטל בת הרב ר׳ יעקב משה הכהן ע״ה
הרב יהודה בן ר׳ נח ז״ל
מרים בת ר׳ משה ע״ה

◄◦►

ר׳ מרדכי דוד בן ר׳ משה צבי ז״ל
גולדה בת ר׳ שלמה ע״ה
ר׳ אברהם מאיר בן ר׳ משה אהרן בנימין ז״ל
חנה גיטל דבשע בת ר׳ זאב וולף ע״ה

There is so much to say about them that volumes would not do them justice, but if their greatness had to be encapsulated in one word, that word would be אמונה. They lived with total faith in Hashem and they radiated it to all who knew them, or even observed them. Their emunah fortified them during trying times and exhilarated them in good times, because they knew that everything flowed from Hashem and that it was good, whether they understood it at the time, or not.

It is fitting, therefore, that this sefer be dedicated to our grandparents, who personified its message. Emunah is difficult to attain in our world, which places its faith in science, power, and wealth. We must seize every opportunity to let our children see that Hashem is present in our world, every day, all the time.

Young people will grow in emunah as they read these true stories and discover how we can see Hashem's Hand in our lives. This sefer will give them the inspiration to deal with the challenges that come with life, and it is our hope that as they mature they will progress to the classics of mussar and yirah. May the lessons of this sefer be a z'chus for our grandparents, for our family, and for Klal Yisrael.

Table of Contents

Introduction by Chana Nestlebaum	11
1. Nothing to Worry About	15
2. It Didn't Just Happen by Itself	19
3. Be THAT Person	22
4. Make His Name Great	25
5. Be a Hero	28
6. No More Second Guessing	31
7. Is Hashem's Hand Too Short?	34
8. A Real Eye-Opener	38
9. Take Time to Notice	41
10. When the Going Gets Tough	45
11. Darkness to Dawn	49
12. Need Money? No Problem!	52
13. Getting in Good With Them	56
14. You're On	59
15. Every Little Bit Helps	62
16. "A" for Effort	65
17. A Gift Wrapped in a Hardship	68
18. "I'm With Him"	71
19. Crowd Out Troubles	74
20. Feeling Around in the Dark	77
21. Nothing but Kindness	81
22. First Accept, Then Pray	85
23. Take It Personally	89
24. Training Our Eyes	93
25. Today's Itinerary	97

26. There's Just One Goal	101
27. There's No Harm in Asking	104
28. My Most Reliable Friend	107
29. Pray for the Power to Pray	110
30. Just Because	113
31. Who's It All For?	116
32. Some Day We'll Find Out	119
33. "I Can't Do It Without You!"	122
34. Keep It Coming	125
35. Follow the Leader	128
36. What's Yours Is Yours	131
37. The 120-Year Lease	134
38. Let Hashem Do the Math	137
39. You Can Choose to Be Happy	140
40. A Menu for the Whole World	143
41. Enough Is Enough	146
42. You Can't Lose	149
43. You Don't Scare Me	152
44. Go to the Chief	155
45. "It Just So Happened…"	158
46. Don't Ruin the Cake	161
47. What's My Part?	164
48. Never Say Never	167
49. Until We Are Awakened	170
50. Just Because You Asked	173
51. An Impossible Family Reunion	176
52. It's Not What You Think	179
53. Believe It Will Be Good	182
54. Impossible? For Whom?	185
55. Doing Hashem's Advertising	188
56. Gam Zu L'Tovah: It's Real!	191
57. If It's All Good, Why Pray?	194
58. Trust the Driver	197
59. The Big Question	200

60. Ask the Manufacturer	203
61. Why Get a Berachah?	206
62. It's on the Way	209
63. Round-the-Clock Security	212
64. "Is This the Thanks I Get?"	215
65. One Hundred Times Over	218
66. Don't Let Your Arms Go Numb	221
67. Not So Fast!	224
68. How Do You Keep Going?	227
69. What's My Job?	230
70. If It's Good, Why Pray?	233
71. There's Always an Option	236
72. Perfectly Under Control	239
73. No Appointment Necessary	242
74. What Do You Expect?	245
75. Hashem's Treasure	248
76. Can You Pray to Be Good?	251
77. Someone Else's Problem	254
78. Hashem Chooses the Winners	258
79. When Your Father Is Rich	261
80. When the Difficulty Persists	264
81. Beyond Our Grasp	267
82. Helping Helps	270
83. Wait Until You Find Out	273
84. "I Knew You'd Need This"	276
85. A Hug From Dvir	279
86. Building Our Strength	282

Introduction
By Chana Nestlebaum

"**G**ood morning, Reuven. I just want you to know that today, your friend Yaakov is going to say something that will seem thoughtless and insulting. But don't worry. If you overlook it, then I'll make your toothache into a little cavity instead of a root canal, which is what it really should be. Remember, whatever happens, it's coming from Me. I'm looking out for you."

"Good night, Leah. Listen, I know you feel badly about the C you got on your *Chumash* test, and the D you got in *Navi*, and all your other grades. But don't worry. Pretty soon someone is going to suggest that you transfer to a different school. That's where you're going to be successful and also meet your best friend for life. Forget about the grades and go to sleep. Remember, Leah, I love you."

Imagine if throughout the day, you found messages from Hashem. When you faced a challenge, He would let you know that He sees what you're going through and has the whole situation in hand. When something good happened, it came with a note attached that said, "This is something special, just for you."

There would be no greater source of courage, comfort and joy in our lives. We would have no worries. We would feel pampered and protected at all times, even in the midst of something that would otherwise be unpleasant.

If you can imagine living like this, then you can imagine what life is like for someone who lives with rock-solid *emunah*. *Emunah* is so essential to our happiness that you can see it yourself. Who are the people you know who are positive, helpful and caring, the ones who rarely have a negative word to say? They are the people who believe in the essential lesson of *emunah* — that Hashem is all good, and therefore there's good in everything that happens and in everyone born into the world. They are the ones who feel Hashem's love and therefore, feel lovable.

On the other hand, who are the people who are bitter, who complain and worry about everything? They are the ones who feel that they have to scratch and grab for whatever they want in life. They believe that no one is taking care of them. They feel unloved and deprived and therefore, they have little to give. To them, the world is a dangerous, competitive place where anything can happen if you don't watch out.

It's no wonder, then, that thousands of Jews around the world have jumped on the bandwagon of Rabbi David Ashear's **Living Emunah**. In this book, now on its third volume, we find out how to uncover the messages that Reuven and Leah received in our imaginary opening scenario. These messages don't come to us by text, email or postcard. They come to us in the events of our lives. Rabbi Ashear has taught thousands of Jews worldwide to "read their messages" and discover Hashem's love and guidance in everything that happens in our world.

These books have inspired and encouraged countless Jews and given rise to an "*emunah* revolution" that includes Daily Emunah emails read by tens of thousands, as well as *emunah shiurim* heard by people around the world. You might wonder how many ways there are to deliver the basic messages of *emunah*: "Hashem is good; Hashem loves us; Hashem runs the world and whatever He does is for the good." The answer is that the subject of *emunah* is not like the subject of algebra, about which you might say, "Once you know it, you know it."

Rather, it's like playing violin; you have to practice every day or you begin to backslide. There can never be too many books on *emunah*, because every Jew needs to re-energize himself everyday.

The book you are about to begin is your own special gateway to this all-important mitzvah. It's a gift to young Jews everywhere who are just beginning their journey into adulthood, who have yet to encounter the challenges of earning a living, raising children and the many other *emunah* challenges that arise as life moves forward. You, too, deserve to have a daily dose of inspiration that, bit by bit, day by day, will help you "read the messages" and build a life of meaning, confidence and happiness.

This book, based on **Living Emunah Volume I**, brings the ideas of *emunah* to life in a way that reflects your experiences. How do you face the challenges of school, family relationships and friendships? How do you deal with the disappointments that cloud every life — the summer job you wanted but didn't get, the must-have item you can't have, the learning that just won't penetrate?

Living Emunah for Teens helps you build a foundation of *emunah* that will change the way you view your challenges and help you to find Hashem's love and goodness in your life. It blends real-life stories, thought-provoking scenarios, plain, clear explanations and the wisdom of Chazal, *Tehillim,* the Torah and *Neviim* to reach into your mind and heart and make a difference in your life.

You can become that person people love to be around. You can be the one who feels blessed; who feels so loved and cared for that he always has plenty to spare for others; who lives in a good world surrounded by good people, directed moment-by-moment by a loving Father.

Make the *emunah* that you gain through this volume into your constant companion; feed and strengthen it every day of your life. This, Chazal tell us, is ultimately the job we are in this world to do: "Chavakuk came and established the entirety of Torah on one principle: 'And the righteous will live by his faith'" (*Chavakuk* 2:4, *Makkos* 24a).

May each of you be inspired to live by your faith, to always feel Hashem's love and to experience all the sweetness with which He surrounds us every day. And may the "*emunah* revolution" of which you are now a part be the merit the Jewish people need to usher in the *Geulah,* when we will no longer have to search for Hashem's light behind the clouds, but rather, it will shine bright for all the world to see.

1
Nothing to Worry About

Chovos HaLevavos says that trusting in Hashem is the only way for a person to live a life that's not weighted down with worries.

Everyone wants to be happy. This is such a powerful goal that our whole economy is built on it. Just think about everything you see advertised, whether it's a new flavor of tortilla chip or a terrific new yeshivah or the latest style of clothing. What's the message behind it all? "This will make you happy. You'll look better. You'll feel better. You'll learn better. You'll taste something delicious." Rabbi Ephraim Wachsman points out that these messages bombard us constantly, everywhere we look.

People believe the message and spend their lives trying to earn enough money to buy all the "happiness" they see advertised. If you ask the average American high-school student why he studies, he'll say, "So I can get good grades and get into a good college." That is so that he can get a good job, so that he can make a good salary, so that he can afford all the things he believes will make him happy. He imagines the sleek car he'll be driving, the big house he'll own and the fantastic vacations he'll take with his family and he assumes that with all of these, he'll be happy.

The truth, however, is that he is living under a false illusion. He might have all that he imagines and be miserable — weighted down with all kinds of worries, disconnected from his wife and children, maybe even disappointed that he doesn't have more. And what if he doesn't achieve these dreams? That would be even worse; he would feel that he has failed in life.

What this person doesn't know, and what you are about to learn, is that happiness is always there, right at our fingertips, ready for us to grasp and keep. *Emunah* is the secret to happiness, but to a Jew, it's really not a secret at all. Every time we recite *Bircas HaMazon,* we remind ourselves, *"Baruch hagever asher yivtach baShem* — blessed is the person who trusts in Hashem." The trusting person's life is a constant blessing, free of worry and full of gratitude. He sees whatever he has in life as an amazing gift.

Imagine if all day long, the UPS man was delivering gifts to your door, all from the same wonderful benefactor who loves you so much that he just can't stop giving to you. You'd feel like the luckiest person on earth. And that's how a person who lives with *emunah* feels. Even if once in a while, the benefactor asks you to do something you find difficult, you would never doubt for a minute that it's coming from his love for you. Doubt and bitterness wouldn't enter into the picture. You'd know that everything will work out for the best.

We learn from the *Chovos HaLevavos* (in the introduction to *Shaar HaBitachon*) that trusting in Hashem is the only way for a person to live a life that's not weighted down with worries. Without that trust, even small problems turn into huge ones in our minds. We imagine all kinds of possibilities, even when we have no real reason to believe something terrible will happen. For example:

> ***A scenario:*** *A girl comes home from seminary and starts applying for jobs. She's got her heart set on a certain job that pays better than any of the others for which she's applied. It's between her and one other applicant, and she waits tensely to hear the verdict. All the time she's waiting, her thoughts are running wild: "If they wanted me, they'd have told me right away. I'm probably not going to get the job. What if I don't get any job? I'll never get married! Everyone will think I'm a loser because I'm just sitting home doing nothing. Who would marry*

someone who can't even get a job? I wonder how long it's going to take me to find my bashert? What if I'm one of those girls who doesn't get married? How will I be able to face going to my younger sister's wedding?"

This girl has assumed the worst and extrapolated from there a whole lifetime of miseries. You can be sure that this type of thinking doesn't just apply to big things like getting a job. She no doubt has spent her high-school years worrying about her appearance, her grades, social status and everything else that comes along with life. Her default mode is worry; even if she manages to paste a smile on her face for her friends, her heart is churning. She can't enjoy the unexpected free time she has on her hands as she waits for a job to come through. She's abrupt and moody with her family.

Compare her inner world to that of someone with *bitachon*. Let's imagine that instead of a post-seminary girl waiting for an answer about a job, the subject is a *yeshivah bachur* who has just come back from Eretz Yisrael and is waiting for an answer on a local yeshivah where he can resume his learning. He has applied to several different yeshivos and so far, none have worked out. The *z'man* is starting in three days.

Easily, he could be overwhelmed with all the same worries that are plaguing the young girl in the first scenario. However, he realizes that Hashem will direct him to the place that is best for him. He hasn't gotten into his first two choices, and he could easily feel, "I'm doing my best to get into a good yeshivah. Why isn't Hashem helping me?" But instead, he leaves it up to Hashem to show him what a "good yeshivah" is for him. He remains upbeat and enjoys the last days of *bein hazmanim* with his friends and family. When friends ask him, "Where are you learning next *z'man*?" he answers calmly, "I don't know yet. I'm waiting to see what works out."

What is the difference between these two people? We might think, "Well, one is a pessimistic type and the other is an optimist. That's their natures." But the real difference is in where they place Hashem in their lives. To the girl, He is far in the background, almost invisible. To the boy, He is running the show.

Worry eats up our happiness. It ruins our relationships with others, robs us of self-confidence and clouds our vision. We become like someone who stands on top of a beautiful mountain and instead of admiring the breathtaking view, he thinks about how easy it would be to fall off the cliff.

When we work on our *emunah,* we free ourselves of these problems. We can feel cared for and secure because we know that Hashem, Who loves us and delivers countless gifts to our door every day, is running our lives. We trust Him, knowing that He sees the full view and always leads us in the direction that is best for us. The more we look at life this way, the happier we will be and the calmer we will feel in our hearts, no matter what life brings.

MAKE IT REAL:

Make a list of five things you worried about that never happened, or did happen but you managed to deal with the results. Imagine how much happier you would have felt during those times of worry if you had simply trusted that Hashem would work things out for you.

2
It Didn't Just Happen by Itself

> *"A person does not even stub his toe down below unless it was decreed upon him from Above."*

A scenario: One morning, Moshe's alarm clock goes off at its usual time of 6:45 a.m. However, Moshe had only fallen asleep at 3 a.m. He knows he has to get up anyway and get himself to Shacharis, so he gets out of bed, still half-asleep, and scuffs his way across the still-dark dorm room. That's when his foot bashes into his roommate's 20-pound weight, which was left in the middle of the floor after a late-night workout.

"Ouch!" he cries out. "Dovid! What's wrong with you?" he screams at his still-sleeping roommate. "Look at my toe. It's turning blue!"

"This is going to be a bad day," Moshe thinks to himself. "I can feel it. Why do I have to go around all day with a swollen toe because this guy can't put his stuff away?"

Most of our days are filled with routine experiences. We get up, get dressed, go through our day and come home. Some things go right and some things go wrong. It's not the material of a great dramatic play. But the Gemara (*Chullin* 7b) teaches us that in truth, every moment of our lives is directed from Above as a scene in the greatest drama of all. It's the story of Hashem's creation and perfection of the world, and everything that happens to us is part of that story.

In the words of the Gemara (*Chullin* 7b), "A person does not even stub his toe down below unless it was decreed upon him from Above." A stubbed toe or annoying little paper cut or other minor injury doesn't seem like much of a message, but as this Gemara tells us, the small things also count. It goes on to say that the little bit of blood you might draw from such an injury actually rises to Hashem like the blood of a *korban* and gives you a *kapparah* for some *aveirah* you may have done.

Elsewhere in the Gemara (*Arachin* 16b), there's a discussion about the definition of suffering. In Hashem's kindness, He has many ways to bring about the *kapparah* a person might need in small, manageable proportions. Rabbi Elazar says that if you bring an item of clothing to a tailor for alterations and when you get it back it still does not fit as you wish, that is suffering. A second rabbi adds that if you're served a drink that is not at the temperature you like, that is suffering. A third rabbi says that if you accidentally put your shirt on inside out and now have to take it off and put it on again, you, too, have suffered. Rava gives the famous example that if you reach into your pocket for three coins, pull out only two and have to reach back in for the third coin, that is defined as suffering.

All of these instances of "suffering" let us know that we are still on Hashem's radar. He hasn't given up on us and is still nudging us along our path in life, correcting our course whenever we start heading in a slightly wrong direction. The Gemara offers these examples because if someone goes through a 40-day period in which nothing goes wrong in his life, he has to be concerned that he might be receiving his entire reward in this world, with nothing left for *Olam Haba*. This only happens when Hashem has given up on a person's ability to improve himself and earn an eternal reward. Therefore, it's reassuring to know that even such small irritations as the ones listed are counted as suffering.

You might wonder how an absence of annoyances could be interpreted with such certainty as bad news from Above. What if a person hires competent tailors, gets his coffee from a place where it's always served at the right temperature, dresses carefully each morning and pays close attention when he removes coins from his pocket? Does that mean he has no *Olam Haba*?

The fact that these small aggravations are the examples the Gemara chooses to give us teaches us just how far Hashem's supervision of our lives extends. None of the people involved in these examples has full control of his performance. If Hashem deems that someone makes an error in order to provide us with a small but potent inconvenience, then that is what will happen.

We hear stories about people who face incredible challenges with courage and faith. We hear about people who smile through painful illnesses, turn tragic losses into a springboard for *chesed* and give to others when it would seem that they have nothing to give. Sometimes when the going gets very tough, we manage to rally our resources and rise to the occasion. But what happens when we stub our toe, or our coffee is cold or our suit doesn't fit? What happens when someone keeps us waiting or cuts us off in traffic or forgets to give back something he borrowed? Do we see those, too, as coming from Hashem, or do we assume that they are too insignificant to be the doings of the Master of the World?

If we remember that these small inconveniences are also from Hashem, then we can view them with gratitude as a tremendous opportunity to repair something that is wrong in our lives and get back on track without a great *nisayon*. We can give Hashem our *korban* with a smile, knowing that it is being lovingly accepted.

> ## MAKE IT REAL:
> *Think of one ongoing irritation in your life and pre-set your mind to accept it and view it as a korban whenever it happens. Ask yourself, "Am I really so perfect that I don't need any kapparah in my life?"*

3
Be THAT Person

Every good middah has its roots in the belief that Hashem runs the world and does everything for our good.

You know that person who everyone loves? The one who's happy for you when something good happens, and knows just what to do or say when you're down? He's the one who just shrugs and says, "O.K., no problem," when you turn him down for a favor — and he really means it!

Maybe you wish you could be like this person, but you think, "That's just not the way I am." You might even think he gets stepped on or taken advantage of because of his pleasant, tolerant nature. The fact is, though, he doesn't feel stepped on at all. He's never angry at anyone. How does he do it?

This person's happy, lovable personal traits all come from the same source. It's called *emunah*. Every good *middah* has its roots in the belief that Hashem runs the world and does everything for our good. Looking a little more closely, we can see how a negative *middah* can never exist in the same place as *emunah*.

- **Jealousy (*kinah*):** This is the quality that, according to Shlomo HaMelech, decays our bones. According to

Rabbeinu Yonah, it weakens our heart. If you ask a doctor, he'll agree that stress (and what causes more stress than jealousy?) is the heart's biggest enemy.

But a person with *emunah* is immune to jealousy. If he believes that Hashem gives him exactly what he needs to fulfill his mission in this world, he has no interest in other people's talents or possessions. They're of no use to him. If he's trying his best with the tools Hashem has given him, he doesn't look for more.

- **Anger (*ka'as*):** We become angry when events or people do not rise up to our expectations. Out of anger, we often say or do hurtful things that drive our friends and family away. On the other hand, one of the appealing traits of "that person" we describe above is that he takes everything in stride.

  That is the result of *emunah*. When you tell yourself that Hashem is directing the action, you have no reason to be angry at anyone. The challenge the other person is putting into your life is a challenge Hashem wants you to have for your good — so why be angry?

- **Arrogance (*ga'avah*):** Someone who is arrogant about his belongings, talents or accomplishments is forgetting that he would have nothing at all if Hashem hadn't provided for him. He's like someone who borrows an expensive suit to go to a fancy wedding. There's nothing wrong with liking the way the suit fits and feels, but if he walks into the wedding hall and starts thinking, *Look how cheap that guy's suit is*, then he's a fool. He's only wearing what his friend loaned him; what sense does it make to let his pride get inflated because of it?

  When we carry around in our hearts a real awareness that everything we have is "on loan" from Hashem, we're not arrogant. We don't put other people down or treat them as if they're less than we are. Instead, we're humble — and grateful too — because we realize how lucky we are that Hashem has given us these gifts.

We all have the opportunity to be "that person," the one every loves to be around. The path to this goal is paved by *emunah,* and the more we try to stick to that path, the sooner we can start becoming the very best version of ourselves.

> ### *MAKE IT REAL:*
> *Think about one middah that you feel needs strengthening in you.*
> *How can emunah bring you success in strengthening it? Think of an emunah motto or lesson that you can tell yourself when you feel yourself slipping in this middah.*

4
Make His Name Great

> When a Jew acts with kindness and dignity, his behavior speaks volumes about the greatness of Hashem and His Torah.

Imagine that you stop at a coffee shop before school, put your bagel and coffee down on the counter to pay, and then, the cashier knocks over the cup. The cover pops off and the coffee splashes all over your clean shirt. Now you have to go home and change. You'll be late for school. Your morning is ruined all because of the cashier's careless move.

Would you throw an angry fit and scream, "Look what you've done"? If you did so, you would humiliate the cashier and get everyone else in the shop talking about his carelessness.

Perhaps you would hold your tongue but be boiling inside. You might stomp out of the coffee shop with an angry look on your face — and who could blame you?

But what would happen if, instead, you said, "Don't worry. Baruch Hashem, I'm O.K. Accidents happen!" In that case, everyone would be talking about your amazing calmness and patience. Someone might even comment, "Whoever raised him did a good job."

A person who has *emunah* automatically reflects well on his Father. When a Jew acts with kindness and dignity, his behavior speaks volumes about the greatness of Hashem and His Torah. If you have trouble connecting with this idea, think about the opposite. Imagine seeing someone you admire — perhaps a rebbi or an important member of the community — completely lose his temper. You might wonder, is it possible to be a *talmid chacham* and still be angry or selfish?

These *middos* are a *chillul Hashem* that cast a shadow over Hashem's greatness. It's hard to respect someone who is screaming in anger or sulking over a setback. And if you can't respect the person, how can you respect what the person believes in?

With *emunah*, we make Hashem's Name great among other people. Avraham Avinu was the first to show us how this is done. He taught the world *emunah* — belief in Hashem — and what that meant in terms of day-to-day behavior. He was loved and respected by all because of his dignified, calm manner in all situations. His regal bearing, which came from his *emunah*, won him the title "a prince of Hashem." When a person knows that Hashem is running the show, he doesn't look around for someone to blame for mistakes and problems. He realizes that everything is unfolding exactly as Hashem wants, even if it's not what the person himself wants at the moment.

People with *emunah* not only handle little annoyances with a smile and patience, but also, they handle big challenges in the same way. When a person is wheeled into the emergency room with a broken leg, he's in pain. But if he has *emunah*, he's not going to find people to blame for his pain and lash out at them. He will be able to see the kindness of those who are caring for him and thank them for their help. Rather than feeling persecuted and bitter, he will do his best to accept what has happened and find the good in it. Everyone who sees him will respect and admire his attitude, and by association, they will respect and admire Hashem, Who has "raised" him to respond this way.

As Jews, we know that we have an obligation to make a *Kiddush Hashem* wherever and whenever possible. We make that task a lot easier for ourselves when we build up our *emunah,* so that rather than struggling to rein in our runaway emotions, we are truly calm inside. Then, like Avraham Avinu, our words and actions will be an example that teaches the world the power of living with Hashem.

> ## MAKE IT REAL:
> *The next time you are in a situation that you find irritating, imagine that the people around you are going to judge your family according to how you react. Try to grab on to your best character traits to respond in a way that will reflect positively on them.*

5
Be a Hero

> *"He has no fears… Important and distinguished people are afraid of him."*

Did you ever find yourself feeling nervous in front of someone you wanted to impress? You're thinking, "This is the person who can get me into the yeshivah I want." Or "This is the person who can get me the job I want." Or "This person is very popular and I better not make a fool of myself in front of her."

You might flatter that person by saying what you think he wants to hear, even if it's an out-and-out falsehood. You might agree to go somewhere with that person even though you don't feel right about going, or perhaps listen to that person's lashon hara to make him feel that you're his confidant. All this you do because you're afraid that if you are true to your real beliefs and feelings, this person will somehow harm you.

There's a big difference between trying to make a good impression on people — something we should all strive to do — and fearing them, believing that they're holding your fate in their hands. You might think that this is a habit people outgrow as they become older and more confident, but unfortunately, that is often not the case. Even in the adult world, people can build up a tremendous amount of fear about their boss, their finances, their future or what others think of them.

But a person who has *bitachon* is a true hero. "He has no fears," says the *Chovos HaLevavos* (*Shaar HaBitachon*). On the contrary, "Important and distinguished people are afraid of him. And even the stones upon which he walks seek to please him."

We fear someone because we think he has power over us. We think he can hurt us or deny us something that we want and feel we need. But with *emunah* and *bitachon,* this fear cannot exist. We know deep down that the twists and turns in our lives are all laid out by Hashem. Someone might be an instrument in pushing us along a particular road in life, but Hashem alone paves that road for us.

Of course, we are required to do our *hishtadlus* toward achieving our goals. That means we have to live in a normal way and take normal precautions. Therefore, if you're trying to get into a certain school, you have to prepare for your interview, dress appropriately and treat the interviewer respectfully.

In fact, even if we have nothing at all to gain from another person, we have to treat him well, praising him and making him feel good. As *Reishis Chochmah* (*Shaar HaYirah,* Ch. 12) tells us, when we leave this world we will be asked, "Did you make your fellow a king?"

But what we do as normal *hishtadlus* and what we do to honor other people should have nothing to do with fear. *Emunah* means that we fear no person. The only useful place for fear is in our relationship with Hashem, because He is the Only One Who can actually do good to us. He is the One we need to please.

Living with *emunah* means living free of self-consciousness. It means living honestly, being comfortable with who you are. People with *emunah* are sincere in what they say and they are true to their beliefs. So if you want to be a hero, someone who is truly not afraid of anyone, *emunah* is the only equipment you need.

> **MAKE IT REAL:**
>
> *Is there someone you find intimidating? Mentally practice having an interaction with that person in which you are sincere and confident, realizing that this person has no power to harm you in any way.*

6
No More Second Guessing

> *"To everything there is a season and a time for every purpose under Heaven."*

"I wish I had gone to the other high school. Then I wouldn't be stuck with this impossible math course!"

"I should have never offered to give my friend a ride. Now look how late I am for yeshivah!"

"If only I had walked along the other side of the street, I never would have been pickpocketed."

"I could have gone to my cousin for Shabbos and had such a great time. Instead, I stayed home to keep my little brother company. What a mistake!"

No one sets out to make a mistake. Most people take whatever information they have on hand, think about what their goal is and make the best decision they can. But what happens when you end up regretting that decision? What happens when you are sure that, had you done things differently, your life would be better right now?

That can be a heavy burden to bear. You feel that you're suffering unnecessarily, and every aspect of your situation irks you because in your mind, it didn't have to be this way!

But what if you knew that in fact, it *did* have to be this way — that your decision was meant to be as it was, and you are following the path Hashem chose for you to follow? You might still have to deal with the results of your decision, but you wouldn't have to suffer regret.

Take one of the examples above: the person who decides to stay home with his little brother rather than have an enjoyable Shabbos at his cousin's house. If he sits around on Shabbos imagining the fantastic time he would be having eating his aunt's incredible food and singing *zemiros* with his eight cousins, he will be miserable. But the image he holds in his mind is nothing more than a fantasy; if it should have happened, it would have happened. But it didn't. He might as well be imagining a Shabbos on Mars.

On the other hand, if he realizes that he is where he is supposed to be, where Hashem has placed him, there's nothing to regret. He can relax and enjoy making his little brother happy. His acceptance of the situation won't make a quiet Shabbos into a lively one, but it doesn't matter, because that lively Shabbos at the cousin's house was not meant to be.

Regretting a decision is no more logical than mourning over not winning the lottery. It would make no sense to think, I *wish I had picked those numbers instead of the ones I picked.* Even if you were off by just one number, winning is winning and everything else is not. Were you meant to win the lottery, you would have chosen the right numbers.

Even when we have made a poor decision, Hashem is placing us in a situation in which we can learn something we needed to learn. For example, if someone slacks off throughout high school and then cannot get into the seminary of her choice, she may have used poor judgment during high school, but regret won't fix the problem. The only way to move is forward, in the best direction possible based on the situation as it stands: "This is where Hashem has placed me. Where does He want me to go from here?"

Sometimes we feel that had we acted differently or sooner, our problems would have been resolved long ago. "If I had gone to the doctor and gotten medicine a week ago, I'd be over this sore throat by now!" To this, Shlomo HaMelech offers one answer: "To everything there is a season and a time for every purpose under Heaven" (*Koheles* 3:1). This means that Hashem has chosen the time for your strep throat to go away, for your sister to get married, for each of us to be born and each of us to leave this world. When we overlook an opportunity that could have helped us, it's because the time has not yet come for us to be helped. Even the overlooking is from Hashem.

A bumper sticker on a car in Eretz Yisrael expressed this important point of *emunah* concisely: "To trust in Hashem is to trust in His timing." When we live in a world in which we know that everything is as it should be, we save all the energy we would have spent on regrets and pour it into making the next step and the next decision the best it can be.

> ## MAKE IT REAL:
> *Think of something you regret. Name some of the good things that have come out of that situation. (Perhaps you became close to someone who helped you, or learned something that you've used since, or used your experience to help someone else, etc.)*

7
Is Hashem's Hand Too Short?

> *Asking Hashem for everything we need, without limits, is a great expression of emunah, and will be rewarded by Hashem.*

A young lady had been waiting several years for a shidduch. People were already telling her that perhaps she was being too picky. She should face the fact everything she wanted was not going to be found in one boy. But the girl was determined. She wasn't asking for the impossible — just someone she could truly admire. To keep her emunah strong, she put a sticker on the family refrigerator. It said, "HaYad Hashem tiktzar?" (Bamidbar 11:23)

These were the words Hashem said to Moshe when Moshe questioned how He could provide 30 days' worth of meat to the Jews in the Wilderness. It means, "Is Hashem's hand too short?"

She believed that Hashem could do anything, including finding her a husband she would be proud and happy to marry. And indeed, Hashem reached into her life — with no exertion at all — and brought her bashert.

When we ask people for favors, we make a calculation. Is this something they can do? Is it something that comes hard to them? Do they have the time, money or energy to spare? Are we on good terms with them?

Then we make the error of thinking that praying to Hashem for the things we need in life runs on the same system. *I can't ask for all this. It's too much!* Or, *I can't ask Hashem for something so small and petty.* Or, *How can I ask Hashem for help when I don't deserve it?*

None of these considerations count when we're speaking of Hashem. He can do anything, and He loves us so much that He wants to give us everything we ask for. When we tone down our requests or hold back because we think Hashem won't be willing or able to help us, we are thinking in the wrong direction. *Emunah* teaches us just the opposite; Hashem is the *only* One to ask for everything.

There is a maxim that says, "Instead of telling Hashem how big your problems are, tell your problems how big Hashem is." When this is our viewpoint, we never need to feel that we're beyond help.

For instance, when we pray for someone's recovery from illness, we pray for a *refuah sheleimah* — a complete recovery. We pray for this even if the person is very ill, even if a complete recovery would seem to be inconceivable. Never would we think to ask Hashem, *Could You just make him a little better? Say, 50 percent better?* If we believe that Hashem has the power to make the patient 50 percent better, then why would we doubt for a moment that He could grant a complete recovery?

Asking Hashem for everything we need, without limits, is a great expression of *emunah,* and will be rewarded by Hashem. In *Tehillim* (81:10), after Hashem tells us that He is the One Who took us out of *Mitzrayim,* He says, "Open wide your mouth and I will fill it." First He reminds us that He can do anything; He saved us from the Egyptians and parted the sea for us! Then He urges us to open our mouths wide — tell Him everything we want and need — and He will fill those requests.

When we ask people for favors, we may feel that we are bothering them. That is because we're taking something from them — either time or effort or money. People's resources are limited, and therefore, when we take something from them, they have less. While it's true that they are gaining greatly from the mitzvah of *chesed* they are doing, we certainly don't feel as if we are doing them a favor. Because of this, we try to be careful about what we ask others to do for us.

For example, if you go out for pizza with your friend twice, and both times you're short on money and must borrow from him, you might not feel right asking him a third time. This is especially so if you still haven't paid him back for the first two times.

But Hashem's resources are completely without limits. He has all the time, money and strength there has ever been and will ever be. Asking Him for everything we want is not a bother to Him — it's the greatest praise. It says to Hashem, "I know that You control everything. You can do anything. And You are the only One Who can help me." We are telling Hashem that we believe in Him, and that is what He wants from us more than anything else.

> *Rabbi Elazar ben Pedas was very poor. One time, he fainted and Hashem appeared to him. He used that opportunity to ask why he was poor, and Hashem explained that he was born under a mazal of poverty. Hashem offered to destroy the world and start over so that Rabbi Elazar could be born under a different mazal, but Rabbi Elazar didn't want that. Hashem was pleased with this response and offered to give him "thirteen rivers of afarsamon oil in the Next World."*
>
> *Rabbi Elazar then told Hashem that he wanted more. He knew Hashem could give him a million rivers if He wanted — and still have plenty left over for the other tzaddikim who merited such a reward. Hashem appreciated Rabbi Elazar's answer and patted him lovingly on the forehead (Taanis 25a).*

Rav Shimshon Pincus (*Nefesh Shimshon* — *Emunah* 244) mentions that a pat on the head is not Hashem's ultimate show of affection. A kiss is even better, but Rabbi Elazar didn't earn a kiss. Rav Pincus explained that he should have argued when Hashem told him that he was stuck under the influence of his *mazal*. He should have insisted that Hashem give him money despite his *mazal*. Then, with that complete and total statement of Hashem's unlimited power, Rabbi Elazar would have gotten a kiss.

We might not be in a position to have arguments with Hashem or receive his loving pats and kisses. But we can remember this story, and remember that our heartfelt, all-out, nothing-held-back prayers for Hashem's help are music to His ears. When we ask for the moon and the sun, it only makes Him love us more.

> **MAKE IT REAL:**
>
> *What is your highest hope for yourself or someone in your life? The next time you daven, concentrate on asking Hashem to fulfill this request to its maximum, knowing that He loves hearing your words.*

8

A Real Eye-Opener

Even the ability to see Hashem in our lives is a gift from Hashem.

A rabbi tells the following story:

I was preparing a speech on bitachon and looking for just the right words to say. I thought that maybe I could use something I had said in a previous class, which was recorded on a CD. But I had five recorded classes and I didn't know which CD had the segment I needed. There was no time to listen to all five, so I hoped I would find it quickly.

I listened to the entire first CD, but it wasn't the right one. Then I put on the second, and soon after it started spinning, it stopped. The readout said "error." I took it off, dusted it and tried it again. Again it wouldn't work. With no choice, I skipped to the third CD and the same thing happened. Twenty seconds of sound and then it stopped. So, I tried the fourth CD, and shortly after it began, I heard the words I was seeking. The "broken" CDs had saved me more than an hour of listening time and led me to exactly what I needed.

I was sure that Hashem had interceded to help me out, and my belief was soon proven true. When I retried the two "broken" CDs, both worked perfectly.

Why didn't the rabbi credit this sequence of events

to good luck or coincidence? The reason is because when a person knows that Hashem is actively involved in his life, he constantly sees more and more proof of that fact. The more we look, the more we see, and the more we see, the more Hashem shows us. Little by little, we come to feel that we are being carried through life in Hashem's protective arms. He is caring for our every need like a doting father, even in the midst of the struggles He sends our way.

It all starts with opening our eyes. For example, you're on your way to school when you pass by a bright red car parked on your block. Because you never saw it before, you notice it, and because you notice its unusual bright color, you suddenly remember the red folder you left at home — the one that contains a report that is due today. You turn around and get the folder and arrive at school just in time.

You could tell this story two ways: "I was walking along when I saw this red car parked on the block. I thought, *Hey, where did that come from*? And then all of a sudden I remembered my red folder sitting on the kitchen table. It's a good thing I remembered because otherwise, my report would have been late and I'd have lost points."

In that version of the story, everything happened in a natural, *Olam Hazeh* way. You saw something unusual; it jarred your memory and you were saved from a problem.

But you could also tell the story — and see the story — in a completely different way. "Hashem is so good to me! I would have gotten into big trouble if I forgot my report, but Hashem didn't let it happen. He made it so that the Levines' cousin was visiting and his bright red car was parked right on my block. So of course I noticed it, and of course that reminded me of my red folder, and *Baruch Hashem,* I had just enough time to run back and get it."

The second version, the event is seen as a mini-miracle. Hashem moved many pieces in the universe quite subtly to protect our forgetful student from a costly mistake. He created the circumstances that caused the Levines' cousin to come to town. He had him drive a bright red car. Perhaps two years ago, when the cousin bought his car, one of the reasons he selected a red one was just for this moment. Hashem also had the student select a red folder, so that she would associate the car with it. He made sure she left the house early enough to have time to turn back and retrieve the folder. There are, of course, other reasons why the Levines' cousin came to town and had a red car. This is just one of many calculations that Hashem made in setting up this circumstance.

We can never see all the moves being made behind the scenes as Hashem directs our lives. We can, however, see the results, and when we do, it's our job to acknowledge it and share our story with others. "Speak about all his wonders," *Tehillim* (105:2) urges us. In this way, we not only build our own *emunah,* but we spread it as well.

Imagine if every day, 10 people told you stories of *hashgachah pratis*. In a matter of just a few days, you'd feel as if the world was saturated with Hashem's presence. Everywhere you would turn, you would be seeing Hashem's Hand. Nothing could make you feel more secure and calm.

"Open my eyes and I will see..." (*Tehillim* 119:18). Even the ability to see Hashem in our lives is a gift from Hashem. It's the step that starts off a lifelong cycle of experiencing, recognizing and attracting Hashem's *hashgachah pratis,* creating for each of us the happy life of a trusting, beloved child.

> ## MAKE IT REAL:
> *The next time you hear yourself saying that, "it just so happened that...," stop yourself and think about how Hashem was working behind the scenes.*

9
Take Time to Notice

Gratitude and happiness are inseparable partners. You won't find one without the other.

A scenario: One January afternoon, great news swept through the school. With the snow piling up rapidly outside, school was closing early! The buses were already lining up in the driveway to take the students safely home.

Shmuelly and his friends piled onto the bus and Shmuelly quickly claimed a seat by the window. Finally, after everyone was on board, the bus slogged its way out to the street and toward Shmuelly's neighborhood. The ride was slow. A few times, the bus was stopped in its tracks behind cars that had become stuck in the snow. Shmuelly was becoming impatient. His day off was dripping away minute by minute!

Then, peering out the window, he noticed an elderly couple carrying a few bags of groceries. They were walking along on the slushy sidewalk, struggling to take each step. The wind was blowing hard and their heads were bent down to protect their faces. How far had they walked? How far did they still have to go?

Suddenly, the heated air inside the bus seemed like a soft warm blanket around Shmuelly. The cramped bus seat seemed like a luxurious couch. The bus itself, a pretty old, rickety vehicle, seemed like a royal coach *carrying the students through the cold, wet and wind completely protected. "Baruch Hashem for this old bus!" Shmuelly thought.*

In this story, Shmuelly learned a secret of greatness — to recognize every single little thing Hashem gives us. We might feel that Hashem hasn't done anything special for us lately. Everything has been normal. Our parents didn't win the lottery. We didn't get all A's on this term's report card. No one we're close to is getting married. No new babies have been born. The people we know who are sick are still sick; they haven't been cured by a miracle. So it seems that Hashem is just waiting on the sidelines while we play inning after inning on our own. But as Shmuelly realized, Hashem is providing tremendous gifts for us at every moment. We just don't notice.

Learning to notice is one of our most powerful tools for becoming happy people who enjoy a feeling of closeness to Hashem. It is also the key to receiving more and more of Hashem's gifts and blessings. Sometimes, unfortunately, we only notice the good we receive when it's taken away. You can be sure that if Shmuelly didn't have the luxury of a bus ride and had to walk home instead, he would arrive at his house full of gratitude. He'd thank Hashem for having a house to live in, heat coming out of the radiator, a cup of hot cocoa to drink and dry clothes to put on. He would thank Hashem for his parents, who bought the house and keep it running.

All of a sudden, the things he barely notices every day would be under a bright spotlight, all because he had to endure a half-hour of sloshing through freezing cold snowdrifts, slipping and sliding and feeling his hands and feet turning numb from the cold. If Hashem wanted to say, "Shmuelly! Be grateful for your parents and your home!" this would be one sure way.

How much better is it to learn to appreciate our gifts without having to suffer first! We only have to make up our minds to notice the good and thank Hashem for it, and we will soon be feeling as if we've got the best life in the world.

One perfect time to turn our focus in this direction is when we say *Modim* in the *Shemoneh Esrei*. We can make *Modim* real by stopping for a moment to think of some of the many things for which we truly want to thank Hashem.

There is a true story of a *yeshivah bachur* who was very careful to recite the *Shemoneh Esrei* word for word with focus and meaning. But whenever he finished *davening* and looked over at his rebbi, he would see that his rebbi was not yet finished. What was his rebbi saying that took so much more time? It didn't seem that there could be anything more to the *davening* than what the *bachur* was already saying. One day, he decided to ask his rebbi why his *Shemoneh Esrei* took so much longer.

The rebbi's answer could be summarized in one word: "*Modim.*" He explained to his student that before he bowed and thanked Hashem for all his wonders, he took stock of what he was thankful for. *I think about my wife, each of my children and grandchildren, my house, my parnassah, the privilege of being able to learn Torah and I think, Hashem, You have given me so much!* Then I bow and recite "*Modim.*"

The rebbi was not only building his *emunah* each time he did this, but he was also tapping into a powerful merit described by the *Daas Zekeinim* (*Devarim* 10:12). We know that a Jew is obligated to recite 100 *berachos* a day (*Menachos* 53b; *Shulchan Aruch Orach Chaim* 46), but perhaps we might worry that on some days, for some reason, we don't fulfill this obligation. The *Daas Zekeinim* reveals that the numerical value of the word "*modim*" is 100, and therefore, a person who recites it with real meaning and sincerity is considered to have said his 100 *berachos*.

Whether by saying "*Modim*" with feeling, or concentrating on the meaning of the *berachos* we recite throughout the day, or simply taking time to notice the abundance of gifts in our lives, the more we recognize Hashem's goodness to us, the more we attract it into our lives. *David HaMelech* says "*Mizmor l'sodah...ivdu es Hashem b'simchah...*" (*Tehillim* 100:1). First is the song of thanks — *mizmor l'sodah*. Then, once we've filled up our hearts with thanks, we arrive at "*ivdu es Hashem b'simchah,*" serving Hashem with joy. Gratitude and happiness are inseparable partners. You won't find one without the other.

MAKE IT REAL:

List seven things for which you are deeply grateful. Assign each item to a different day of the week, and concentrate on it with your full attention when you say Modim on that day. For example, on Sunday, think of how much your parents do for you. On Monday, think of your physical health and strength, and so forth throughout the week.

10
When the Going Gets Tough

Accepting Hashem's will not only brings us closer to Him, but that closeness brings us berachah and often solves our problem.

Before soldiers are sent off to war to face the enemy, they learn how to fight. Before doctors are allowed in the operating room to operate on live human beings, they must master the skills and knowledge they need. Before firefighters are sent into burning buildings, they learn and practice how to rescue people and put out fires. Difficult, dangerous jobs require preparation.

In life, difficult times are sure to arise. No one sails though life without suffering disappointment, pain and loss. These are the times when our *emunah* is tested. It's easy enough to feel that Hashem loves us as we're flying off on an exciting vacation or standing under the *chuppah* with our *bashert* or holding a healthy new baby in our arms. But how are we to make it through the difficult times with the same sense of Hashem's love?

Gratitude is how we "train" for these situations. When we have filled up our hearts with the knowledge that Hashem loves us, cares for us and heaps blessing after blessing upon us, we have trust in Him. Then, when something difficult happens, we can call upon that trust.

Did you ever see a baby get an injection at the doctor's office? The baby's mother is holding him down so the doctor can get the needle in and out quickly. Imagine how the baby feels: "That's my mother and she's holding me down so this man can stick a needle in me! I thought she loved me!" For a moment, the baby may truly feel confused and even betrayed. But instantly, something amazing happens. The injection is over and the baby is crying on his mother's shoulder. She soothes him and he soon cuddles comfortably in her arms and drifts off to sleep.

Why does the baby seek his mother's comfort when she's the one that just put him through pain? It's because he knows her as the one who feeds him, bathes him, rocks him to sleep, smiles at him and showers him with love. He trusts in her love, even when, for a short while, she seems to be allowing someone to hurt him. He cannot understand why the shot is necessary for him and how it will protect him from much worse suffering. He only knows that his mother loves and cares for him, and that's enough.

When we take the same approach to the suffering that comes our way, we earn tremendous merit for ourselves, says the Rebbe of Komarno: "I don't know what You're doing, Hashem, but I know that You love me and I know that this is the best thing for me and I know You are with me every step of the way." When this is our approach, he says, our soul becomes so elevated that it is as if we have been fasting for 300 years. In other words, by accepting a difficult challenge with love, we can accomplish what would otherwise be impossible.

This is like an elevator up to the top of the spiritual mountain. We know that if we are capable of learning Torah, we can reach the highest levels by doing so. But what if learning comes very hard to a person, or he must earn a living and can't spend his days immersed in Torah? How is he able to serve Hashem? The Baal Shem Tov tells us that for such a person, there is still a way to reach the highest levels. "Take it upon yourself to be satisfied with your lot and content with the way Hashem deals with you in all matters."

A person who can do this finds a level of connection to Hashem that brings him tremendous inner strength and happiness. This is not just a theory, but a fact that's been experienced by people who have had to go through terrible struggles.

Rav Yechezkel Abramsky, a leader of Russian Jewry in the oppressive Communist period, was at one time sent to a Siberian prison camp. He was taken away without his *tallis* and *tefillin*, without any kosher food to sustain him, without any *sefarim* — without even a coat! He recalled after his release that one morning in prison, he began to say, "*Modeh Ani*," but as he recited the words, he fell into despair. What did he have to thank Hashem for? He had nothing. He could not even do a mitzvah. But when he arrived at the words "*rabbah emunasecha* — great is faith in You" — he found comfort. "I said to myself, *I have my emunah. I have something with such tremendous power, and no one can take that away from me.*"

The person to whom Rav Abramsky told this story, the *Maharyatz*, commented that for the sake of reaching that level, the Rav's struggles had been worthwhile. In other words, this level of closeness to Hashem was a spiritual treasure that far outweighed the physical pain.

Accepting Hashem's will means facing challenges with trust that what is happening is for our benefit, and that Hashem is there with us in our time of need. Sometimes our thinking runs in the opposite direction; we feel that if we want our troubles to go away, we had better scream and yell to Hashem and tell him why this whole situation is not fair. By accepting the difficulty, we might think we're saying, "This is just fine with me, Hashem. I don't mind at all."

However, the truth is that accepting Hashem's will not only brings us closer to Him, but that closeness brings us *berachah* and often solves our problem: There was a man named Reb Levi Yitzchak of Vizhnitz. He and his wife were so poor that they would go to bed hungry. One day, Reb Levi set off to visit his Rebbe, Reb Mendel of Riminov. His wife, sick and tired of their life of poverty, warned him that he had better get a *berachah* for *parnassah* from the Rebbe. "Otherwise," she warned, "don't bother coming home!"

Reb Levi Yitzchak traveled to Reb Mendel and sat there learning and *davening* for several days, happy to be in the *tzaddik's* presence. Somehow, he forgot about getting the *berachah*. It seemed like such a petty thing in this holy environment. When he set out for home, however, he remembered his wife's warning. He sat back down again in the Rebbe's *beis medrash* and resumed his learning, trying to find the right moment to bring up his little problem.

Then one day, Reb Mendel called for him. He asked Reb Levi Yitzchak how things were going at home. "*Baruch Hashem* I have *kol tov v'tuv* — every blessing," he replied. The Rebbe laughed. "Do you think I don't know that you're starving? But your answer cut straight through the heavens and sustained me and the entire world. In this merit, you will have great wealth for all generations."

When a person fills himself with *emunah,* his thoughts create an empty container for Hashem to fill with blessings. Not only do we have a lifeline to sustain us in times of trouble, but we also have such immeasurable *zechus* that our troubles may be replaced by *berachos* we could not even imagine.

MAKE IT REAL:

Whether you are Baruch Hashem facing only the normal troubles of daily life or you have chas v'shalom some larger challenge facing you, take some time every day to think about your challenge through the perspective of emunah. Tell yourself that you can trust Hashem and turn to Him for comfort, just as the baby turns to his mother.

11
Darkness to Dawn

For a person facing a time of trouble, his most desperate moment is his most powerful time to pray.

A scenario: "Hashem, You're my Father and I know You love me. So please listen to what I have to say. I know I haven't paid much attention in yeshivah all this time. I'm not a great learner and I'm already in eighth grade, and it's going to be hard for me to get into mesivta. But here's the thing: I really want to do better. I really don't want to feel like a big loser, and be the one guy who gets rejected from every decent yeshivah. If I get into a good mesivta, I'm going to work very, very hard. Please, please, please, Hashem, let me get into one of the yeshivos I applied to, and you'll see, I'll really prove myself."

Baruch's intentions were all pure. His promise was sincere. His request was for something truly *l'shem Shamayim* — that he should have an opportunity to improve himself in his Torah learning.

But as the acceptance letters began arriving at his friends' houses, all he received were polite rejections. He prayed again, this time more fervently. "I can't take it, Hashem! Please help me get into a good yeshivah! It's all I want!" He even began to learn an extra 10 minutes every night — which for him was not easy — to show Hashem how serious he was.

It was August, a few weeks before yeshivah was to start, and Baruch still had nowhere to go. "Hashem, why did You forget me?" he cried. His heart was breaking. He had thrown his worries onto Hashem's shoulders and they had crashed right back down on him. What did this mean?

The one thing it did *not* mean was that Hashem had forgotten about Baruch. Hashem doesn't fall asleep on the job; He never takes a break, as *Tehillim* (121:4) teaches us: "Behold, the Guardian of Israel neither sleeps nor slumbers." There is never a moment in which Hashem isn't looking out for Baruch's well-being, even when Baruch himself is distracted by other thoughts or fast asleep on his pillow.

Sometimes our lowest point is the turnaround, just as the tide has to get to its lowest point before it begins rising again, and the moon has to disappear from the sky before it begins to wax again. At that very moment when the low point is reached, the reversal begins. For a person facing a time of trouble, his most desperate moment is his most powerful time to pray. This desperation is the force that squeezes our most beautiful, humble and sincere prayers out of our hearts.

We see this throughout the Torah. For example, Chanah suffered for 19 years without a child. Everyone had given up hope, including her husband Elkanah, who tried to console her by asking, "Aren't I better than ten children to you?" (*I Shmuel* 1:8). With those words, she realized that she was utterly alone in her quest to become a mother. Her powerful longing wrested a prayer from the deepest place in her heart, and this prayer was answered with the birth of her son, Shmuel HaNavi.

Moshe Rabbeinu faced another seemingly hopeless situation in which Hashem Himself had pronounced doom on the Jewish people after the sin of the Golden Calf. How can there be hope when the decree comes from Hashem? Moshe didn't give up. The Gemara (*Berachos* 32a) says, "Moshe strengthened himself in prayer." Just when all hope seemed surely to be lost, he redoubled his efforts and begged for the Jewish nation's survival.

Why does a situation sometimes have to get so bad before it can get better? We can understand this by learning about the nature of *yeshuos* — Hashem's salvation. In the second *berachah* of the *Shemoneh Esrei,* we call Hashem "*matzmiach yeshuos* — the One Who makes salvation sprout." The word "sprout" teaches us that Hashem's *yeshuos* follow the pattern of the plants that grow from the ground. The seed goes into the earth and then — two weeks of nothing. We check out our garden every day and all we see is dirt. But under the moist soil, the cover of the seed is decaying. It's literally rotting away, while at the same time, the tiny sprout is beginning to take shape. If we keep watering the plant, the seed will dissolve; we will finally see the sprout pop out from the soil and begin its climb toward the sun.

Our prayers are like the water that the gardener keeps faithfully pouring onto the soil. Day after day, he sees no results. But he knows that the water is helping the seed to disintegrate. He realizes that the seed must dissolve further toward nothingness, and then the plant can begin to grow. So our situations sometimes get worse and worse; our prayers seem to bring nothing but further decay. But that is only so that in time, a fresh, strong *yeshuah* can sprout. Our job is not to look at the dirt and despair, but to trust that beneath the surface, new life is taking form.

MAKE IT REAL:

Take your most stubborn problem — the one you simply can't seem to overcome — and imagine that every time you daven to Hashem about it, the "seed" is dissolving a little further so that the solution can soon rise to the surface.

12

Need Money? No Problem!

Our only concern is to try to apply our time and resources to worthy matters, to accept that only He knows what is really beneficial for us to have.

> A man came to the Brisker Rav, Rav Yitzchak Zev Soloveitchik, to ask for a berachah. He was on his way to America to raise money to pay a debt.
> "Isn't there enough money here in Israel?" the Rav asked the man.
> "Well, I've been trying, but it hasn't been working," the man answered.
> "When is the money due?" the Rav asked.
> "In three weeks," said the man.
> "Three weeks? Why are you worrying now about money you need in three weeks? The money I need for my yeshivah usually comes in the day before it's due!"

If you had a big debt due in three weeks, would you face it like the Brisker Rav, or like the man who came to him for a *berachah*? That depends on your level of *bitachon*. For people who live with a deep, complete belief that Hashem will make sure they have what they need, there is no point in worrying "ahead of time" about money. Money can come a million different ways at any time. If Hashem wants you to have it, because having it will be best for you, nothing will stop the money from coming. On the other hand, if Hashem wants to withhold the money from you — also for your good — nothing you can do will bring it to you.

Even before we begin supporting our own families, money often plays a big role in our lives. Having it means having a choice of which camp we attend, the clothing we wear, the hobbies we can pursue and sometimes, unfortunately, in the friends and social circles to which we have access. If we come from families where money has always been a struggle, we might fear that our own lives will be just as difficult. If we come from families where money is plentiful and our lives have been privileged, we might feel that we can only be happy if we can maintain that standard.

Being a *baal bitachon* means living without these worries. It means truly believing that Hashem apportions each person's *parnassah* on Rosh Hashanah and no human being can influence that decision. Our job is to make a reasonable effort to earn a livelihood, and Hashem will then give us what He already allotted for us. Only through *tefillah* and mitzvos can we sometimes add to our allotment, and only through our own *aveiros* can we lose what was coming to us.

When we are doing Hashem's work, He makes sure we have what we need. We are part of His "business" and He is an entrepreneur with unlimited funds at hand to pay for everything and anything that will make His enterprise run better. If He isn't funding a particular activity, it's because He doesn't see it as a benefit. Our only concern is to try to apply our time and resources to worthy matters that Hashem will want to fund, and to accept that only He knows what is really necessary and beneficial for us to have. When we live with this trust, money is no longer a cause of worry. We value what we have and trust that we will always have what we need. This gives us a tremendously greater balance between spirituality and material concerns in our life, bringing us peace of mind and happiness.

Rav Yosef Shlomo Kahaneman, the Ponevezher Rav, saw this fact as clearly as we see the sky above, as this story illustrates:

> The Rav wanted to open a school, and he needed property on which to build it. There was one property

available, but it cost 100,000 rubles, much more than the Rav had. The owner, however, needed cash and was willing to cut the price in half. This was too good an opportunity for the Rav to turn down, but he only had 25,000 rubles available. He offered to turn over that amount immediately and pay the remaining 25,000 within three weeks.

The landowner was willing to agree, but only if the Rav would forfeit his deposit if he didn't make his second payment on time. It was a great risk; the Rav had no idea where the other 25,000 would come from, and if he didn't have it, he'd lose the first 25,000. The Rav and his wife discussed the situation and decided that because the community was in such desperate need of a school, the risk was worth taking.

They weren't operating on dreams alone. Practically, they knew that once people heard that a school was actually going to open, they would be willing to donate to the cause. If the Rav got the ball rolling, they were sure, the rest would come.

Unfortunately, that wasn't the case. No one was responding to his fund-raising efforts. The night before the money was due, on a Motza'ei Shabbos, the Rav turned to Hashem. "I did my hishtadlus (effort). I leave the rest in Your hands," he said. Then, with a light heart, he went to learn.

When he returned home at 2 a.m., two of the town's wealthiest men were waiting for him. They explained that they had just completed a shidduch, and had 25,000 rubles that were set aside for the couple. They wanted to leave the money with the Rav to hold. Rabbi Kahaneman asked if he could borrow until it was needed for use. The Rav laid out the terms of repayment, and the men agreed. The next day, the Rav brought 25,000 to the landowner, right on time.

When the Rav got home, he found out that the shidduch had been broken. There would be no rush to repay. It took him a few months to raise the money to pay back the loan, and thus the story ended.

This was a story of risk, drama and just-in-the-nick-of-time rescue. But because the Rav knew that the burden was on Hashem's shoulders and not his own, it was not a story of worry or anxiety or accusations. Had Hashem decided that the Rav would lose the 25,000 rubles, he would have accepted the outcome with the same tranquility that he felt as he left his home for the *beis medrash,* not knowing what would happen next.

When we put our trust in Hashem and realize that He can provide for us in ways that we cannot even imagine, we can relax. We can feel a true sense of security in our lives and our futures, and that's something that no amount of money can buy.

> ### MAKE IT REAL:
> *Imagine being a Jew in the midbar, living on mann. What would it be like to get only what you need for each day? What would it be like to have only today's food in your refrigerator, or only today's clothing in your closet?*

13
Getting in Good With Them

With a firm grasp of emunah, we realize that no one has any real power over us.

A scenario: There's someone new in your class. Not just any someone, but the son of the wealthiest man in town. He lives in a house the size of a hotel. He has an inground pool that his friends get to swim in all summer long. His family goes to Eretz Yisrael every Succos and he's allowed to bring two friends! Most important of all, getting in good with him means having a good chance at getting into the best mesivta in the area. His father owns it.

So you start hanging around this boy. You discover that despite all his advantages, he's not very nice. He uses words you would never use. He talks about things you would never talk about. He sometimes insults you. But you laugh at his jokes and nod at his opinions and let him believe you're a good friend, because there just seems to be so many advantages to being in his circle.

If you would follow the same path as the boy in this scenario, you would be running your life without the benefit of one very important piece of information: no one can do you any good — or any harm — unless it's what Hashem wants for you. People work hard to impress people who they think might be able to help them. People put up with rudeness and even abuse from the most popular, the wealthiest, the coolest person in their group, hoping that this will somehow make them more successful. But the truth is that with a firm grasp of *emunah,* we realize that no one has any real power over us.

Whatever we are meant to have in our lives — even a Succos in Eretz Yisrael or a free pass to the best school in town — is determined only by Hashem. This is the first of the Rambam's 13 Principles of Faith (*Ani Ma'amim*), which we find in our *siddurim*. We say, "I believe with perfect *emunah* that the Creator, blessed is His Name, creates and governs everything that has been created and that He alone made, makes and will make all things." This means there's only One Boss.

No one can keep us from receiving what Hashem has in store for us, nor can anyone give us something He doesn't have in store for us. Therefore, it really is useless to strive to please and impress people for the purpose of getting benefits out of the relationship. The benefits you are going to receive in your life are not in their hands.

This is a fantastic piece of truth to absorb into our bones when we're young. It saves us from falling into a wide array of people-pleasing traps that await us as we make our way in adult life. Certainly it's good to try to please others by treating them with friendliness and respect. It's also good and important to try to please bosses or customers by working hard, doing a good job, being pleasant and honest. This is all part of *bein adam la'chaveiro,* and the *hishtadlus* we do to earn a *parnassah*. However, if you believe that all these people hold your fate in their hands, you'll wear yourself out with stress and anxiety trying to be who they want you to be.

There's a saying: "It's not what you know, it's who you know that counts." This is a cynical saying that means people get further through their personal connections than they do through their skills, talents and knowledge. It so happens that this saying is absolutely true, but only if your big, important connection is with the One Above.

MAKE IT REAL:

Is there anyone who you feel you "need" to be friends with in order to gain status or some other benefits? The next time you're interacting with that person, tell yourself "he/she has nothing for me." Instead of putting yourself in an inferior role, try letting that friendship re-establish itself on an equal footing.

14

You're On

Hashem is always there behind the scenes, setting the exact challenges before us that we need to improve ourselves and hoping that we'll succeed.

You come home from school dead tired. What a day! All you want is to plop down on your bed and read your book. You're picturing that "aaaah" moment as you walk through the door, say hello to your mother and head up the stairs. Then you open the door to your bedroom, which you share with your younger brother, and what do you see? A Lego city, made up of hundreds of little pieces, is sprawled out across your bed! Your brother looks up excitedly to tell you about his masterpiece, but quickly catches the furious expression on your face. What do you do next?

You wouldn't think of this as a high-stakes moment in your life. It's not as if you're heading down a ski slope competing for the Olympic gold medal. It's not as if a panel of judges are watching your performance, ready to rate your grace under pressure. It's just your annoying little brother being thoughtless. It's just you, a regular eighth-grade boy getting annoyed at him, just as he deserves.

But stop! This *is* the Olympics! This is *your* moment — one among thousands of opportunities that you'll have throughout your lifetime to pass or fail a test. When that heat begins to rise in your heart and your mind starts to scream, "This isn't right! This isn't fair!" recognize the signs; the time has come to shift into high gear and put out your very best effort to respond in the proper way.

Life tests don't get announced a week ahead of time. They go on all the time. They pop up unexpectedly. They aren't labeled "TEST." Instead, they come to us looking like bad luck, thoughtless people, a bout of illness, a disappointment or some other everyday difficulty. The only studying we get to do is the work we put in throughout every day of our lives to increase our *emunah*.

Sometimes tests even come to us in the form of good luck, nice people and positive events. Rav Moshe Chaim Luzzatto tells us in *Mesillas Yesharim* (Chapter 1) that "All matters in the world — whether good or bad — are tests for a person." For example, you study well for a test and get an "A." Your friend doesn't study much at all and gets a "C." Could you call getting an "A" a real test of your character? Isn't it more difficult to deal with a poor grade? But this is the test Hashem has designed for you, because perhaps you need to learn sensitivity to other people. Will you brag about your "A" to your less successful friend? Or perhaps you need to learn to reach out to help others. Will you offer to help him study for the next test? Will you use your "A" to become a greater person or to become arrogant?

Each test we encounter gives us a chance to raise ourselves to a higher level. We learn this from one of the greatest tests of all time — Hashem's commandment to Avraham to sacrifice Yitzchak. The verse (*Bereishis* 22:1) says Hashem *nisah es Avraham* — "Hashem tested Avraham." The Midrash (*Bereishis Rabbah* 55:1) associates the word *nisah* — which means tested — with *nes*, which means banner. It quotes *Tehillim* (60:6) which says *nes l'hisnoseis* — "a banner to be lifted." Our tests are a means to lift us higher. When we greet them like a nuisance or a terrible injustice, we miss that opportunity. We might stay at our present level, or *chas v'shalom*, sink lower.

So let's go back to the brother whose dream of plopping down on his bed has been destroyed in a flash. He can react according to his immediate impulse and scream at his brother. If he's a really angry type, he might swipe the whole city off the bed and onto the floor. If he's the whiny type, he might march back downstairs to his mother and lodge a complaint against his brother.

But what if he realizes in a flash, *Hey, I get it. This is a test! Well, I'm not going to fall for this one. No one's going to get me to lose my cool. I'm going to ace this thing*? Now all of a sudden he's calm. *I don't know why this had to be the day my brother decided to build Manhattan on my bed, but here it is. O.K., Hashem, I'm going to deal with it.*" His expression relaxes and he compliments his brother on his amazing project. Then he lets him know, calmly, that his bed wasn't such a good choice of location. They work out the situation with no hurt feelings and no anger.

The older brother passes his test with flying colors, and part of the reason he is able to do so is because he realizes it *is* a test. When a person lives life with *emunah*, he realizes that everything that happens to him is orchestrated from Above. He can feel the eyes of the Judge on him as he chooses his reaction. It's his moment to either overcome the challenge or be overcome by it. Hashem is always there behind the scenes, setting the exact challenges before us that we need to improve ourselves and hoping that we'll succeed.

> **MAKE IT REAL:**
> *The next time you face a setback, imagine a spotlight shining on you and a voice announcing, "This is your test. Ready, set, go!"*

15

Every Little Bit Helps

Each time we respond to a situation with emunah, we climb a little higher.

When you finish a lesson in this book, you might think to yourself, *O.K., I get it. The next time things go wrong, I'm going to remember that it's a challenge sent by Hashem for my benefit. I'm going to think about how much He loves me and does for me all the time, and that way I'll handle the situation calmly.*

But then what happens? Something goes wrong. You get upset, maybe even angry: *Why this? Why now? I can't handle it!* Later on when it all works out, you wonder why you lost your cool. Why weren't you able to hold onto your *emunah* when it really counted? What's the use of learning about it if you can't use it when the moment arrives? What's the use of being able to hit home runs during practice if you can't hit the ball in a real game? What's the use of studying until you know all the material if you can't come up with the answers on the test?

When these thoughts occur to you, remember one thing — your learning has certainly made a difference. Perhaps it didn't yet turn you into the kind of *baal emunah* we read about in books, but there's no question that if you learn and believe what you learn, little by little you are becoming stronger.

Emunah is like a vitamin. You might take vitamins every day, and yet, sometimes you still get sick, or you don't feel like getting out of bed in the morning. So you might think to yourself, *What's the use of taking these vitamins every day?* What you don't realize is how many sicknesses come from a lack of vitamins. For example, long ago when merchants traded by sending out sailing ships filled with cargo, the sailors would often become weak and sick during their long weeks at sea. Then scientists discovered that the problem came from a lack of citrus fruit in their diets; they were suffering from a lack of Vitamin C. You might not feel when you eat an orange or take a Vitamin C tablet that you are making yourself healthy, but if you lacked that vitamin, you'd quickly understand what it does for you.

In a similar way, learning about *emunah* on a regular basis protects your spiritual health. It doesn't mean you'll never suffer from the worry, anger, resentment and other negative emotions that come from imperfect *emunah*. It does mean that you'll be strengthening yourself — even when you don't realize it — by the effort you make.

This stop-and-go progress is part of human nature. Not even a highly respected *talmid chacham* can say to himself, *I've reached the highest level of emunah. Nothing can bother me now.* Even at his level, he has challenges; that's how Hashem prods us to grow, and growth is a life-long project, no matter what level a person is on. Rabbi Fischel Schachter tells the following story that illustrates this point:

> There was a rebbi, a talmid chacham, who spent all his time learning, teaching and writing volumes upon volumes of brilliant Torah insights. He wanted very much to have them printed, but the nearest printing press was overseas. He called upon one of his students to take his life's work and travel with it to the printing press. "Guard it carefully," he told his student. The student was petrified to take on such a mission, but he accepted.
>
> Soon after the ship set sail with the student on board, a violent storm broke out at sea. The ship began to capsize. The student survived, but the rebbi's papers were lost. He returned home and told his friends what had happened. How would he break the news to the rebbi? The students thought of a plan.

The next day in class, a student asked the rebbi, "The Mishnah (Berachos 6b) says we have to bless Hashem for the bad just as we bless Him for the good. How can anyone feel the same about a disaster as he feels about a happy event?"

The rebbi answered that since everything Hashem does is for the good, there is no "bad." One by one, the students asked the rebbi the same question in a different form. How can we bless Hashem for getting sick? How can we bless Him for losing money? How about war? What about if our house burns down? The rebbi repeated his point over and over, with growing emotion, trying to get this vital point across.

Finally, the boy who had lost the rebbi's papers informed him of what happened. The rebbi promptly fainted. When the students revived him, they apologized for their behavior and explained that they had hoped to prepare him for the news. "I guess it didn't work as we thought it would," one boy said.

"What do you mean?" the rebbi replied. "At least I woke up! Who knows what would have happened if you hadn't prepared me!"

The rebbi recognized, as all of us should, that there are thousands of levels of *emunah*. Each time we respond to a situation with *emunah*, we climb a little higher. We may not even notice it at the time, but that doesn't mean that our effort isn't lifting us, bit by bit, to new heights.

MAKE IT REAL:

Think of an ongoing challenge in your life that has been a long-term problem for you. For example, are there people who rub you the wrong way? Are there chores you dislike doing? Is there something you are afraid of? Compare how you handle that challenge now to the way you handled it two or three years ago. Do you see that little by little, you are growing?

16
"A" for Effort

Only Hashem knows exactly what we need, exactly where we stand right now and how much we can achieve if we try.

A scenario: Rena made up her mind that she would make sure to say Tehillim every day for her friend who had not gotten into any seminary. "I'll do it every day right after breakfast," she told herself. But something always interfered. Her little brother missed the bus and needed to be walked to school. Her mother needed her to hold the baby. Once she couldn't even find her Sefer Tehillim. "What does Hashem want from me?" she wondered. "I'm trying to do a good thing. Why is He making it so hard?"

Shimmy started ninth grade with a resolution: "No more fooling around. I'm going to settle down and really put my 100 percent into my learning." Sadly, though he tried, he found that his skills were not up to par. He was having trouble keeping up, and the extra time he spent learning with a chavrusa/tutor just wore him down. "I really want to be excited about learning. Isn't that what Hashem wants? Why did He make it so hard for me?"

Most people have an idea in their heads: *If I'm doing the right thing, Hashem will make it easy for me.* Sometimes this is true, but the fact that something isn't coming easy is not in any way proof that Hashem is working against you. Sometimes it's the struggle that gets us where we need to go. When we have to work hard for something, we value it more. Our achievement is more solid and durable. It won't just drift or fade away.

Nature provides a perfect *mashal* for how this works. Several years ago, there was a massive storm named Hurricane Sandy. It hit the East Coast, and Lakewood, NJ was right in its path. There was one housing development in which each house was identical, and each had the same kind of tree planted in exactly the same spot in the front yard. When the storm finally passed and the damage was assessed, people were surprised to find that some of those trees remained rooted while others were plucked out of the ground like dandelions. Why did the same type of trees, planted in the same spots on the same day, hit by the same winds, have such differing outcomes? Someone figured it out: trees planted in yards that had an automatic sprinkler system were uprooted, while those that received their water from the rain alone had remained firm. Those trees were forced to send their roots deeper into the soil in order to get water. The fact that they were "deprived" of the daily dousing that their neighbors received was what made them strong enough to endure.

If trees could be jealous, the rain-watered ones would have surely envied the sprinkler-watered ones. They had such an easy life! They didn't have to struggle for their life-giving sustenance. Yet that easy life, in the end, weakened those trees to the point where they couldn't withstand the storm.

So what does Hashem want of Rena in our opening story? How can constant interruptions help her to *daven* with *kavannah* for her friend? We may never really know Hashem's plan, but we do know that if Rena accepts the situation without resentment and looks for a way to work with it, she will become greater. Perhaps she must learn to prioritize: "Can I have two minutes to say *Tehillim* and then I'll hold the baby?" Perhaps she needs a little more self-discipline: she could get up a few minutes earlier and fit her commitment in during a quieter part of the morning. Perhaps she just needs to build stronger empathy for her friend so that she isn't so easily distracted from her pain.

And what about Shimmy? How can Hashem give him the obligation to learn Torah but not the patience, focus and ability? Like Rena, if he accepts his challenge rather than kicking at it, he will grow in many ways. Perhaps he'll make a great connection with a *chavrusa* who will inspire him for life. Perhaps he'll learn to appreciate small successes, which will give him satisfaction in his learning no matter what his level. Perhaps he'll strengthen himself in other areas of *avodas Hashem* and become a great *askan* or *baal chesed*.

In both situations, Hashem imposes the specific struggle that will build the strengths each person needs in order to fulfill his purpose in life. Struggles are not obstacles designed to stop us; they are hurdles designed for us to jump over. They're placed at exactly the right height to force us to try harder and improve our abilities. If they were too difficult, we'd give up. If they were too easy, we'd gain nothing. Only Hashem knows exactly what we need, exactly where we stand right now and how much we can achieve if we try. When we dig down deep and make the effort, we build the strength to withstand the "Hurricanes" that come our way.

> **MAKE IT REAL:**
> *Think of something you wish came easier to you. Now write down five ways you can potentially benefit by working on that goal despite the difficulty. You can make these benefits as dramatic as you want, even if right now they seem unlikely.*

17
A Gift Wrapped in a Hardship

We all need to go through trials in life. Some respond with a smile and others will be bitter. It's my experience that the people who smile live happier lives.

If the mailman came to your door with a box wrapped in paper, stamped with the words: "HANDLE WITH CAUTION, HARDSHIP INSIDE," would you accept it? Of course not. Who wants to accept something guaranteed to give you a hard time?

But what if there was a treasure inside that box?

When Hashem sends us difficulties, our first impulse is to refuse the delivery. "Take it back! I don't need this!" However, we have to train ourselves to think again, because when a box of troubles comes to our door, we can be sure that somewhere inside, there's a treasure. What is that treasure? It's a massive, magnanimous lightening of our load.

We can learn this from the experience of the Jews' wandering in the Wilderness. After they received the Torah, they were a three-day journey from Eretz Yisrael. Instead, because of their complaints, the journey took 40 years. But the *Sfas Emes* asks how they could have conquered the land after just three days of travel when we know that that Eretz Yisrael can only be acquired through *yissurim* — hardships (*Berachos* 5a). Does a three-day trip count as *yissurim*? It wouldn't seem so, even though journeying through the desert with large families and livestock doesn't seem to have been easy.

Rabbi Shalom Arush explains that those three days *could* have been enough for the Jews to deserve their land — if they had accepted the trials and tribulations of those three days with love and *emunah*.

One of the greatest treasures we receive within the box marked "hardship" is protection from more difficult problems. When small troubles pop up and we accept them with love, Hashem allows them to take the place of far greater troubles that might have been coming to us. When we keep this in mind, it changes our entire approach to the small setbacks and irritations in our lives.

Instead of "Oh, no!" our response becomes, "Thank You, Hashem!" For instance, you leave something at a friend's house and have to go back to get it. You need to reach someone on the phone and they aren't available. You are supposed to meet someone and he keeps you waiting. Someone breaks a possession of yours. In all these cases and so many more like them, our best response is to thank Hashem for bringing *yissurim* to us in such a gentle way. Who knows what suffering is being avoided through these mishaps?

Those who are highly attuned to the workings of *Shamayim* immediately look for the message in even a small mishap. Once, a bottle of milk spilled in Rav Yisrael Salanter's home. He asked his wife if she had any idea why that might have happened. She replied, "Yes, I just remembered! Last week I forgot to leave money for the milkman." We might not be able to figure out the message in each mishap of our own lives, but we can stay calm by remembering that each of these inconveniences gives us a lot of "mileage." A scraped knee — accepted with love — could be preventing a broken leg.

The Chazon Ish once said, "We all need to go through trials in life. Some people will respond to them with a smile and others will be bitter. It's my experience that the people who smile live happier lives."

It's important to remember that accepting *yissurim* doesn't mean we can't *daven* for relief. However, when we *daven,* we should turn our eyes toward the future rather than complaining about the past. For example, someone who is having difficulty finding a *shidduch* can say to Hashem, "I haven't found my *zivug* yet and there must be a good reason. I fully accept that with love. But please let me find my *zivug* soon."

When we do that, then the reason for our troubles might just disappear. With love and acceptance of our situation, we become greater, and with that new stature, perhaps our troubles are no longer necessary. At the very least, as the Chazon Ish remarked, "The people who smile live happier lives."

> **MAKE IT REAL:**
> *Make up a motto that will help you accept small troubles as a gift. Get into the habit of saying it to yourself or out loud whenever you encounter those irritating, but far from devastating, situations.*

18
"I'm With Him"

Accepting challenges with joy and love is the key to earning abundant berachah.

A scenario: *You're on a thrilling, high-adventure camping and hiking trip in the Rockies. You've never done anything like this before, but fortunately, your group is being led by an experienced guide. "I know this terrain like you know your street," he tells everyone. "So just follow my directions and pay attention and everyone will stay safe."*

Knowing that there are rock slides, steep cliffs, a harsh sun, bears, snakes and various poison plants to beware of on this hike, your basic attitude toward your guide's instructions would be, "Whatever you say." You know that if you follow his instructions, he'll make sure that you have the best experience possible. You also know that if you try to defy him, thinking that you know better, you'll only be harming yourself: That amazing cliff you want to step out on to get the view isn't stable. That easier path through the woods that you want to take is riddled with poison ivy. The creek you want to dive into is lined with sharp rocks. He knows, you don't and you just have to accept that.

In *Pirkei Avos,* Chazal tell us that we should trust Hashem just as we would trust this mountain guide. "Make His will like your will." Whatever He says, we're on board, because the terrain of life in This World contains too many hidden dangers for us to mark out our own path. The second part of Chazal's statement is, "So that He will make your will like His will." As a result of our holding onto Hashem and following Him wherever He leads us, we will arrive at the best possible place — the place in life where we really want to be.

This means that if you have a plan that doesn't work out, you have to find it somewhere within yourself to think, *Hashem didn't want this for me, and therefore, it wouldn't be good for me. I only want what He wants for me.*

Because we are dealing with Hashem rather than a mountain guide, there is another vital part of making Hashem's will our own; we have to do so with love. No one in the Torah knew more than Avraham Avinu about breaking his own will to go with Hashem. He was commanded to sacrifice his own son! But what made this and his other nine tests so remarkable was that he didn't just do what Hashem commanded; he did it with his whole heart (*Chovos HaLevavos, Shaar Cheshbon HaNefesh*). It wasn't just "Well, You're Hashem and if that's what You want, I'll have to do it." It was with joy and peace of mind, and as we've learned, accepting challenges with joy and love is the key to earning abundant *berachah*. There are many reasons why this is so, but one of the main reasons is that it is so difficult to do. As *Pirkei Avos* (6:26) teaches us, "According to the effort is the reward."

The *Chozeh* of Lublin, a great Chassidic Rebbe, was able to actually see the power of acceptance in action. Once, a chassid came to visit him, having traveled many days. As soon as he walked into the room, the Rebbe told him he should go home. The chassid did as his Rebbe instructed, but he was miserable. He hadn't even had the chance to get a *berachah*. What had he done to be sent home?

On his trip home, he stopped at an inn where he met a group of chassidim on their way to see the Rebbe. They saw that he was depressed and asked him why. When he told them what happened, they cheered him up. "If this is what the Rebbe told you to do, you should be happy. You're doing Hashem's will!" They even made a special meal to honor the man for his great deed of loving acceptance. Then they told him that he could turn around and go with them back to the Rebbe.

This time, when the Rebbe saw the man, he was amazed at the change. "When I saw you yesterday, I noticed that there was a heavenly decree of death against you. I instructed you to go home immediately so that you could die peacefully, surrounded by your family. But because you accepted Hashem's will with such joy, the decree was annulled."

Only Hashem knows when we're headed out on a dangerous cliff or a path on which snakes and bears are lurking. He may take us miles out of our way to avoid the danger. He may send us on a steep path in the hot sun, or prevent us from taking that refreshing dip in the creek, all to help us ultimately arrive at our goal and mission in life. When we trust the Guide, even when we cannot see what He sees, we are showing Him that we truly believe He knows all and He knows best. That's *emunah,* and that alone is worth tremendous rewards.

> ## MAKE IT REAL:
> *If you don't accept Hashem's will, does that change what is happening to you? Ask yourself that question the next time you find yourself in a situation that annoys or upsets you.*

19

Crowd Out Troubles

Every time we thank and praise Hashem, we're making a Name for Him in the world.

A scenario: Your friend was supposed to meet you to walk home from school together. You wait and wait. Then you wait some more. You're in a hurry to get home. You're hungry for dinner and besides, you've got a busy night ahead. What's wrong with her? Why is she always late? Why doesn't she have one single bit of consideration? Your mind is churning out dozens of honest, well-deserved criticisms to deliver to her the second she shows up.

All of a sudden you see her coming. She's got a big smile on her face and she's walking as fast as her legs will carry her. When she gets to you, before you say a word, she launches into a story. "Sorry I'm late. But I was talking with Mrs. Deutsch about the play and we were both just talking about you! She says the scenery never looked so stunning and I told her what a fantastic artist you've been ever since I've known you and she was also saying that she really appreciates all the extra time you've been putting in. You really deserve the applause!"

Now what? Are you going to interrupt her to tell her that she shouldn't have kept you waiting? Are you going to be angry at her? Of course not. How can we return praises with a reprimand?

This idea illustrates a key for neutralizing the suffering in our lives: As long as we are busy praising Hashem, He will not send suffering out way: "It is not proper for My children to be cursed while I am blessed" (*Devarim Rabbah* 4:1).

Once a man wrote to the *Sfas Emes* seeking help for his miserable lot in life. The Rebbe told the man to praise Hashem at all times, even when things were going wrong. Acknowledge that Hashem knows what He's doing and runs the world perfectly. Then, said the *Sfas Emes,* the troubles will disappear, because Hashem cannot bear to hear His praises while His children are suffering.

Focusing on problems and letting them drag us down is in fact a sure way to sink even further. Complaints are like a clog in the pipe that brings Hashem's gifts into our lives. Recognizing that Hashem is in charge and always acting for our benefit is a way to dissolve that clog. With that awakening, blessings and even miracles are free to flow (*Divrei Yisrael, Parashas Behar*).

One of the reasons gratitude is such a powerful way to drive away troubles and attract blessings is because it fulfills the purpose for which Hashem chose the Jewish people. Every time we thank and praise Hashem, we're making a Name for Him in the world.

Imagine for example that people often admire your clothes, and every time they ask you where you bought some particular item, you mention the same store. They would begin to have great regard for that store; they might even shop there themselves. After a while, the store might want to give you clothing for free or at half-price, knowing that you'll be giving them great advertising.

Obviously, Hashem doesn't need our endorsement or our advertising. However, He tells us in clear, direct words that this is what He wants from us. "I have created this nation for Me, that they should speak My praises" (*Yeshayah* 43:21). When we show Hashem that we recognize the good that is in everything He gives and does for us, we become a means for drawing people to Him and keeping His name shining bright. We're telling the world, and ourselves, "That's where I go for everything I have." No wonder He wants to entrust us with even more.

We see that there's everything to gain and nothing to lose by keeping our mouths and minds occupied with gratitude to Hashem. In this way, we create the perfect balance, in which we bless His Name and He blesses us.

> **MAKE IT REAL:**
> *Try one time to derail a complaint. Grab it with both hands (figuratively), turn it around and send it in the opposite direction, finding something to praise and appreciate instead. Talk up the positive until your negative feelings are weakened. Start with something minor and then try it with something that's more important to you.*

20
Feeling Around in the Dark

When things happen that seem bad — even horrifically bad — we must believe that they are for the good.

When you walk into a dark room on a Shabbos hoping to find the book you want to read or the shoes you left somewhere on the floor, all you can do is feel around. If you don't find what you're looking for, you may begin to doubt it's there. You have to wait until you can turn on the light to see it.

The same is true when we're looking for Hashem's goodness in the darkness. When we believe it's there, we keep searching, and sometimes we find it. Sometimes, however, we don't find it. Then we might wonder if it's even there. The darkness of *galus* confuses us, and only Hashem can switch on the light.

When *Mashiach* comes, the good that was hiding in the dark will be clear to see. "You shall say on that day: I thank You, Hashem, for having been angry with me" (*Yeshayah* 12:1). We will see that all our troubles were for our benefit and we will see what that benefit was. We will be grateful for our troubles.

Our challenge is to trust that the good is there, even before *Mashiach* comes. We have to keep poking around in the dark, seeking comfort even when we can't see it. Adopting this approach to the challenges in our lives is an enormous source of merit for us. In fact, we learn that if Iyov had trusted that good would come from his troubles, he would have been counted as one of the *Avos,* along with Avraham, Yitzchak and Yaakov (*Yalkut Shimoni, remez* 908).

Building that confidence in the hidden goodness of everything can be a very major challenge. Going back to the analogy of searching for something in a dark room, imagine how much more difficult the search would be if you didn't even know what the object looked like. You didn't even know for certain that it was there. You had never seen it with your own eyes. In that case, you'd be much quicker to throw up your hands, walk out of the room and say, "It's not there."

That's why we actually have to train ourselves to say that our difficulties are for the good even when we don't feel it. Those famous words, *gam zu l'tovah,* are the "training program" that helps us believe in the good of Hashem's every act, even while we still live in the darkness of *galus.* There's no debate about this point anywhere in our Torah or commentaries. In fact the Rambam says that any "intelligent person" can figure out on his own that everything Hashem does is for the good. It's an absolute.

We might think that the challenge of saying *gam zu l'tovah* comes up only when things are really bad. Often, however, it's just the opposite. When a big challenge comes up, we feel unable to handle it on our own and we naturally turn to Hashem to help us. But Hashem doesn't limit His involvement in our lives to the big dramas like severe illness, making or losing fortunes, marrying and having children, war and peace. We can build our ability to "see in the dark" by practicing on the small things that might appear perfectly normal and natural. It's just as important to accept that there is good in a missed bus or a stubbed toe as it is for something more dramatic. The more we train ourselves to realize that nothing happens by chance and that everything is for our good, the more access we will have to the great merit of accepting Hashem's will.

Another way to train ourselves to see the good, even before the light of *Mashiach* reveals it clearly, is to read and listen to stories of clear *hashgachah pratis* in other people's lives. Rabbi Moshe Sherer, one of the major figures in American Orthodox Jewry in the 20th century, told the following *emunah*-building story about his mother:

As a boy, Rabbi Sherer became very ill with a dangerously high fever. A doctor prescribed medicine for him, but Mrs. Sherer couldn't afford it. She took every bit of money she had in the house and ran to the pharmacy, hoping the pharmacist would give her a break on the price. When she got there, the pharmacist was out, but his assistant felt for her plight and offered to help her. He filled up a glass bottle with the life-saving medicine and she took it and ran home. However, in her haste and worry, she tripped. The bottle shattered on the sidewalk and the contents spilled out.

Now she was truly distraught. She didn't know if the pharmacist would help her again, but she had no choice except to ask. She had to save her son! She gathered up the broken glass and ran back to the pharmacy; this time the pharmacist was there. With tears coursing down her cheeks, she explained her situation. He kindly agreed to give her a new bottle of medicine, but first, he took a piece of the broken glass from the first bottle and smelled it to determine what medicine she had been given. As soon as he inhaled the odor, he turned to Mrs. Sherer and said, "It seems you must have angels protecting you today. My assistant gave you the wrong medication. It could have made your child seriously ill."

On retelling this story, Rabbi Sherer said that his mother would always stress the lesson it taught; when things happen that seem bad — even horrifically bad — we must believe that they are for the good.

This belief is central to our success in life as people and as Jews. Yet it slips out of our hands easily, like a balloon suddenly hit by a stiff wind. The more we practice our *emunah* on the small stuff, the more we tell and listen to stories of *hashgachah pratis,* the firmer our grasp becomes. Eventually, instead of a stiff wind of resistance pulling *emunah* from our hands, our *emunah* will carry us along on the current and take us where Hashem wants us to go.

MAKE IT REAL:

Start with something small that bothers you — something for which you cannot find a positive purpose. Make that your first "gam zu l'tovah" project in which you accept that this situation has to happen, it's happening for a good reason and you might just have to wait for Mashiach to find out what that reason is.

21
Nothing but Kindness

If a person trains himself to say things are good, then Hashem says, "I will make things even better for you!"

We know Hashem loves us" and that everything He does is for our good. We also know that Hashem shows Himself to us in two different ways. There's the *rachamim* — mercy — which we see and feel when we enjoy all the wonders of our world. There's also the *din* — strict judgment — which we see when illness, destruction and death enter into the picture. No one would say that life is always rosy.

Even so, the central pillar of our faith is that Hashem is One. This is what we attest to twice a day when we say the *Shema*. Even within the words of that one phrase we see the two sides of Hashem's interactions with us. We say, *"Shema Yisrael, Hashem Elokeinu, Hashem echod."* We call Hashem by two different names — Hashem and *Elokeinu*.

Each of these names represents a different attribute. The four-letter Name of Hashem represents His mercy; the name *Elokim* represents *din* (*She'eiris Menachem*). Yet we say in the *Shema* that "Hashem is One." This means that *din* and *rachamim,* on a higher level, are one and the same. When we cover our eyes to say these words, we are telling Hashem that although we don't see this unity with our own eyes, we trust that it is there.

This is an important part of the puzzle as we try to build

our *emunah*. Just knowing that Hashem is good through and through — that there are no multiple personalities or conflicting qualities within Him — helps us to frame our reactions to events in our lives. When we see this as the rock-solid reality, then the only thing that makes sense is to accept all that happens as an expression of *rachamim*: something Hashem has done out of His love and mercy.

Sometimes it's easy. We wake up well rested, the sun is shining, the smell of coffee is emanating from the kitchen and all is right with the world. Opening our mouths to say *Modeh Ani* in these circumstances is a joy. We feel the blessings literally raining down upon us.

Other times, however, it's not that easy. We had a terrible night's sleep, the wind is whipping the rain against the bedroom window, the house is cold and the day seems doomed before it starts. Then saying *Modeh Ani* is an act of blind faith. "I'm thanking You for waking me up, Hashem, but I'd really much rather stay in bed." In that case, our job is to say, "I don't know *how* all this shows Hashem's love for me, but since that's all He ever has for me, I know that this *has* to be out of love."

We also have a role to play in helping the *rachamim* shine forth from what feels like *din*. That is to accept whatever Hashem sends our way. The person waking up too early from a restless night's sleep, thinking about walking out into the cold, wind-driven rain, has in front of him the task of putting away his complaints and gratefully accepting the day that's been given to him. This brings blessing.

He can put on warm clothes and be grateful for the comfort it gives him. He can eat a good breakfast to try to shore up his low energy. He can step out into the rain under a good solid umbrella or raincoat and make his way to the bus stop feeling like a hero. He can climb onto the bus and feel happy to see his friends also on their way to school. Comfort, warmth and friendship can make the day a great one. What seemed like *din* when the alarm clock rang has shown itself to have *rachamim* at its core.

"If a person trains himself to say things are good, then Hashem says, 'I will make things even better for you!'" (*Divrei*

Yisrael, Parashas Vayishlach). We can see even in our own lives that when people are grateful and satisfied with the gifts we give them, we are encouraged to keep on giving. On the other hand, if nothing we give is ever quite good enough, we eventually give up trying.

> *There was a young wife who received a birthday present from her new husband. He had never gone out to buy her a present all on his own before. He handed it to her a little nervously. He thought she would like it, but what if she didn't? The wife opened the box. It was a bracelet. She never wore bracelets; she didn't like the way they got in the way of her busy hands. "I saw you didn't have any bracelets," the husband said shyly, "so I thought you'd really be able to use this."*
>
> *She paused for a minute, wondering how to react. At last she said, "I love it! It's perfect! It's so beautiful that I think I'll save it only for Shabbos. It will be my special Friday-night jewelry." Knowing that Friday night, she wasn't typing, driving, cooking, washing dishes and so forth, she could manage to comfortably wear the bracelet. Her husband was delighted. He felt honored that she set his gift aside for Shabbos. He looked forward to the next gift-giving occasion; it was so wonderful to be able to make his wife happy!*

Had the wife complained about the gift, even politely, her husband would have lost his desire to give. Next time, he would probably ask her to pick something out for herself. She would have missed the pleasure of knowing he had thought about her and taken time to choose something she would like. Instead, this wise young woman put aside her complaint and found a way to cherish the gift that had come to her with love. Now the pipeline of giving was open.

Likewise, when we tell Hashem, "It's good," He wants to give us more. By keeping in mind that whether it looks like *din* or it looks like *rachamim,* everything that comes to us is rooted in Hashem's love, we can truthfully say it's good — even when it's difficult.

MAKE IT REAL:

When you cover your eyes to say the Shema, think about the idea that everything that happens springs from one Source.

22

First Accept, Then Pray

We can and should go to Hashem with our needs. Before we ask for what we need, we must first accept with love everything that has happened until this moment.

A scenario: You spend your summer working as a counselor in an overnight camp. You have the youngest bunk — 8-year-olds. They need help with just about everything. At any given moment, at least one of them is crying to go home. You give the job your all, acting as Mommy, Daddy and child psychologist to your campers. Visiting day comes along and you meet two kinds of parents:

One type says to you, "Thanks so much for everything you do for our child. It's amazing how much effort you put in. It can't be easy to keep up with 12 third-graders. There's just one thing, though. Could I ask you to make sure he eats his supper? He says he's hungry at night."

The other type says to you: "I'm glad we finally get to meet you. There are a few things we need to address. Our son has been complaining to us all summer that you keep them out in the sun too long. I can't believe you're not more careful. It's so dangerous! I've called the head counselor about it but it seems that nothing has changed. You must make sure he doesn't get overheated!"

You can imagine how different your reaction would be to these two different types of requests. One type is sincerely grateful for what you've done. These parents express their appreciation wholeheartedly, without criticism. Then they ask for your help going forward. There are no recriminations: "You let our child go hungry!" There's only thanks for everything you've done so far, and a request for help to remedy a situation in the future.

The second type, however, is full of complaints about how you've handled things so far. These parents only notice what's missing. There's no appreciation for your hard work, for the difficulty of your job or for anything you've done for their child. Instead, you get accusations of being neglectful and endangering the children's welfare. You also find out that a complaint has been lodged with the head counselor.

It's clear which kind of request would receive a more enthusiastic response. Yet when we make our requests of Hashem, especially about the things that seem wrong in our lives, we often follow the pattern of the second type of parent. We tell Hashem that He hasn't been taking proper care of us, that He isn't fulfilling our needs. We are full of requests, demands and tears over all we've gone through.

Is this wrong? Aren't we supposed to cry to Hashem when we are in need? Aren't we supposed to turn to Him for comfort when we're hurting? Isn't that actually coming from true *emunah*?

There seems to be two contradicting ideas; to accept everything Hashem sends our way, and to *daven* for Him to fulfill our needs. If we accept our situation and believe it is the best for us, how can we pray to change it? And on the other hand, if we are supposed to turn to Hashem for everything, how can we refrain from registering our complaints with the only One Who can help us?

For example, a boy has a very difficult time learning Gemara. His grades are terrible. He finds yeshivah depressing and confusing. His self-esteem is suffering. He wants to tell Hashem how unfair it is that he wasn't blessed with a quicker mind. He wants to say, "Why can't I be like everyone else? Why is yeshivah so hard for me? You see that I try and try, but nothing helps!" Should he just accept that he'll never learn well?

Our camp counselor in the beginning scenario can solve the contradiction for us: The best way to address a need is to accept what's in the past and ask for what you desire in the future. The first type of parents did not say one negative word about what had gone on until visiting day. Instead, they thanked the counselor for everything he had done. Then, they asked for what they needed in the future. Feeling that what he had done so far had been appreciated, the counselor was more than happy to fulfill their request.

The second type of parents dwelled on everything that had upset them. They were saving up their complaints for visiting day, using it as an opportunity to vent their frustrations. The counselor should try to do what was best for the camper, but he could be 99.9 percent sure that no matter what he did to appease these parents, they'd only find other reasons to complain. He certainly wouldn't feel any need to go "above and beyond" to make them happy.

Certainly, we can and should go to Hashem with our needs. This *is emunah*. The *Shemoneh Esrei* provides us with many opportunities to put in our personal pleas for ourselves, and includes many pleas on behalf of Klal Yisrael. But before we open our mouths to ask for what we need, we must first accept with love everything that has happened until this moment.

The boy who had trouble learning could therefore say something like, "Hashem, I accept that up until now, it's been the best thing for me to struggle with my learning. But please, starting now, open up my mind and help me learn better."

People who first sincerely accept their situation and then request Hashem's help often find their problems resolving before their eyes. They know that as they climb to higher levels of *emunah*, their situation changes. The difficulties that Hashem deemed good and necessary for them yesterday might not be necessary tomorrow. For that, we can always pray.

MAKE IT REAL:

Work on one personal request you can make of Hashem during Shema Koleinu. Think of how you can sincerely accept the challenge you've experienced so far and ask for an improvement in the future.

23
Take It Personally

Besides the good we see, there's all the good we don't see.

A scenario: Your family went out of town for a cousin's aufruf. Your aunt has prepared all the food for the Shabbos meals, at which your whole extended family will be present. She's really gone above and beyond, with platter after platter of fish, meat, side dishes and delicacies emerging from the kitchen.

When Shabbos is over and your family is on the way home, your brother fondly reviews the menu. "Aunt Naomi treated me like royalty!" he says. "She made all my favorite food. Spicy salmon, kneidlach, roast, sweet kugel — even Dr. Pepper! I gave her a big thank-you before we left. I really enjoyed everything."

"She didn't cook it for you," you correct your brother. "She was making a big seudah anyway. I mean, it was nice and everything, but it wasn't such a big deal."

As we noted earlier, there are two kinds of guests (*Berachos* 58a). The good guest says, "Look at everything the host did for me. The food and drinks — it was all done for me. I'm so grateful." The bad guest says, "What's the big deal? He was preparing anyway. He didn't do anything for me."

If we want to build our *emunah* and *bitachon*, we have to be good guests in Hashem's world. That means noticing everything Hashem does for us and taking it personally. We can't just notice that the sun is shining; we have to appreciate that it's shining for us. We get the benefit of its light and warmth. We get to go swimming today because it's not raining.

By constantly reminding ourselves that Hashem is involved in every detail of our lives, that He is loving and full of compassion for us, and that every bit of enjoyment we have comes from Him, we reach greater and greater levels of *emunah*. It might seem strained and awkward at first to thank Hashem that the ice-cream shop's flavor of the month is your favorite; that your lost keys turned up in your raincoat pocket (thank Hashem for the rain!); that your friend invited you for Shabbos; or any bit of goodness that comes your way.

You might think to yourself, *Can't things sometimes just happen? Pistachio Coconut Medley is bound to be the flavor of the month at least once a summer. It's not exactly a miracle from Shamayim.* But that kind of thinking misses the point; Hashem uses nature and coincidence to hide His involvement in our lives. In reality, it's all Him, and it's all for each of us individually, in the way that is best for us.

What does it take to be aware of all the small blessings Hashem is always sending our way? David HaMelech tells us that it takes wisdom: "Whoever is wise will guard these and contemplate the kindnesses of Hashem (*Tehillim* 107:43). Ironically, we sometimes only have that wisdom when it comes to other people. Your friend complains about his terrible day and you say, "What are you complaining about? You got an A on your English test. And you're leaving in a week for Eretz Yisrael. Boy, I wish I had so much to complain about!" The annoyances of his day quickly bury the happiness and gratitude he could be feeling, yet it's so obvious to you.

The reason you see and he doesn't is not necessarily that you are more attuned to Hashem's kindness. Most likely it is simply that you are not suffering from the challenges he's experiencing at the moment. Your vision isn't clouded as his is. When it's your turn to be down and cranky, that same friend might just be the one to show you the bright side.

The more we get used to noticing all the gifts, great and small, with which Hashem fills every day, the more goodness He sends us. Every "thank you" is like a *korban todah* — a thanksgiving offering brought to the Beis HaMikdash (*Tehillim Rabbah*). It's that precious to Hashem, and yet it's so easy to do once we shift our focus. The alarm clock doesn't ring, but you make the bus anyway: Thank Hashem! A glass falls but it doesn't break: Thank Hashem! You got a flat tire in a dangerous neighborhood and got back on the road safely: Thank Hashem!

Besides the good we see, there's all the good we don't see. We have no way of knowing how, behind the scenes, Hashem is working to save us from our troubles and create the conditions for our success.

> *A wife was feeling a little disappointed. Shavuos was coming and she just didn't have the time to prepare for a tableful of guests. She had kept it simple. Just her, her husband and their single son. No married kids, no grandchildren, no neighbors. It was all she felt she could handle, and yet, she missed the anticipation of big family meals with lots of special Shavuos dishes.*
>
> *On Shavuos morning, her husband came home from learning all night in shul and opened the refrigerator to get a drink of water. Strangely, nothing in the fridge was very cold. Then he noticed that the motor wasn't making any noise. He bent down to check the controls and saw that the temperature gauge was set at "OFF." He told his wife, and she suddenly remembered that their little grandson, who had been with her in the kitchen on Erev Yom Tov, had opened the refrigerator and was fiddling around inside. "He must have turned the dial," she concluded.*
>
> *"But guess what. We already ate our first meal. The food for the second meal can stay cold for another few hours until it's time to heat it up. Tonight we're eating at our daughter's house and tomorrow at our neighbor's. So there's nothing to worry about!" The disappointment of a quiet Shavuos turned into a blessing. "Thank You,*

Hashem, for keeping me from preparing pans of food that would have been ruined. Thank You for keeping me from having to wonder how to feed loads of guests. Thank You for that little grandson of ours and his nimble little hands."

Hashem is always on the job, doing for us, saving us from disasters big and small. We have a job too — to praise Him and thank Him for all He does for us. The more we do our job, the more we are able to see Hashem doing His.

MAKE IT REAL:

Set aside just one minute a day — at a set time, such as right after supper or right before bed — to thank Hashem for specific gifts you received that day. Anything, even as small as "Thanks for having my mother make schnitzel for supper" can be part of our list.

24

Training Our Eyes

What we see when we look at our lives also depends on what we think about.

What we see has a lot to do with what we think about. For instance, when a photographer looks at a majestic mountain, he notices the lighting and thinks of how he would frame the picture to capture the grandeur. A skier looking at the mountain notices how steep it is and thinks about how he'd navigate it. A geologist looking at the mountain notices what type of rock it consists of and thinks about how it was formed.

What we see when we look at our lives also depends on what we think about. When a person who has *emunah* looks at life, he sees Hashem's hand. A person with a lesser level of *emunah* sees the same events as natural occurrences or coincidences. He doesn't realize that every instance — every person he meets, every experience he encounters — is Hashem speaking to him, guiding him on his trip through life.

People say, "If I could only see Hashem, it would be so much easier to believe in Him." A person with strong *emunah* might answer, "How can you *not* see Him?" The photographer doesn't understand how someone can look at the mountain and not notice the shadows and sunlight. To him it's so obvious because it's what he looks for. He can't even stop himself from noticing it; this perspective is ingrained in him. Likewise, the more we think about Hashem's involvement in our lives, the more we see it, until eventually it becomes so ingrained in us that we can't ignore it even if we want to.

The trick is to start noticing. The photographer isn't born with his special perspective. He has to learn how to see the world from a photographer's eye. We, too, have to learn to see the world from the eye of a believing Jew, of a *baal emunah*. As we learn, we begin to hear the messages Hashem is sending us through His interactions with us. He is saying, "I'm here!" a million ways each day.

> *Eliyahu had been seeking a shidduch in America for more than a year, but he was having a great deal of difficulty even getting a date. He just didn't fit in anywhere. He was no longer in yeshivah, but he was sincere and serious about his avodas Hashem. It seemed that the more sincere girls were not interested in a boy who was working.*
>
> *He went to Eretz Yisrael to attend a friend's wedding. He planned a stay for two weeks, during which several friends had lined up shidduchim for him. He went out with three different girls, but none of them were quite right. It was time to go back to America. But on the way to the airport, Eliyahu began to feel sick. He couldn't imagine flying for 11 hours with the fever and stomach pain he was having. He told the cab driver to bring him back to the house where he had been staying — the home of Moshe, his former yeshivah roommate, and his wife Leah. Eliyahu felt better almost as soon as he got to his friends' house.*
>
> *It was a Thursday, and Eliyahu was clearly going to be with his friends for Shabbos. They had another guest coming as well — an 18-year-old Israeli boy named Eyal. Shabbos was pleasant, and Eyal and Eliyahu really hit it off. They seemed to have a lot in common and very similar personalities.*
>
> *As soon as Havdalah was over, Leah said, "No one go anywhere. We're going to all sit down right now and think until we come up with a shidduch idea for*

Eliyahu." Eyal suddenly lit up. "My older sister has a friend who I think Eliyahu would like."

The contacts were made, the first date was arranged, and three weeks later, Eliyahu and Chaya were engaged. She was from an entirely different community in an entirely different city in Israel. Their paths, under normal circumstances, would never have crossed. Yet Hashem had brought Eliyahu halfway around the world, stricken him with a mystery virus that kept him from flying home and brought Eyal to his friend's house for Shabbos all so this couple could come together.

With events like *shidduchim,* we have a greater tendency to retrace all the steps that led to the big event and observe Hashem in action. "Eyal *just happened* to be coming for Shabbos. Shlomo *just happened* to be stuck at his friend's house because he was too sick to fly home. It was all Hashem's plan!"

But Hashem is talking to us all the time, putting people and opportunities in our path in order to lead us to our destiny. There is a story of a woman who was shopping with her mother in Brooklyn when it started to rain. They had traveled by bus, but now that they had a lot of bundles to carry and the weather had changed, they wished they had a car ride home. They stopped into a coffee shop and the woman opened her *Tehillim* and asked Hashem to send them a ride. Moments later, an old friend of the woman walked into the coffee shop. "Is everything all right?" she asked. "I see you're saying *Tehillim.*"

"I was *davening* for a ride home," the woman said. "And now here you are!"

That would be enough of a *hashgachah pratis* story, but there's another part to it. A few years later, the second woman, who had provided the ride, was feeling down about life. Someone gave her a book about *emunah* to read, hoping it would help her feel encouraged. As she read the book, she was amazed to discover her own story in it. The story was told from the point of view of the woman who had prayed for a ride and got answered. "Little did I know that Hashem would use my own story to help me with a different problem years later!" she exclaimed.

It's at times like this that we can clearly hear Hashem saying, "See? I'm watching you. I'm with you every step of the way." We just have to train our eyes, like the photographer trains his, to see what's important, to see the world from the expert perspective of a Jew who knows Who runs the world. Eventually, it's no longer hard to see Hashem; it's hard *not* to see Him.

> ### MAKE IT REAL:
> *When was the last time something happened to you that seemed to be clear hashgachah pratis? Tell yourself that story and remember how you felt, knowing that Hashem had set the stage for your success.*

25
Today's Itinerary

Our job is to go where Hashem sends us, look around and ask, "What can I accomplish here?"

You head out to the store to do some Erev Shabbos errands for your mother. You think, *Friday-afternoon traffic! It's going to be bumper to bumper. I'm going to take the side streets. It'll end up taking less time*. The next thing you know, you see your friend standing on the side of the road staring miserably at a flat tire. You pull over and help him out.

Why did you just happen to leave for the store when you did? Why did you just happen to take the same road your friend had set out on just 10 minutes before you? You may have had your reasons, but the real reason, when you think about it, is obvious. You thought you were going out to buy groceries, but Hashem was sending you out to help your friend.

"A man's steps are from Hashem" (*Mishlei* 20:24). Every detour, every missed bus, every rescheduled appointment — even the steps that go as exactly planned and right on schedule — are laid out for us by Hashem for reasons we do not know. Sometimes, the reason is to give us a chance to earn a *zechus* that we will need further down the road. It's as if Hashem is giving us a chance to earn the money for an unexpected toll that's coming up in another 10, 50 or 100 miles.

Here is an incredible true story that shows us exactly how Hashem directs our steps for our benefit:

The Goldberg family's new baby was a cranky little guy. He cried sometimes for hours at a time, and the only thing that helped him fall asleep was a long car ride. One night, Mrs. Goldberg was having trouble settling the baby down for the night, and she asked her husband to take him for a ride.

The husband was happy to help. Besides, he had a deposit to make at the bank. He could drive to the ATM and get two things accomplished at one time. He strapped the frantic baby into the car seat, popped a pacifier in his mouth and set off to the bank. In moments, the baby had quieted down. But once he stopped in front of the ATM, the baby roused. He spit out his pacifier and began screaming again. Mr. Goldberg shut off the engine, got out of the car, opened the back door, picked up the pacifier, put it back in the baby's mouth and got back on the road. He drove for another half-hour, until the baby was fast asleep.

It was a great victory. He walked into the house proudly carrying the car seat with the peaceful baby snoozing inside. His wife gently transferred the baby into the crib and all was well — until Mr. Goldberg began to remove his jacket. He felt inside his pocket. Where was the money? Where was the cash he had been carrying all day? Two thousand dollars had disappeared. "Oh, no!" he thought. "It must have fallen out of my pocket at the ATM when I bent down to get the pacifier!"

He raced back to the bank and began checking the ground all around the ATM. He saw nothing, not a single dollar. "What would I expect?" Mr. Goldberg thought. "That right here in the middle of Brooklyn, $2,000 is going to sit on the ground and no one is going to take it?"

Suddenly, a Jewish man and his wife drove up. "Are you looking for something?" the man asked.

"Yes. I lost a lot of money here. I think it dropped out of my pocket."

The man pulled $2,000 out of his pocket and handed it to Mr. Goldberg.

"We came through here about an hour ago and saw

> *the money scattered all over the ground. We figured someone dropped it and would be coming back for it, so we gathered it all up and waited around. But when no one came, we ran to do a couple of quick errands and now we were just checking back again, and here you are!"*

The couple thought they were headed out to do some errands. However, their itinerary in *Shamayim* read: 9:37 p.m.: Arrive at bank. Choose whether or not to earn *sechar* of returning fellow Jew's lost money. The couple chose to do the mitzvah to which Hashem had led them. They knew they had driven up to the ATM just at that moment for just this reason. They took the time to gather up the scattered bills and wait around for the owner. When he didn't show up, they did what they needed to do and then took the time to come back again. At that point, Hashem rewarded them with the successful completion of the mitzvah they had taken upon themselves.

They knew there was a reason for them to have arrived on the scene when they did. But they didn't know how much they would need the *sechar* they were earning.

> *Two days after they returned Mr. Goldberg's money, the couple's daughter, who was expecting a baby soon, began having terrible stomach pains. Her doctor sent her to the hospital, where she was diagnosed with a very infected appendix. She needed emergency surgery. Baruch Hashem, both the mother and the baby came out of the life-threatening situation perfectly healthy. Of course the parents hoped and prayed for a good outcome, but they did so with greater optimism, because they had the zechus of that special mitzvah in their pocket, just as Hashem had planned.*

Sometimes, our immediate reaction when we're waylaid from the agenda we have planned is to be annoyed. *How am I ever going to get my homework done if I have to go look in on my grandmother? Why can't someone else babysit for my little sister for once?"* With only two days of Chol HaMoed, why do I have to waste one on a family trip? All my friends are going to Great Adventures!

When these feelings rise up inside us — when Hashem is taking us on a route we didn't plan — we have a tremendous chance to build our *emunah* by realizing that although we *thought* we were going to be doing one thing, Hashem *knew* we would be doing something else. For a good reason. For our benefit. For something good that we can get out of the situation. Our job is to go where Hashem sends us, look around and ask, "What can I accomplish here?" The answer is often right in front of our eyes.

> **MAKE IT REAL:**
> *The next time your plans get changed, especially when the change is not to your liking, say to yourself, "This is where I was meant to go today. Let's see why."*

26

There's Just One Goal

There's no Hashem and Us. There's only Hashem.

There are 613 mitzvos. There are 120 years of a person's life. One of the big questions people have asked themselves throughout history is, *What's it all for?* Certainly, each of us has a unique purpose in the world. Our mitzvos and our everyday actions are the way we fulfill our purpose. But all of our individual missions are really part of one grand mission: to recognize that Hashem created us (*Ramban, Parashas Bo*) and that He alone runs the world (*Daas Torah, Parashas Behar*).

Simple — yet very complicated. That's because while we're serving Hashem and thanking Him for everything He gives us, we're also doing our *hishtadlus* to succeed in life. We're putting our effort into learning how to learn, into building our intellectual skills, our *derech eretz*, our talents, our physical strength and our health. When you run three miles every morning, it's hard not to take credit for your incredible energy and endurance. After all, you worked hard to build it. When you are at the top of your class, it's hard not to take credit for the hours of study and focus you put into getting there.

So while we're here on earth trying to fulfill our mission of recognizing Hashem, we're busy with all the endeavors — good, positive endeavors — that bring recognition to our very own selves. How are we supposed to become accomplished people while at the same time living up to the one goal: recognizing that everything we accomplish comes from Hashem?

Hashem gave us one mitzvah that powerfully teaches us how to balance our *hishtadlus* with our belief in Hashem's control of everything. That mitzvah is *shemittah*. A farmer was once asked how he had the strength to let his land lie uncultivated for an entire year. How could he not be worried about his livelihood? Could you imagine your parents taking a year off from their jobs and just assuming that the money will come from somewhere else?

That's exactly what a farmer must do. This farmer was able to do it with a calm heart because he knew that even when he was planting, fertilizing, watering and tending his crops, they only grew because Hashem made it so. If Hashem was in charge of his success anyway, then there was no problem in his mind about leaving the land alone when Hashem commanded that he do so. Hashem would find another way to support him, just as He had supported him through his crops.

What farming is to a farmer, success in school is to a student. If we work hard, we tend to think we get good grades because we're so industrious and intelligent. Rav Ephraim Wachsman suggests that if a person starts to feel pride in his brilliance, he should realize that just opening the book to start learning takes more computations from our nervous system than all the human thinking that's gone on since the beginning of time. Our nervous system is so vastly complex, involving so many chemicals, molecules, enzymes, proteins and intricate, lightning-fast processes that our greatest intellectual feat is nothing by comparison.

The more we attribute our successes to Hashem, the more we are fulfilling our purpose of recognizing that we are His creations and that He runs the world. This opens our hearts to serving Hashem. We do His mitzvos with the sense that we are serving the King, the One on Whom everything depends. We're not doing Him a favor and hoping for a reward; we're recognizing that we're only in this world, and the world is only here, because of Hashem. There's no Hashem and Us. There's only Hashem.

Here is an example of someone who took this message

completely to heart: Rabbi Gershon Liebman, a French rabbi who led 80,000 Jews to become *baalei teshuvah,* had a group of students who compiled his lectures into a book. When it came out, they gave it to him to read. They were surprised to hear their very humble rebbi exclaim, "Wow, what beautiful *chiddushim!*" When they asked him why he had given his own book such a rave review, he replied quite simply: "Just because Hashem put a *chiddush* into my mind, does that mean I did anything?"

Rabbi Liebman could compliment the insights in the book because he didn't lay claim to them as his own. They were Hashem's insights, which He kindly allowed Rabbi Liebman to introduce into the world. Surely, Hashem chose the *shaliach* based on his ability to understand the Torah and express the insight, but another perhaps even more important qualification Rabbi Liebman had was his humility. He recognized that his brilliant mind would not exist without all the biology and chemistry with which Hashem formed and maintained it, as well as the *rebbeim* and environment that Hashem provided him so that he could learn Torah.

In *Parashas Shemos* (19:5), Hashem says *ki li kol ha'aretz* — "for the whole world is Mine." These are the words we must keep in mind when we put in our effort and arrive at success. They are also the words to remember when our efforts *don't* succeed. Because it really is simple: As long as we remember that it's all Hashem, we are fulfilling the purpose of our lives and our *avodas Hashem.*

MAKE IT REAL:

Raise your awareness of ki li kol ha'aretz by remembering to give Hashem credit whenever you feel pride for an achievement or receive a compliment from someone else.

27

There's No Harm in Asking

These tefillos are the real keys that unlock the berachah. Hashem created a world in which tefillah is hishtadlus.

You have a friend whose family is always short of money. He comes to you one day and says, "Good news! I found a job for the summer! The only thing is, I have no way to get there. I really need a bike. Do you think you could loan me $100 to buy one and I'll pay you back after I get paid from my job?"

Since he already owes you for several other loans you made to him, you're not feeling very positive about his request. You give an excuse and turn the conversation to another subject.

Two days later, he asks you again. "Sorry, I can't right now," you say.

"Well, when do you think you can?" he asks.

"I don't know. Probably I just won't be able to help you out. Sorry," you repeat.

He waits another week, and since you're his richest friend, he figures he'll try you again. You're beginning to get annoyed. When is enough enough? Why doesn't he take the hint?

What's in your friend's mind as he rallies what seems like bottomless chutzpah to keep after you about this loan? Simply this: "There's no harm in asking. If he says 'no,' then I'm not any worse off than I was before."

Most people have a sense of boundaries regarding how much

they can ask of other people and how often they can ask. No one wants to feel that he's being a pest or imposing on someone else. But there is one place to which we can always turn with absolutely no limitations; one Source of help that not only permits us to keep asking and asking, but *wants* us to do so. This is Hashem.

We never have to be embarrassed to tell Hashem our problems because he already knows us inside out. He knows about one person's hot temper, another person's anxiety, someone else's self-centeredness and another person's weak willpower. And with everything He knows about us, He still loves us more than anyone in the world could possibly love us. There's nothing He cannot do for us; He's never out of money or time. Nor is He ever out of patience.

In fact, our prayers are the operating system that Hashem installed in Creation to make things run. Three times a day — Shacharis, Minchah and Maariv — He calls on us to step into His "office" and tell Him what's on our mind. We can ask for the same things three times a day every day and not only does it not wear Him down, but rather, it pleases and delights Him. Every time we ask Hashem for something we need, it's as if we're saying, "Hashem, I believe in You. I believe that You are the real Source of anything and everything I need." If we imagine a *tefillah* as a thread that connects us to Hashem, we can see that each *tefillah* adds yet another thread until we are connected to Hashem by a thick, strong, unbreakable cord.

It's not just the areas mentioned in the *Shemoneh Esrei* that draw Hashem's attention. It's anything and everything: "They should ask Him...Who has in His hand the potential and the ability, for everything they need, because He will answer from the Heavens to everyone who calls out to Him sincerely," says the *Sefer HaChinuch* (431). Hashem isn't bored by our small problems nor is He annoyed by the problems we might have brought upon ourselves. He's not up there in *Shamayim* saying, "You want me to help you pass English when you haven't been grasping the material? It's your own fault!"

Asking is the key that opens Hashem's storehouse and brings His gifts into the world. We know there's no limit to what He *can* give, but what He *does* give depends on our prayers. We learn this from *Bereishis*. Even though plants and trees were created on the third day of creation, they didn't sprout and become visible above the soil until the sixth day, when Adam was created. Rashi explains that this is because the *berachah* of trees, grass, fruits and vegetables had to wait until there was someone to pray for it.

Many people think of *tefillah* as a means of asking Hashem for miraculous solutions to our problems. "When all else fails, pray!" In reality, however, everything happens only because we pray. We stay healthy because of *Refa'einu Hashem* and we have *parnassah* because of *Bareich Aleinu*. *Shema Koleinu* gives us the opportunity to ask for needs that aren't specifically mentioned in the *Shemoneh Esrei*.

These *tefillos* are the real keys that unlock the *berachah*. There's no dividing line between *tefillah* and *hishtadlus*. Hashem created a world in which *tefillah* is *hishtadlus*. In fact, it's the most powerful, effective *hishtadlus* we can do.

We have no idea what wonderful gifts Hashem holds in store for us. We can only find out by asking Him for what we want and need. Every time we pray with a sincere heart, truly connecting to Hashem like a child coming to his father for help, we are bringing ourselves a little closer to Him and making ourselves a little more worthy of the very things for which we are asking. When the One we ask is Hashem, there is truly "no harm in asking." In fact, it's exactly what He wants us to do.

MAKE IT REAL:

Choose something you really want from Hashem and ask for it during Shema Koleinu in Shemoneh Esrei. Ask as if you're speaking to a rich, powerful person who you think can do anything for you and only wants what is best for you.

28
My Most Reliable Friend

We can pray for Him to fulfill our need, but it's not our place to tell Him how to fulfill it.

A scenario: "I'm trying to get to Glatt Galaxy and the traffic is unbelievable," a girl tells her friend as she crawls along in Erev Shabbos traffic and talks on her hands-free cell phone. "It's closing in 20 minutes and I don't even know if I'll get there in time!"

"Yeah, traffic is pretty terrible on Friday," her friend commiserates.

"It'll be a disaster if I don't get there in time. My mother's challah didn't rise and I have to buy some. We're having a bunch of guests."

"Well, good luck," the friend says.

"Good luck? That's all you can say?"

"Well, I don't know how to make the traffic go faster, so yeah, good luck!"

In the realm of personal needs, getting through a traffic jam doesn't rank very high, and yet it's more than this friend can provide. What if, instead of asking her friend, the driver had addressed her troubles to Hashem: "Hashem, please get me to the store on time!"

There are people who consider that idea foolish, as if they're going to the president of the United States to purchase some postage stamps. Sure, the stamps come from the government, but a president doesn't bother himself with selling stamps.

There are other people, however, who would naturally turn to Hashem when the traffic gets snarled, when a big test is coming up (Please may I do well!), when they're setting out on a vacation (Please may it be a safe and enjoyable trip!), when they're going on an interview (Please may I make a good impression), when they're left taking care of their siblings (Please may they behave and stay safe!) and even when they're going out shopping (Please may I find what I'm looking for at a good price!).

This is more than *tefillah*. It is living with Hashem, feeling His presence throughout our day in every situation that comes our way. For people who develop this kind of relationship with Hashem, praying isn't something they do; it's who they are. This is exactly what David HaMelech means when he says, "*Va'ani tefillah* — and I am prayer" (*Tehillim* 109:4).

Living with Hashem means never being alone in your dilemmas and never being without a supporter for your goals. Even when you do something good that no one has noticed, you can tell Hashem, "I did this for You. I hope You like it!" In that way, you're never without recognition for your mitzvos and *chesed*.

Imagine you have a decision to make; should you take a job as a camp counselor for the summer, or should you take a job in your father's office? You just can't decide. There are many pros and cons on either side. Your friends all give you differing advice. So you turn to Hashem. "What should I do, Hashem? Which job would be better for me? Please help me decide."

Suddenly the fog of confusion lifts. Just by turning the matter over to Hashem, you feel more relaxed and focused. Perhaps you'll do some more thinking and suddenly feel clarity, or perhaps someone you trust will give you advice that sounds just right. Regardless of how your decision ultimately gets made, because you turned to Hashem for help, you'll feel that your decision is the right answer for your dilemma.

Part of relying on Hashem for all our needs is relying on His judgment and timing. We can pray for Him to fulfill our need, but it's not our place to tell Him how to fulfill it. Hashem has many ways to help us, and we may have no inkling of what they are. Just when it seems that all avenues of help are closed off, He can open up an avenue we never knew existed. This true story illustrates the point:

> A boy was learning in a post high-school yeshivah that was designed for talmidim who wanted to attend college or work in the afternoon. He was an excellent learner, but he was determined to work on a college degree as well. Much to his disappointment, he discovered that the schedule for his first semester of college courses — all of which were required — would not fit in with a morning learning seder. He went to the dean to ask for an accommodation, but the dean refused.
>
> The boy informed his rebbi at the yeshivah that he would not be able to learn there in the coming z'man. "I did the best I could but it didn't work out," he said.
>
> "Have you been praying to Hashem to work it out?" the rebbi asked.
>
> "No, but it doesn't matter now anyway. It's too late to change my schedule," he answered.
>
> "You never know what Hashem might choose to do," the rebbi told him. He took the rebbi's advice and asked Hashem, "Somehow, please make it so that I can learn first seder in yeshivah and still go to college."
>
> A few days later, the boy called the rebbi. "I'm coming!" he said. "You'll never guess what happened. The dean retired after serving the school for 40 years and the new dean who just came in let me reschedule my classes!"
>
> Living with Hashem means living in a world of encouragement, support and security. The more we turn to Him, the more we see how He turns the wheels of the universe to give us just what we need.

MAKE IT REAL:

When you think to yourself, "I hope that..." or "I need...," rephrase it. Turn it from a hope or desire in your mind to a tefillah on your lips and ask Hashem to fulfill your request.

29

Pray for the Power to Pray

When we're having trouble praying with focus and sincerity, He wants us to pray for the ability to pray.

A scenario: The parents left for a wedding in a city two hours away from home. They wouldn't be back until the wee hours of the morning. They left their 15-year-old daughter, Leah, in charge, with 13-year-old Yitzy as second in command. It was up to them to oversee dinner, baths and bedtime for the younger six children. Although Leah had babysat for her siblings often, this was a big job even for her.

"Leah, don't try to be a hero," her mother said. "If one of the kids gives you trouble or wakes up in the middle of the night, I'm sure you can handle it. But if everyone wakes up everyone else and it's getting chaotic, call Mrs. Kaufman next door. She knows you might be calling. Don't worry about waking her up. She's happy to help."

At midnight, the 3-year-old woke up crying. He roused the baby, whose screaming awakened the 5-year-old. The 5-year-old, not wishing to suffer alone, ran to her 7-year-old sister's bed and shook her until she, too, was wide awake.

Leah and Yitzy were running from room to room, soothing one child, holding another, getting drinks for another. Eventually, the entire household was up and *everyone was crying. That's when Leah's parents opened the door.*

"Leah! What's going on here?" her mother asked. "Why didn't you call for help?"

Surely, Leah's mother would see that her daughter was up against a lot of opposition in her effort to do the job she had been given. But the mother's compassion was dampened by the fact that Leah didn't ask for help when help was available. Why did she struggle alone, letting everything fall into chaos, when she could have had calm, competent Mrs. Kaufman by her side helping her put everything right? In a way, Leah had been neglectful.

When Hashem sends our *neshamah* down into this world to do its job, He knows there are going to be plenty of challenges. We all have that bright, pure spark of holiness inside us that wants to do the job it's been sent to do: Torah, mitzvos and *ma'asim tovim*. But the job isn't easy. Other people pull us in the wrong direction: "Who do you think you are? The Rebbe?" Our own desires pull us as well, causing us to justify going places, doing things, eating food or looking at sights that deep inside, we know are pulling us downward. Sometimes the *yetzer hara* comes disguised as humility: "That's for a big *tzaddik*, not for a normal person like me."

Perhaps we could handle one challenge at a time. But struggles are never that cooperative. More likely, many challenges will "wake up" in us at the same time, one arousing the other, making it seem almost impossible to win. In that case, we may tend to give up the fight.

Because Hashem knows what we're up against — and it's all part of His plan — He leaves us with the one phone number we need to call when the job becomes too difficult for us to handle alone. "Call on Me!" He tells us.

It is precisely when we feel disconnected from Him that He wants us to dial His number. When we're having trouble praying with focus and sincerity, He wants us to pray for the ability to pray. When we're feeling lax and uninspired, He wants us to pray for inspiration. When Torah learning can't seem to sink into our minds, He wants us to pray for our minds to open. He wants us to turn to Him for help in serving Him. Even though it's our job to overcome the challenges and tests, Hashem is willing to give us the power to pass the tests — but we have to ask.

We might think that when our spirituality seems to be at a lower level, this is the exact wrong time to ask Hashem for help. On what merit is He going to give a shot of inspiration to someone who can't even get himself up for *minyan* in the morning or someone who just can't resist the lure of a video she knows she shouldn't be watching?

Those kinds of thoughts are an example of the "false humility" we mentioned earlier. They are thoughts that derail our growth, and we know they are false because true humility is a powerful boost to spiritual growth. Hashem never sees us as too lowly to help. The proof of this is in the generation of *yetzias Mitzrayim*. They were at the 49th level of impurity — one level away from spiritual oblivion — when Hashem performed the most remarkable miracles in history for them.

"I am Hashem your G-d Who took you from the land of Egypt; open your mouth wide and I will fill it" (*Tehillim* 81:11). With these words, we learn that just as Hashem lifted us out of the impurity of Egypt and lifted us up all the way to *Kabbalas HaTorah*, He will take anyone who has sunk down and lift him up. The only condition: "open your mouth wide." Pray. Ask for help. The wider we open our mouths, the greater the opening we create for Hashem to fill — and He will fill it, with exactly the help we need to do what we are in this world to do (Rav Chaim Shmulevitz, *Sichos Mussar, Maamar 28*).

MAKE IT REAL:

When you're feeling uninspired, rather than allowing your heart to close up, open your heart and your mouth wide and ask Hashem for inspiration.

30

Just Because

He will never reject us as long as we turn to Him with a sincere heart.

A scenario: A mother scooped her 2-year-old son Dovi off the floor where he was flailing about screaming for another cookie. He was still kicking and screaming as she held him close to her and gave him a tight hug. She kissed his head, which was damp from all his exertion. He was a real 2-year-old, putting his whole heart and soul into showing his Mommy who was boss.

As she held him, he calmed down and snuggled into her shoulder. He was so cute, so smart and stubborn. She looked at his chubby tear-stained cheeks and gave him another kiss. "You know why I love you?" she said to him. "Just because you're my Dovi."

The wise mother of a toddler can take a step back from the noise and disruption he brings into her life and see a dear child struggling with the challenges of toddlerhood. She loves him all the same. She loves him even more when he seeks comfort from her — the very person he's bent on defying.

We can learn from this mother and child. When we struggle against the darker side of our human nature, when we kick and scream about the obligations that seem too heavy or the pleasures we must occasionally bypass, Hashem is not standing by waiting to punish us. He is watching us like this mother watches her child, knowing that we are struggling with the struggles of human-hood. He is filled with love for us anyway — just because we are who we are. We are creations in His image. Our souls are connected to Him. All He wants is to scoop us up and help us calm down, to give us a shoulder on which to find comfort.

That's why we are never too lowly to pray to Hashem. He will never view us with disdain. He will never reject us as long as we turn to Him with a sincere heart. Rav Moshe Feinstein is quoted as saying that Hashem's love for the worst sinner is greater than our love for the greatest *tzaddik*. In fact, Hashem will even help a thief who prays to Him for protection as he embarks on his crime (*Berachos* 63a). The only factor that makes him deserving is the faith he shows in Hashem when he turns to Him for help (*Pri Tzaddik, Eikev, Os* 19).

There is another, related reason why people sometimes don't pray for what they need. That is the fear that if they are answered, this will decrease their merits in *Shamayim*. They will have to "pay" for the help they receive, leaving less merit for future needs and for their life in the Next World. However, Chazal teach that anything Hashem does for a person through the normal channels of nature does not decrease his merits. Only a miracle might do so.

But even a miracle, when it's the result of our prayer for help, can be considered the normal course of nature because Hashem created the world to run on prayer (*Maharsha, Kiddushin* 29b). Just as it's no miracle that gas propels a car, it's no miracle that prayer produces results.

One other reason people hold back from praying for what they need is that they don't want to feel obligated to Hashem. This is perhaps the least sensible reason of all. How can anyone feel that he isn't obligated to Hashem for every single thing he has?

> *A scenario:* A guest shows up for Shabbos. He's given a spacious beautiful room with a luxurious bed, thick towels, a stack of reading material and a small fridge filled

with water and snacks for him to take as he pleases. The meals are over the top, plentiful and delicious. Because he lives far away, his hosts invite him to stay Motza'ei Shabbos as well, so he doesn't have to travel late into the night. In the morning, they make him a deluxe breakfast with eggs, bagels, lox, fruit and four kinds of cheese.

"Would you like some milk for your coffee?" the host asks him.

"Oh, no, I wouldn't want to bother you," he replies.

Imagine the host's reaction at these words. He might want to say, "Are you serious? After I put you up for two nights in a luxury suite, saw to your every need and served you a five-star hotel breakfast, you think milk for your coffee is a bother for me? What do you think all the rest of this was?"

Not only is the idea ludicrous, but it's insulting. The guest doesn't understand how deeply obligated he already is to his host.

In the same way, if we try to avoid "bothering" Hashem, we are ignoring the fact that everything we have is already coming from Him. We are already obligated to Him in every way possible, and whatever we need from Him now is just a drop in the bucket compared to what He has already done and continues to do for us at every moment.

The message in all of this is that if we ever hear our inner voice trying to talk us out of praying to Hashem for what we need, we should not accept what it is saying. We are not too far gone; we are not losing our merits; and it is impossible for us to owe more to Hashem than we already do. All He wants is to be the One Whose shoulder we seek, the One to Whom we turn, not because we've been good or because of our merits, but just because He loves us.

MAKE IT REAL:

If there are things you want Hashem to do for you but you have not asked, think about your reasons for not asking.

31

Who's It All For?

Hashem gives us everything, and then He gives us the privilege of using it to serve Him.

A scenario: *You really try to be a good daughter. You help your mother in the kitchen, keep your room spotless and bring home excellent grades. Parent-teacher night is pure nachas for your mother as your teachers sing your praises.*

That's why it just doesn't seem fair that your parents won't let you go to Eretz Yisrael for the summer with your cousin's family. After everything you've done for your parents, why can't they do this one thing for you? They have a million reasons, but they're all just excuses. The bottom line is, you deserve this trip.

This girl's thinking might seem pretty reasonable, except that it's based on one completely false premise: that the parents owe their daughter anything. They have given her everything, starting with her existence in the world. Without her mother's constant care, she would not have survived a day of infancy. Without her parents' hard work throughout the years, she'd have nothing to eat and nowhere to live. Without their encouragement and support, her intelligence and talents would have had no way to emerge.

All her helpfulness at home and hard work at school are not gifts to her parents; they're gifts to herself. Through these efforts, she learns and grows into a mature, responsible, capable person. Even though she does what her parents want her to do, they aren't indebted to her because they are the ones who make it all possible.

The mistake in this girl's thinking echoes the thoughts that might at times arise in our minds when we consider our service to Hashem. Look at all we do for Him! We shut off our phones and computers every Shabbos. We pass up the hundreds of great restaurants out there in the world and confine ourselves to the few that are kosher. We spend long days in yeshivah when most kids our age have afternoons to spend in whatever way they choose. We learn Torah, we give *tzedakah* and do *chesed*. We're literally working for Hashem 24/7.

So when we want something in return, it seems only right that we should get it. That's especially so when we take on something extra.

But if we think that way, we are like the girl in the opening story. We're forgetting that we're only able to serve Hashem 24/7 because He gives us what we need to do so. Try learning Torah without a pair of eyes and an intelligent mind. Try enjoying Shabbos without a *seudah* on the table and nice clothing to wear. Try giving *tzedakah* without money. Hashem gives us everything, and then He gives us the privilege of using it to serve Him. He lets us feel that we're earning our keep, when in fact, we could not begin to earn even one second of our existence.

Then, after we've served Him for our entire lifetime, He lets us keep every bit of the *sechar* for ourselves. It's as if an investor sets someone up in business and then, when the business starts earning a profit, instead of taking back his loan he says, "Never mind. You keep it."

Even with all this kindness from Hashem, we sometimes feel He's asking too much of us. We get tired and stale in our *avodas Hashem* and it starts to feel like a burden when in fact it is all for our own benefit. "What does Hashem want of us?" the Torah asks (*Devarim* 10:12), and it answers that He wants us to observe His mitzvos "for your own good." It's all for us, so that we can earn a reward.

> *A scenario: After 30 years on the job, the carpenter wants to retire. His boss, a contractor, doesn't want to lose this*

talented worker. He begs him to stay on the job, but the carpenter says he's tired of work and besides, his wife wants him to spend more time at home.

After some discussion, the boss makes an offer: "I have one more project I need done and I want you to do it. Can you just stay one more year until this project is done?"

The carpenter discusses it with his wife and they decide that he'll remain on the job until this last project — a large, beautiful house — is completed. But the carpenter's heart isn't in it. He cuts corners and tries to get it done quickly so that he can start his retirement. The one-year project is done in seven months. The tiles are laid in crooked lines and the corners of the walls don't quite meet in some spots. The carpenter feels a little guilty, but he didn't ask for this job. It's the boss's own fault for keeping him on when he wanted to quit.

At the end of the job, the carpenter goes to his boss and says, "O.K., it's done. That's it for me."

"There's just one more thing," says the boss as he hands a set of keys to the carpenter. "These are the keys to the house. It's yours to keep — a parting gift for you."

(Rabbi Dovid Hoffman, Torah Tavlin)

Had the carpenter known he was building his own house, there's no doubt that he would have built it in the best possible way. He thought he was working for his boss when in fact, he was working for himself.

Likewise, our *avodas Hashem* isn't really a service to Hashem; He doesn't need anything from us. In reality, we are building ourselves a "home." If we could keep that in mind as we perform Hashem's mitzvos, we would build something extraordinary — something that reflects the very best we have to offer.

MAKE IT REAL:

The next time you are about to do a mitzvah in a half-hearted way, think of the carpenter. You're building your own house!

32
Some Day We'll Find Out

When Mashiach comes, there will be no more mystery; His kindness will be clear for everyone to see.

A scenario: *In the summer after 10th grade, Menachem was a counselor at an overnight camp. He was to receive $400 as payment for the summer. It would arrive, said the head counselor, sometime in September.*

Then, a few weeks into the school year, Menachem heard the shocking news. The camp had gone bankrupt; no one would be getting paid. So much for the mountain bike Menachem had planned to buy with his pay. After awhile, he accepted what happened and moved on.

The big surprise came a week before Pesach. It was $400 from the camp director, with a short note saying, "Thank you for making our camp's final season something special. Sorry for the delay in payment. Chag Kasher v'Sameach." Menachem would have a mountain bike for Chol HaMoed!

The next day, Menachem was carrying a heavy carton of Pesach dishes into the kitchen. Without looking, he dropped it down onto the kitchen table, right on top of his sister's laptop. It was crushed. He would have to buy her a new one. There went the $400.

When things like this happen, we wonder. *If Hashem was going to take the money from me, why did He give it to me in the first place?* It almost seems cruel to put something in our hands and then swipe it away. In reality, though, Hashem did Menachem a great kindness by giving him the money to pay for the mistake he was going to make. Rather than struggling to pay off his debt to his sister, he could make good on it right away.

Wouldn't life be so much happier and easier if we could see Hashem's kindness even when the things that happen to us appear negative? This clarity is the essence of the happiness we will experience when *Mashiach* comes. We each long for *Mashiach* for various personal reasons — everyone will get along, no one will get sick, no one will be poor — but all of those problems come down to one thing, which is that in this world, Hashem's kindness is often hidden. When *Mashiach* comes, there will be no more mystery; His kindness will be clear for everyone to see.

For now, however, it takes a Jewish soul filled with *emunah* to see that when Hashem gives us money and then takes it back, He is actually giving us the money to pay our debts to Him. It's as if you owe $100 to your friend and he gives you the $100 with which to pay him back. You wouldn't complain about returning the $100; you'd marvel at your friend's generosity.

Hashem's account books are a mystery to us. We have no idea how our merits and our debts stack up against each other. Because of that, we sometimes see cruelty where there is infinite love and kindness. Only our emunah keeps us from becoming resentful and falling into the trap that this feeling sets for a person's heart, mind and *neshamah*.

Not only are we often blind to the good in the seemingly bad experiences, but also, we are blind to the full extent of the good that Hashem does for us constantly. We walk down the street and are not mugged by the robber who is standing on the corner looking for victims. We breathe in a lungful of flu virus, unaware that our immune system is fighting it off and keeping us in perfect good health. Just the fact that a person is born in America in the 21st century is a magnificent kindness: seldom in history has life been as secure and free for the Jewish people.

These constant, ongoing kindnesses and miracles are what we are thanking Hashem for three times a day when we bow down and say *Modim.* With the words *al nisecha she'b'chol yom imanu* we recognize "the miracles He performs for us each day."

And there's still more goodness in Hashem's goodness. Although we do recognize when something good happens to us, and we may even feel gratitude for Hashem for His kindness, we cannot begin to imagine just how much kindness He is sending into our lives.

For example, when you were born, your parents surely got many heart-felt "*mazal tovs.*" A new baby is such an open miracle that it fills parents' hearts with seemingly limitless joy. But your birth was just the beginning. You began to grow up and learn Torah, do mitzvos, do *chesed* and contribute to Klal Yisrael. Your parents' *zechus* mounted higher. When *iy"H* you get married and have children of your own, your parents will have a true empire of *zechus* as you continue in your *avodas Hashem* and train your children to go on that same path. In a few more generations into the future, the *zechus* will be beyond human calculation. But all of this and more, to the end of time, is contained in the kindness Hashem performed for your parents when you were born.

We only see the tip of the kindness Hashem does for us, the tiny part that is visible in this world at any given moment in time. Our job for now is to believe in the full extent of Hashem's goodness and thank Him for it, until the time when everything becomes clear.

MAKE IT REAL:

Think of one good thing that has happened to you and make a list of all the good that has come from it and will iy"H come from it in the future.

33
"I Can't Do It Without You!"

We're obligated to put in our best effort but we are fooling ourselves if we believe that it's our efforts that bring success.

There's a lot we need to get done every day. Since first grade at least, we've been hearing that if we want to be successful, we have to put in our best effort. Try hard. Be on top of the situation. Be prepared. Be persistent. This is all necessary and all true.

However, it's possible to do all that and get nowhere. Whether or not we actually get to our goal depends on one thing alone: Hashem's will. If He helps us, our efforts will pay off. But if for some reason He does not want our plan to be fulfilled, no matter what we do and how hard we try, it won't happen.

"If Hashem doesn't help the builders, their work is all for nothing," David HaMelech tells us (*Tehillim* 127:1). He is warning us never to forget Who makes things happen. We're obligated to put in our best effort — our *hishtadlus* — but we are fooling ourselves if we believe that it's our efforts that bring success.

There is a story of a successful but very aggressive businessman who *davened* with great *kavannah*. His Rav commented to him that it seemed strange for someone who feels so close to Hashem to be so ruthless in business. The man replied, "Rabbi, you misunderstand. I can handle my business on my own. I'm just praying to Hashem that He stays out of my way and doesn't ruin things for me."

It isn't difficult to see the foolishness of this man's attitude. We might even feel like laughing at it. But very often, we fall into the same kind of thinking. For example, a person might plan a vacation down to the last detail. She might save up her money for a year, book the flight, reserve the hotel and organize a perfect itinerary. She expects that this will ensure her of a perfect vacation. But all of that preparation will amount to zero if she breaks her leg two days before she's scheduled to leave. Her vacation will only happen if Hashem wants it to happen. Therefore, her most important preparation is to *daven* for her plans to succeed.

We see this concept in action in every area of life:

- Two children come down with strep throat. They are prescribed the same medicine. It works for one child, but not for the other. Without Hashem's help, medicine doesn't heal.

- A pizza shop opens up in a busy shopping area, but it never catches on. Another person buys it, but it still doesn't get enough business. Then a third person buys it, changes nothing at all and yet, does a booming business. Without Hashem's help, the customers won't come.

- Two students graduate college with a perfect average, hoping to become doctors. One goes on to become a successful heart surgeon; the other can't get into medical school and can't seem to settle on a different option. Without Hashem's help, his academic achievement doesn't bring him success.

- A couple plans to attend a wedding. But after calling every possible babysitter in town and finding no one to stay with the children, they are forced to accept the fact that they won't be going. Their plans won't come through if Hashem doesn't allow it.

- A grandfather books a flight to Eretz Yisrael to attend his grandson's *bris*. The airport workers go on strike and all flights are canceled. Even with money to buy the ticket and time off from work to travel, he won't be at the *bris* without Hashem's help.

Knowing that success is in Hashem's hands alone can help us face frustrating situations with a calm feeling inside us. When people struggle uselessly to accomplish something, we say they're "banging their head against the wall." We can visualize the image of someone feeling the painful thump, thump, thump of banging his head, never stopping to realize that this simply cannot succeed in knocking down the wall. The person is not only foolish, but self-destructive as well.

It's the same for us when we inflict on ourselves the pain of trying to force an outcome that simply is not going to be. If, instead, we stop for a moment and realize that "it's not *bashert*" — it's not what Hashem wants for us right now, because it isn't what is good for us right now — then we can take a deep breath, change our mind-set and look for the next reasonable option.

Whether we are blessed with success or we experience a setback, our job is the same. That is to acknowledge that what has happened is all Hashem's doing. *Davening* for success in our endeavors is our most important *hishtadlus*. When things don't go our way, we can remember that our setback was meant for our good, and we can look for the message that is surely there for us within the disappointment. When things do go our way, we must know Who to thank, for without Hashem's help, we'd have achieved nothing at all.

MAKE IT REAL:

Think about a goal you are working toward. Put Hashem in the picture by davening for Him to grant you success and thanking him for the things that you've already achieved.

34

Keep It Coming

We have a daily opportunity to recognize Hashem for what He gives us. Shemoneh Esrei's berachos are each like a tap that opens the flow of a specific life necessity.

A scenario: *Yehudah always had a great voice and perfect pitch. He was the one everyone counted on to lead the zemiros and davening in yeshivah. When his friends started to get married, he was the one they wanted to sing during the chuppah. To Yehudah, his vocal talent was as natural as breathing.*

Then, the day of his close friend's wedding arrived. He was looking forward to the occasion and planning to introduce a new melody for "Mi Adir" in his friend's honor. The tickle in his throat that he felt when he woke up got him a little worried, but he assumed it would clear up. Instead, it became a severe case of laryngitis. Yehudah had no voice. How could it be that Yehudah the Singer couldn't sing?

When we wake up every morning and say *Modeh Ani*, we are reminding ourselves of the lesson Yehudah learned that day. Nothing is guaranteed. In *Modeh Ani* we thank Hashem for putting our *neshamos* back into our bodies for another day. We went to bed alive, but that doesn't mean we will wake up alive. *Modeh Ani* reminds us that nothing happens all by itself; Hashem keeps the blessings coming.

Losing one of these blessings that we take for granted is one sure — although painful — way of remembering what Hashem has given us. Yehudah never considered his voice a continuous blessing from Hashem. He thought of it as part of the "standard equipment" with which he was sent into the world. Just like some cars come with a keyless ignition and some do not, Yehudah figured that some people come with musical talent and some do not. However, neither the ignition nor his voice could operate correctly for one split second without Hashem's constant maintenance.

> ***A scenario:*** *Leah davened fervently every day that she would be admitted to Beis Tov Me'od, the best high school in town. One day, she received the good news — an acceptance letter! She thanked Hashem with all her heart for giving her what she wanted. The school year started and she found her place in her new class. She made friends, got good grades and truly felt that she had it made.*

Under Leah's circumstances, she would most likely not be *davening* any more for success in school. She wouldn't think that *continuing* to be in Beis Tov Me'od, *continuing* to get good grades and *continuing* to be liked and admired by her friends were ever in doubt. She was doing everything she could to be a good student; why should she not rest comfortably with her success? What she doesn't realize is that moment by moment, day by day, Hashem is giving her all the elements of a wonderful school experience — and it could vanish just as easily as it materialized.

> *A new student enters Beis Tov Me'od. She's from a well-known family and carries herself like a celebrity. For some reason, the other students, and even some of the teachers, are mesmerized by her charms. Leah isn't inclined to follow the crowd; the girl senses Leah's reserved attitude toward her and doesn't like it. Soon, Leah is on the outside of her class's social circle. She begins davening that Hashem somehow resolve her situation and ease her pain.*

There is a saying that, "You don't know what you have until it's gone." For a Jew, however, gratitude for what we have doesn't have to come with the pain of loss. It can come with the joy of thankfulness. We have the *Birchos HaShachar* to remind us every day that Hashem keeps us going in every way, every day.

If we pay attention as we say these *berachos*, we will not take anything for granted — not our intelligence, nor our ability to stand and balance, nor our physical energy, nor our eyesight, nor our clothing, nor dry land on which we set our feet — nothing! When we say the *berachah* "*she'asah li kal tzarchi*" — Who gives me all my needs — we recognize the fact that we are like someone who stands empty-handed in front of his father every morning and receives just what he needs for that day. We have nothing until Hashem gives it to us.

Not only do we have a daily opportunity to recognize Hashem for what He gives us, but we have three opportunities a day to ask Him to continue providing for us and to request that which we feel we still need. *Shemoneh Esrei's berachos* are each like a tap that opens the flow of a specific life necessity. Our health, *parnassah*, intelligence, spiritual growth and *yeshuos* for the entire Jewish people come to us on a daily basis because we ask Hashem to keep it all coming.

When we start out on a new venture — like Leah starting her high-school career — we are attuned to the idea that we need *siyata d'Shmaya*. We don't know how things will turn out, so we *daven*. But once we are comfortable with what we have, it's even more important, and yet more difficult, to recognize that it is all an answer to our *tefillos*. With that grateful recognition, we keep all those taps open, and keep the *berachah* flowing into our lives.

MAKE IT REAL:

Take one of the Birchos HaShachar or Birchos Shemoneh Esrei that's particularly relevant to you and think of a way — an image or a thought — to connect to it more powerfully when you recite it.

Keep It Coming ❖

35

Follow the Leader

The more we recognize Hashem's kindness, the happier we will be.

A scenario: Reuven's group of first graders followed along behind him on the camp's trip to the zoo. He had mapped out their entire route, making sure there would be places to rest, places to refill water bottles, a spot to sit and have lunch, and most importantly, enough time on the schedule to linger in the "big cats" section where the lions, tigers and leopards roamed in natural-looking surroundings.

Some of the kids were perfectly content to follow Reuven. They knew their counselor would give them a great time and they felt secure with him. Others had their own ideas. "We want to rest now!" cried out four cranky children, plopping down on a bench on a hot, tree-less path. "No, not here," Reuven said. "It's too sunny. In a few minutes we'll stop." The boys sulked as Reuven guided them by the hand back to the group.

In our lives, we are sometimes like the balky first graders. In His infinite kindness, Hashem has laid out a perfect plan for us, but we don't exactly see it that way. We have our own ideas about where we want to go and what we want to do, and in our mind, kindness would mean letting us have our way. However, we are very ill equipped to resist Hashem's plan, because like these first graders, we lack the foresight, insight or the intelligence to know what is truly good for us from a higher perspective.

We only know what we see in front of our eyes and what we feel at this moment. When the little children are hot, they want to stop right where they are. They don't have the capacity to judge whether or not this is the best place to stop. They don't know that two minutes further up the path is a shady area with plenty of benches and a water fountain. Neither do they understand that if they were to sit down in the hot sun for five minutes, they'd be too drained to enjoy the rest of the trip.

Because they are not getting what they want, they see the counselor as being mean; he is not letting them rest. But in reality he is being very kind. He is willing to force the issue, even if he has to listen to them complaining and spend time arguing with them, all for their sake.

There is so much going on in *Shamayim* that we can't see or understand, and yet these are the gears that make the wheels of our lives go around. When we resist the path Hashem is laying out for us, we're doing so without any idea of what is really happening. We're trying to tinker with the machinery when we don't even know how it works. As a result, we end up angry, sulky and exhausted.

The best way to live a calm, happy life is to be like the happy campers in the story who trusted their counselor and followed him willingly. To be able to do that, there's one fact we have to believe: that Hashem is always kind. The more we recognize Hashem's kindness, the happier we will be.

David HaMelech reminds us of Hashem's kindness time and time again throughout *Sefer Tehillim*. Even when he was running for his life, suffering from the rebellion of his own son Avshalom and fighting brutal wars with Israel's enemies, he still saw a world that was built on Hashem's *chesed* (*Tehillim* 89:3). He endured some of the most difficult challenges a person could experience, but through it all he recognized that "the kindness of Hashem fills the earth" (33:5). There is not one square inch that is empty of Hashem's *chesed*. The battlefield, the hospital room, the jail cell are all included in this description.

The only way to believe with our hearts what we don't always see with our eyes is to recognize that we are not equipped to understand Hashem's ways. Because Hashem gave us intelligence, it's hard for us to accept that we are so limited. It seems that if we just thought hard enough and learned enough Torah, we would be able to understand. After all, the human brain has an incredible capacity!

Nevertheless, we are limited. We accept our limitations in terms of our physical strength: a person can become very strong, but there is no way, not matter how strong he might become, that he could lift up a high-rise office building with his bare hands.

The ability to understand Hashem's ways and see the kindness in our difficulties is that high-rise building we can never lift, no matter what. There's certainly much merit in looking for the good and finding as much of it as we are able. But the bottom line is that we, like little children, can achieve our greatest happiness by simply trusting that Hashem acts toward us only out of kindness, and that wherever he leads us is the place that is best for us to go.

MAKE IT REAL:

"Let's see where Hashem is taking me." These are powerful words you can use to help you build trust in Hashem the next time you face a disappointment or challenge.

36

What's Yours Is Yours

You will get what you're supposed to have.

A scenario: A man arrives at a yeshivah dinner where he is one of five honorees. Arriving a few minutes late, he goes to sit at the dais where the other honorees are seated, and finds that there are no more empty seats. One of the school's big donors has apparently helped himself to a seat of honor.

A girl comes home from seminary and begins applying for jobs. She is called for an interview and everything goes perfectly. The owner of the business says he just has to discuss her salary with the bookkeeper and then he can make her an offer. After a week of waiting and unreturned calls, the girl finds out that the bookkeeper's daughter has taken the job.

A boy saves up his dollars and cents in a shoe box in his room. His goal is to buy a tent so he can go on a camping trip with his friend's family. One day, a worker spends some time in his room installing a new window. The next day, when the boy goes to put his allowance into his shoe box, he finds it empty.

All of these people have been deprived of something that seemed rightfully to belong to them. All of them were victimized in some way, although perhaps, in some cases, not intentionally. No one would blame them for feeling that what happened was unfair. But from the viewpoint of *emunah*, they would understand that they were not deprived at all; they will always get exactly what Hashem plans for them to get.

"They will call you by the name you're supposed to be called; they will have you sit where you're supposed to sit; you will get what you're supposed to have, and no one can touch that which belongs to someone else, even by the width of a hair." This is the strong statement the Gemara makes (*Yoma* 38a) to inform us that there is no basis for shouting, whispering or even thinking, "That's not fair!" If the honoree was supposed to have a seat at the dais, it would have been empty and awaiting his arrival. Likewise, the girl would have the job and the boy would have his money.

People who trust in Hashem are not troubled by the ups and downs of honor and money. They don't feel threatened when competition comes along. They do what they're supposed to do and enjoy the certainty that they will get what they're supposed to get. In fact, Hashem will make sure that they get it: "The blessings will come to you and catch up to you" (*Devarim* 28:2).

> *Rabbi Yaakov Yagen used to learn all night long with the great Kabbalist, Rabbi Sharabi. They would then daven Shacharis, learn some more and then at 11 a.m., Rabbi Yagen would open his soap and perfume shop in Machaneh Yehudah. Since most of the shops opened earlier, Rabbi Yagen's wife suggested that perhaps he was losing business by opening so late. However, Rabbi Sharabi advised him that Hashem could send him parnassah any time of the day.*
>
> *At one point, someone noticed that people lined up in front of Rabbi Yagen's shop at 10:30 in the morning, waiting for him to open. The man decided to open a larger, more elegant store selling exactly the same items,*

right next door to Rabbi Yagen's shop. He believed that if he opened earlier, all the people standing in line would become his customers.

However, not one customer deserted Rabbi Yagen's waiting line. The competitor wanted to know why, so he sent out a worker to ask them. "He says thank you when we buy from him and gives us blessings," they explained. To them, that was worth the wait.

Rabbi Yagen wasn't bothered by the man's head-to-head competition because he knew very well that he would get every *shekel* Hashem had designated for him. But what if Rabbi Yagen had lost these customers? What if his income diminished noticeably after the new store opened?

That's when *emunah* becomes a bigger challenge, because he would not only have to have faith that the money could come to him from some other source, but also, he would have to accept that perhaps the money wasn't designated for him in the first place. Perhaps this loss of business would simply bring his income down to the amount set for him on Rosh Hashanah. He would be losing money that he was never meant to have. In either situation, the competitor hasn't done anything to Rabbi Yagen; he can't, because "you will get what you're supposed to have."

Repeating this phrase to ourselves when we want to scream, "That's not fair!" can go far in deflating anger and jealousy. Our anger won't change anything, and our jealousy is misdirected at another person who is also getting what he's supposed to get. Living our lives with this perspective makes us into siblings, friends and, eventually, parents and spouses whom others will honor and love.

MAKE IT REAL:

Has there ever been a time when you lost out on something you felt you deserved? Think about it now in light of the idea that you cannot lose something you're meant to have.

37

The 120-Year Lease

Humility doesn't mean not thinking well of yourself; it means knowing that what you have comes from Hashem.

A scenario: Rivky is going to a wedding of a wealthy friend from seminary. She's embarrassed by her own bargain-basement wardrobe and decides to upgrade her look by borrowing from a few friends. One friend loans her a custom-made dress. Another loans her a diamond necklace and a sapphire ring. She has her make-up and hair done by professionals. When she looks in the mirror, she feels like a queen.

But imagine how foolish Rivky would be if she began to look down on the other guests at the wedding because of their inferior clothing and their lack of fine jewelry. Can a person be haughty over items she's borrowed, and a face that's been painted on? She might enjoy the moment and relish it for her own fun and satisfaction, but there's no basis for her to feel superior because of her borrowed finery. It's not hers.

On a deeper level, however, her real face, hair, clothing, intelligence and talents are borrowed as well. Everything a person has is a gift from Hashem, on loan for his lifetime. Hashem gives us what we need to serve Him and fulfill our purpose in the world. If good looks will help us on our mission, then He will give us good looks. If wealth will help us, He will give us wealth. If intelligence will be needed, then He will give us that as well. The lease on these gifts runs out at the end of our lives, when they are no longer of use to us.

If we use our gifts well, for the mission Hashem has given us, then He may bestow more on us. He might see that we are making good on His investment in us and find it worthwhile to invest more. On the other hand, if we waste or misuse what He gives us, we may soon find it dwindling away.

No matter what our attributes are or to what degree we are blessed with them, we never have ownership of them and therefore, we can't take credit for them. Hashem's purpose is never that His gifts to us should become the basis of arrogance. This trait is the polar opposite of humility, which is the key to every good *middah,* as the *Tomer Devorah* (Chapter 2) explains. He calls humility the "crown jewel and glory of a Jew." It is also the key to being loved by others, because Hashem gives a special *chein* to humble people (*Mishlei* 3:34).

There are many other great rewards for a person who is humble: Hashem accepts his prayers and forgives his wrongdoing; he receives Torah knowledge and becomes wise; he is welcomed in Hashem's presence (*Shelah HaKadosh*) and Chazal add that those who are humble will be chosen as escorts of *Mashiach.*

Clearly, such great rewards would not be designated for an easy task. True humility takes a sharp focus on the thoughts that go on inside our minds. From the time a child is small, he hears "great job," "what a smart boy," "you're so talented," "you're so strong," "what a good helper." In addition, a girl is likely to often hear how pretty she looks. These compliments are meant to build a child's self-esteem so that he'll feel confident, valued and worthy of love.

With this as our basic training, we've got a long way to go before we can add the mature perspective to these compliments, reminding ourselves that we should not feel great; we should feel grateful. When a student does well on a test and his rebbi says, "You really knew your stuff," the student's natural reaction is to hold his head up a little higher. Instead, he can take that moment to thank Hashem for giving him the intelligence to absorb the material. "*Baruch Hashem,* I was able to understand it and remember it."

Every personal asset and every achievement is an opportunity to thank Hashem for loaning us so much wonderful equipment for our journey through life. When we get dressed up in our Shabbos clothes, check ourselves in the mirror and like what we see, we can change that moment of potential *ga'avah* (arrogance) into a moment of gratitude: "Thank You, Hashem, for giving me a nice smile and nice clothes."

Humility doesn't mean not thinking well of yourself; it means knowing that what you have comes from Hashem. We have to recognize our gifts — otherwise we would have no reason for gratitude. But once we recognize what we have, we have to remember Who owns it.

David HaMelech was the king of Israel. He commanded a powerful army and possessed great wisdom and tremendous wealth. If anyone might have been convinced of his own mightiness, it would have been him. Yet he recognized that everything he had was drawn directly from Hashem, just as a baby receives all his nourishment from his mother (*Tehillim* 131:2). This warrior and king viewed himself in a totally dependent, cared-for state, being held and nurtured and carried along by Hashem.

Humility is the "crown jewel of a Jew," even a Jew who actually wears a crown. It's a trait that a person has to work to cultivate, but the work is well worth the effort, because from humility, every other positive trait will inevitably grow.

MAKE IT REAL:

Take a small piece of paper and write down on it three traits or talents you value in yourself. Put it somewhere where you will see it every day, and take a minute to read each item and thank Hashem for it. (Taping it into the Modim page of your siddur can help give you extra kavannah for that berachah.)

38
Let Hashem Do the Math

There are no mistakes; if there's something we are meant to accomplish and we use our time and abilities wisely, we will have what we need to accomplish it.

Hard times had hit the city and the yeshivah was struggling to stay afloat. But the Alter of Novardok didn't let that stand in the way of admitting the many new talmidim who wanted to learn in his yeshivah. What could be better than teaching Torah to so many fine bachurim?

As happy as the Alter was with the big influx of students, the yeshivah's financial committee was in a panic. "Where are we going to put all these bachurim? How are we going to provide for them? We're stretched too thin already and our supporters are all hurting. There has to be a limit!"

But the Alter told the committee members that they had it all backward. If the yeshivah would bring in as many students as possible, Hashem would make sure they would be supported.

In this world, everyone is an accountant. Can I afford this? Can I afford that? For some things, that kind of calculation makes sense and is the responsible way to be. But when it comes to doing Hashem's will, our mathematical formulas don't produce an accurate answer. Hashem has His own formula that will fill in any gaps created by our sincere performance of His mitzvos.

What does that mean to us? It doesn't mean we can go out and buy ourselves a designer watch or take an expensive vacation with expectation that Hashem will refill our bank account. If we're seeking luxuries, then Hashem's promise of *parnassah* is not at all guaranteed.

But what if someone decides, as many do in the secular world, that he has to "save up" to get married? In other words, he won't start dating until he has a certain sum in the bank that makes him feel secure that he can support a wife. This is backward math. Hashem has told us that we should marry. That's our job, and Hashem will make sure we have what we need to do it. "*Berachah* comes into a home only on account of the wife," says the Gemara (*Bava Metzia* 59a). Of course a person has to be responsible and have some type of plan as to how he will be able to support a wife. He just doesn't need to have it "saved up" in advance.

> A family that wasn't poor, but didn't have a lot of extra money, had two children in shidduchim at the same time. "Maybe this isn't wise," the father said. "What if they get married close together? How will we do it?"
>
> The mother wasn't worried. "When Hashem finds both of them their bashert, He will help us with our finances as well."
>
> The son was married first. Since he married a girl from another country, the expense of bringing the whole family to the wedding, on top of the gifts for the bride and other wedding expenses, added up to a huge bill. The parents figured out a way to borrow the money and made a beautiful, memorable wedding.
>
> A few months later, the daughter became engaged. They had borrowed every penny they could for the first wedding and had no idea what they would do now. They took some money from a gemach to get a start on the preparations, but it wasn't nearly enough.

> *One day, as the mother davened, desperation took over. She looked up to Hashem and said, "O.K., what do You want us to do? We're at the end of our rope! Please help us!"*
>
> *That very afternoon, a neighbor, who was also a great baal tzedakah, called the bride's father. "Listen, I'm sure it's not easy for you to make two weddings so close together. I'm going to raise $10,000 for you."*

There are thousands upon thousands of stories like this. When people say, "Hashem, I'm doing Your will and I need Your help," help comes. Of course we have to do our *hishtadlus* in life, but that only applies to obtaining the necessities. Beyond that, Hashem makes sure we have whatever we need to do the jobs He sent us into the world to do.

If we don't have the money for our goal — for instance, someone wants to be a big *baal tzedakah* but can barely pay his own bills — then that means that Hashem hasn't put him in the world to be a *baal tzedakah*. That's not the role Hashem wrote for him in his life. There are no mistakes; if there's something we are meant to accomplish and we use our time and abilities wisely, we will have what we need to accomplish it.

Thinking this way takes away the worry that many people feel when they make choices in their lives. Things might not add up on paper, but if we're doing the job Hashem has given us, the numbers will add up in *Shamayim*. Just leave the math to Hashem.

MAKE IT REAL:

When you think about your future plans, stop and think before you decide that something truly important in life is too expensive. Is this the kind of calculation you should leave to Hashem?

39

You Can Choose to Be Happy

The keys to happiness are not "out there"; they're inside us.

If you want to feel rested, you sleep. If you want to feel full, you eat. If you want to feel energized, you exercise. But what do you do if you want to feel happy? That's the big question that people have been trying to answer for thousands of years.

The answers we usually come up with exist somewhere in the future. "If I get into a good high school, I'll be so happy!" "If I can go on a great trip for Chol HaMoed, I'll be happy." "If I had more friends, I'd be happy." "If my family was rich, I'd be happy."

But the key to happiness doesn't start with "if." It isn't somewhere out there in the future, dependent on us meeting certain goals or enjoying certain experiences or achieving a certain status. The truth is that every one of us has what we need to be happy right now. Thinking about what we're missing, rather than what we have, locks us out of that happy state of mind.

"How can a living person complain?" asks *Yirmiyah* (*Eichah* 3:39). Rashi explains what the *navi* means (*Kiddushin* 80b): How can people complain about their lives after all the *chesed* Hashem does for them? Isn't it enough that He gives them life?

If we felt grateful just to be alive, our whole viewpoint would change. Imagine that you and some friends go on a hike and you get lost in the woods. You wander in circles until you're all exhausted. You're hungry, it's getting dark and it's starting to rain. You finally realize that you've got no choice but to find some sheltered spot and spend the night. Fearing a visit by wild animals, no one can sleep. In the morning, you all set out again. By now you're cold, wet and starving. At long last, you stumble upon a campsite set up around a pond. The campers welcome you, let you dry yourselves by the fire and give you some fruit and cereal to eat.

Do you complain that it's not bagels and lox? Do you feel slighted that they didn't have fresh clothes for you to change into or a soft bed for you to rest on? Not at all. You greet them as if they were a long-lost relative, because you feel as if you've experienced *techiyas hameisim*. You're alive and that's all that matters.

As long as Hashem gives us life, we have the power to choose whether to be happy or to complain. Reb Zusha of Anipoli, the brother of the Noam Elimelech, was renowned for his unshakeable *simchas hachaim*, and it certainly did not arise from all the belongings and privileges he enjoyed, for he lived in abject poverty.

> *A few of the followers of the Maggid of Mezeritch asked their Rebbe a question. How is it possible to bless Hashem for the bad as well as the good, as the Talmud instructs? The Maggid told them to seek their answer from his student, Reb Zusha. They traveled to Anipoli and there they found Reb Zusha poring over a Gemara, his face shining with peace and happiness. He was dressed in ragged, faded clothing and his dire poverty was plain to see. When the visitors asked Reb Zusha their question, he seemed confused. "I'm surprised that my Rebbe, the Maggid, sent you to me for your answer. You should speak to someone who has suffered. I've never suffered a day in my life!"*

The Maggid's followers got their answer. When a person's happiness is based on being able to live in this world and serve Hashem, then no matter what happens to him, he feels fulfilled. If something difficult occurs, he knows that it's an opportunity to rise to the challenge. If something pleasing occurs, he is filled with thanks to Hashem for His gifts.

We hear many stories of seemingly normal, everyday individuals who experience a loss or an illness and still bless Hashem and feel His loving care through it all. These people aren't dancing for joy like a guest at a wedding or screaming with delight like a person on a roller-coaster ride, but they are happy, truly happy in a way that lasts. Happiness isn't the opposite of pain or work or challenge. In fact, it is often the result of summoning up our courage and rising to these tests.

The keys to happiness are not "out there"; they're inside us. We can take those keys in our hand any time we want by appreciating the gift of being alive — and the endless list of wonderful gifts that come along with another day of life.

> ## MAKE IT REAL:
> *Look around you right now. Take a moment to really focus and find pleasure in something in your surroundings. Are you with a good friend? Eating a lunch you like? Is the room you're in keeping you warm on a cold day or cool on a hot day? For this moment, choose happiness!*

40

A Menu for the Whole World

He has taken care of all our needs up until now, and despite our worries, He will continue to do so.

Sit in your backyard or a park on a summer day. Watch the action. You'll see squirrels running up and down the trees. You'll see birds hopping around in the grass pecking at some invisible delicacy. You'll see rabbits nibbling at the clover. If there happens to be a pond, you might see fish, ducks and geese all finding their lunch in the water. You'll see bees sticking their noses into the flowers and legions of ants marching along on the ground.

Who feeds all these mouths?

Each one of these billions of creatures has its meal set out for it every day, exactly to its taste. Hashem feeds everything from the ant to the elephant. Each animal is born with the knowledge of what food is healthy for it to eat, and each makes its home where that food is available. Hashem's bounty is truly astounding.

A zoo once did a study of its expenses and discovered that it costs $5,000 a month — that's $60,000 a year — to feed and take care of just one elephant at the zoo. But the 550,000 elephants roaming the plains of Africa and Asia have no zookeeper to tend to their needs. Hashem does it all.

And if Hashem does all of this for every creature crawling, swimming, flying and hopping upon His earth, then certainly, He does it for His very own children, the Jewish people. All He asks of us is that, unlike all the other creatures, we recognize the Hand that feeds us.

> ***A scenario:*** *A mother spends an hour preparing dinner and everyone sits down, gobbles up the food and walks away without a word of thanks. "What's the point of cooking for them?" she thinks. "They'd be just as happy with a frozen dinner or takeout." The family doesn't acknowledge what they've gotten, or who has given it to them.*
>
> *But imagine another scenario. A mother hears her son say to his friend, "My mother makes the best potato kugel. She's a great cook! That's why I never like to go to friends for Shabbos." This mother feels that her family relies on her for their food and they appreciate what she does for them. That motivates her to do even more to care for them. Takeout just won't do.*

Likewise, the more we rely on Hashem, the more He comes through for us to take care of all of our needs. That's what is meant by the words we say in *Bircas HaMazon,* "*Baruch hagever asher yivtach baShem, v'hayah Hashem mivtacho —* Blessed is the man who trusts in Hashem, and Hashem will be his security" (*Yirmiyah* 17:7).

Sometimes it's difficult to fully trust in Hashem when we're worried about the future. What if what we're hoping for doesn't happen? What if our problem doesn't work out? That's when we have to stop and think about how we've gotten to where we are today. So far, whatever our difficulties have been, they have worked out — because Hashem has worked them out for us. For Him, it's easy. He has everything in the world at His disposal. There's nothing we need that Hashem can't give us. He has taken care of all our needs up until now, and despite our worries, He will continue to do so.

In some ways, the billions of creatures Hashem feeds each day have an advantage over us. They never spend one second of their lives wondering if the bug or leaf or worm they find so delicious will be there for them the next time they're hungry. But a human being can do infinitely better than that. We can use the minds Hashem has given us to appreciate His care and His bounty *and* to work on ourselves to build complete trust in Him.

"Hashem is your shadow at your right hand," *Tehillim* (121:5) assures us. Like a shadow, He moves in accordance with our moves. The more we turn to Hashem for help, the more He turns toward us to help us. The whole world is literally bursting with Hashem's bounty, and He wants to provide us with our share.

> **MAKE IT REAL:**
> *Do as the opening paragraph suggested and watch nature at work. Notice how every single creature has its sustenance and its home.*

41

Enough Is Enough

Satisfaction is a state of mind that we have to work to achieve.

A scenario: *Finally, Leah was remodeling her bedroom. She was 16 and still surrounded by the little-girl colors and designs her mother had chosen for her when she was 6. Her parents allowed her to choose a new carpet and furniture. They had the room painted according to her specifications.*

Now that everything was so new, the old-fashioned ceiling fixture began bothering Leah. She wanted something bigger and brighter. She also realized that her closet door was completely wrong. It needed to be replaced! And with the new sleek look of her room, she certainly couldn't have books stacked on her desk. She needed a bookcase — exactly the kind her friend just bought. Sadly, though, her parents had declared the project finished. She would have to live with these eyesores.

Instead of looking around at her new room and thinking, *Wow! Beautiful!* Leah looks around and sees all the imperfections that mar the perfect look. She sees flaws she never noticed before. Things bother her that, before, were just part of the background. Even though her room has been completely renovated according to her taste, she doesn't feel satisfied and content. She's craving more. This is what Chazal mean when they teach, "A person who has 100 wants 200 and a person who has 200 wants 400 (*Koheles Rabbah*: 1:32).

Always wanting more is obviously no way to become a happy person, and yet it is very much a part of human nature. You go on a family vacation and become upset when your parents won't take you to the attraction you really wanted to see. You go out to a new ice-cream shop and feel a little cheated because the chocolate isn't as chocolaty as it is in the old ice-cream shop. You have a day off from school — great! — but why does it have to be raining?

There is a saying that states: "Don't let the perfect become the enemy of the good." If we're busy searching out the flaws and becoming irritated over them, then instead of feeling happy and content with what we *do* have, we feel irritated about what we *don't* have. The only way to inject that happiness into our hearts and our brains is to learn how to recognize that we do not need anything more than we have. If right now, you are alive and well, housed and fed, loved and cared for, you've got it all.

"Be whole with Hashem your G-d," the Torah tells us (*Devarim* 18:13). The word used in this verse is *tamim,* which means whole or complete. We are under Hashem's perfect care.

What more do we need at the moment? If we do have some further needs, we can trust Hashem to fulfill them for us at the right time in the right way. For now, He is obviously telling us that it is something we must do without. Maybe He's holding back so that we can learn to be more patient, or so that we can learn to appreciate what we already have. Maybe what we want isn't really good for us in the long run. Whatever the reason, we can be absolutely certain that there is nothing missing from our lives. Hashem doesn't forget.

When a person can say, "I've got everything I need," he can enjoy the life he has right now. He's not holding off on happiness until he gets the next thing, and as we have seen in the example above, the next thing will not bring happiness either. It will only lead to a desire for the next thing after that.

People are always looking for new, different, bigger and

better. That's why there are 144 flavors of potato chips. Sadly, more doesn't make us content. The only way to feel satisfied is to take what you have in your hand and appreciate it. You can appreciate something new about your same old stuff every day. You can enjoy wearing your comfortable shoes every time you put them on. You can enjoy your pillow every time you lay your tired head on it.

A scenario: David's Zeidy gave him a fire truck for his fifth birthday. It ran by remote control and made every kind of siren noise a fire truck could possibly make. David waited impatiently as his Zeidy put in the battery and showed him how to use it. The little boy was completely thrilled with his gift. He had been begging his parents for a remote control toy for months.

About 10 minutes after David started running his fire truck around the house, his aunt came over and presented him with another present. This one was a scooter. David dropped his remote control on the floor and ran out to the sidewalk in front of his house to try it out. Zeidy nearly tripped over the fire truck, which was sitting idle on the kitchen floor. Soon, David had left the scooter on the porch and run back into the house. "What else am I getting for my birthday?" he asked.

People grow into adulthood and still think like this 5-year-old child, never arriving at the state of *tamim* — whole and complete. Satisfaction is a state of mind that we have to work to achieve, by holding onto our gifts rather than dropping them and stretching our hands out to grab what's next.

MAKE IT REAL:

Take one day and declare a moratorium (a temporary period of delay) on thinking about wish-list items. If you find yourself thinking about something you want to buy or some place you want to go, tell yourself, "I have enough." How does this exercise change your day?

42

You Can't Lose

Doing for Hashem is the best way to do for ourselves.

A shadchan called Mr. Birnbaum with a suggestion for his daughter. The young man sounded like exactly the type of boy his daughter wanted for a husband, and so, he agreed to allow her to meet him. But when he told his daughter about the boy, she was against it 100 percent. The boy had the same name as her father, and this, she believed, was absolutely not a situation she wanted.

"I'm sorry. I didn't realize you felt strongly about this. But I already said yes to the shadchan," Mr. Birnbaum told his daughter. "If we back out, it will be very hurtful to the boy and his family."

"Well, I don't want to hurt anyone," said the girl. "And I don't want to put you in an uncomfortable position, so I will go out with him just this once."

Later that day, a different shadchan called with a different suggestion. Normally, the shadchan would have been told that the girl was not available at the moment. However, since both father and daughter were sure that the first boy was not going to be "the one," the father accepted a date for his daughter with the second boy. "She won't be available until later in the week," he explained.

Meanwhile, the girl went out with the first boy, and it

so happened that the family of the second boy saw her out on the date. They were infuriated and immediately canceled their son's date. The girl was devastated. She had lost an excellent shidduch just because she wanted to be considerate of the first boy's feelings. But her parents weren't worried. "Hashem saw what you did. You will only gain from the mitzvah."

Several months went by and the girl was not meeting anyone who even came close to the one who had turned her down. Then one day, a shadchan called with a suggestion of a boy who had just started shidduchim. This boy's number-one priority was to find someone sensitive and caring. "I know just the girl," the shadchan replied, and told the boy the "same name" story. Indeed, she did sound like just the girl he was looking for. Today, they are happily married.

We are often faced with decisions — some that don't seem so very significant and others that could be life changing. Many times, the decision is between what we feel we need to do for ourselves and what we know Hashem would want us to do. As the story above shows us, doing for Hashem is the best way to do for ourselves.

Has it ever happened that someone asks you for a favor and you feel that you really don't have time for it? Then perhaps you pull yourself together and do it anyway and — miracle of miracles — you find that you actually do have the time. How does that happen? It happens because Hashem makes sure that you do not lose out by doing a *chesed*. Have you ever felt that you were far too tired to study for a Gemara test; you really just needed to go to bed early? Then you pull yourself together and say, "I'll just study for as long as I can," and — miracle of miracles — you're still sitting there an hour later, pushing yourself to get through to the end of the material. How does that happen? Hashem sees that you're pushing yourself to the limit to learn Torah, and He makes sure you don't run short of energy.

Our idea of the world is limited by what we see. There are 24 hours in the day, $1,000 in the bank, a certain amount of strength in our bodies and in our minds — and that's it. However, when we look at the world that way, we are missing the real picture; Hashem doesn't just make things and set them down in the world like little statues. He is constantly re-energizing everything. We're not using anything up; we are simply sipping from a straw, pulling down more and more of Hashem's endless supply of energy into our lives. When we call on further supplies so that we can do what He wants us to do in the world, He sends us what we need.

This is the secret of *gedolim* who seem to be awake 24 hours a day, learning Torah and handling community affairs and advising those in need of guidance from early morning until late into the night. They don't count on their own strength and energy; they attach themselves to the Source.

We should never fear that we will lose by doing the right thing — by being generous, by working on a good cause, by being honest or friendly or forgiving. "*Shomer mitzvah lo yoda davar ra* — When a person does a mitzvah, no harm will come from it" (*Koheles* 8:5). The *passuk* is telling us that even if it seems that we've lost out, we just need to wait. We will see how much we have gained.

> ### MAKE IT REAL:
> *The next time you think to yourself that you don't have the time or resources to do a mitzvah, push yourself to do it anyway. Then think about it afterward: Were your worries borne out or did it work out fine?*

43

You Don't Scare Me

There is never a need to do or say something that runs against our conscience in order to please someone.

> The Lubavitcher Rebbe was arrested by the Russian secret police. As they brought him to prison, one of the officers held a gun to him. The Rebbe wouldn't be intimidated. "That toy can only frighten someone who has one world and many gods. I have One G-d and two worlds. Put it away. You don't scare me."

With those few short, sharp words, the Lubavitcher Rebbe gave us everything we need to know in order to live a life in which we are not afraid of anyone. First of all, there is only one G-d; that means that anything that happens comes from Him. There are no other powers controlling our fate. No one can harm us in any way unless it is decreed from heaven. People are just Hashem's agents.

Secondly, the ultimate object of most of our fears, which is death, holds only so much power when we understand that our existence will continue in the Next World. For the Russian Communist who did not believe in G-d and heaven, the gun represented the end of everything. For the Lubavitcher Rebbe, it represented a transition from This World to the Next, and that transition would only take place if it was what Hashem in His infinite kindness and wisdom wanted.

In our lives, *Baruch Hashem,* the harm we fear from other people is not at all likely to be a fear of being shot. We live in a mostly safe and civilized country that does a good job of protecting its citizens. But that doesn't mean we don't fear people. We very much do. We fear embarrassing ourselves in front of those we hold in high esteem. We fear being looked down upon by those who hold themselves in high esteem. We fear being criticized, rejected from a school or job, displeasing someone who is important to us and so forth. Other people seem to hold our happiness and prosperity in their hands.

> ***A scenario:*** *There were two spots left for counselors at Camp Chamsin and Reuven wanted one. He regretted telling his friends about the openings, because now three of them were applying as well. "Let the best man win!" one of them joked. But Reuven wasn't laughing. When he went for his interview, he was a nervous wreck. He felt as if everything he told the camp director sounded childish. He could barely look him in the eye. For sure someone else was going to get the job. Why did his friends have to do this to him? Why did the camp director have to look at him as if he had two heads?*

All of Reuven's tension could have been dispelled with one clear thought. *If I'm meant to get the job, I'll get it. It doesn't matter who else applies. It doesn't matter if the director is an ogre or the nicest guy ever. I just have to daven that I get the job and let Hashem take over the worrying.*

This is what the *Chovos HaLevavos* (*Shaar HaBitachon*) means when he tells us that no one can give a person anything or take anything away unless Hashem decrees it. When we worry about what other people will do to us, we are turning our attention in the wrong direction. We are trying to appease someone or defend ourselves against someone who really has no power over us. As the Lubavitcher Rebbe pointed out in the opening story, Hashem is the only One in charge.

Keeping this essential fact in mind at all times prevents us from lowering ourselves by flattering people we think have power. While it's certainly right to be respectful and friendly to others, there is never a need to do or say something that runs against our conscience in order to please someone.

For instance, we might be tempted to listen to *lashon hara* or even add to it if we are looking for approval from the "in-group" at school. We might be tempted to dress in a style we really don't find appropriate in order to impress someone. We might be afraid to admit that we admire someone our friends don't admire; for instance, a teacher, principal or a fellow student. We might voice opinions we don't really hold or keep quiet when we should speak up.

Rabbi Ephraim Wachsman tells the story of Rav Yitzchak Elchanan Spektor when he took his first job as a rabbi. A poor man in town requested that the Rav call the town's richest man to *beis din* to settle a dispute. The Rav summoned the rich man twice and each time got back an arrogant refusal. The third time, the Rav threatened the man with *cherem* if he did not appear. And appear he did — accompanied by the other community leaders, carrying a tray of cake and shnapps to make a *l'chaim* in celebration. The Rav had passed the test! "We wanted to see if you were afraid of us, or afraid of Hashem," they told him.

This is a test we all have to work toward passing. It can be difficult to see past the illusion of power in people's positions, personalities or attitudes toward us. But if we remember that it truly is only an illusion, we can live with courage and integrity. Rather than being afraid of dozens of people and hundreds of possible problems, we can direct our fear in one direction, toward Hashem, Who has it all under control.

> ## MAKE IT REAL:
> *Think about one person who you find a little or perhaps very intimidating. Ask yourself what you are actually afraid of, and add a tefillah to your day that asks Hashem for help or protection in that area.*

44

Go to the Chief

Miracles come to people who can recognize them.

If you were robbed and your father was the chief of police, who would you turn to for help? Would you stop an officer on the beat and tell him your tale, or would you go straight to your father, the chief? Naturally, if you have access to the person at the top, that is the person to whom you go. The officer might listen politely and forget all about you a few minutes later; after all, he's pretty sure they'll never be able to find the robber. But your father will launch a full-scale investigation and turn over every last stone until he either finds the culprit or runs out of options. He'll set a dozen officers on the case if he sees fit to do so.

Going to the one in power makes sense, especially when he loves you and cares about what happens to you. Yet in our lives, we tend to put all our trust in the "officer on the beat," even though we have a direct line to the Chief.

The other side of fearing people and believing they can hurt us is trusting them and believing they can help us. Neither is true. If we turn to Hashem for help, He can enlist the services of anyone and everyone in the world to bring us what we need. He is the Chief, and everyone else is an officer. "Hold yourself back from human beings...for of what importance is he?" says *Yeshayah* (2:24). For whatever we want and need, we can trust in Hashem. Rabbi Eliyahu Falk tells a story that shows just how directly we are able to ask and receive.

An orphaned boy was learning in a yeshivah in Eretz Yisrael. He wanted to get married, but he didn't have the money to begin shidduchim. His friends told him not to worry — find a wife and they would raise the money. That's what the boy did. He met a girl, also an orphan, and they planned to get married. However, between the two of them there was no money for a wedding or apartment.

The friends began trying to raise money, but it was much harder than they expected. After awhile the orphan said, "Enough! I'm going straight to Hashem. I don't want help from anyone else."

He went to the Kosel and spoke to Hashem about his situation. Then he said the entire Sefer Tehillim. When he finished, he turned to Hashem to await his answer, but nothing came. He didn't despair; he simply began again. A little while later, a man tapped him on the shoulder and asked him if there was some way he could help him. The boy turned him down, explaining, "I'm talking to Hashem. He will help me."

He looked up again and spoke to Hashem. "Please help me," he said, "We're orphans and we want to get married and I do not want to leave here until I see your salvation."

When he finished saying those words, he felt another tap on his shoulder. It was the same man. "Your salvation is here!" he declared. "I will take care of everything you need!"

The man explained that he had just arrived in Eretz Yisrael after winning a tax case in court. Had he lost, he'd have been financially ruined. He had promised Hashem that if he won, he would find an orphaned boy and girl who were engaged and he would not only pay for the wedding, but support them as well. "When I heard you talking to Hashem, I knew you were the person I was looking for," said the man.

When we don't see any way out of our difficulties, that is often when Hashem flips the switch and turns our darkness into light. "Hashem's salvation can arrive in an instant" (*Selichos*

R' Tzadok, Sifsei Raninus). All the time that the *chassan* was praying for a way to finance his marriage, all the time that his friends were trying to raise money for him, a court case was going on across the ocean — a case that could not appear to be less relevant to this young man's troubles. Nevertheless, this was the salvation Hashem had planned. It had been in progress for years before this boy even entered *shidduchim,* and it was the complete answer to the *chassan's* prayers.

Why was this young man given such a direct answer to his prayers? It is no doubt because he so clearly recognized that his help would come from Hashem. "The person who trusts in Hashem is blessed," says *Yirmiyah* (17:17). The more we place ourselves and our fate in Hashem's hands, the more openly He cares for us. On the other hand, the more we believe in the forces of nature, the power of other people and our own talents, the more Hashem leaves us under their control. Our lives become limited by what is possible in this world. Miracles come to people who can recognize them.

There are many people in our lives who help us, and we must certainly appreciate them for what they do. However, we have to think just a bit deeper and realize that they are all the "officers" that Hashem has assigned to our case. If we turn to Him, He will make sure we receive all the help we need.

> ## MAKE IT REAL:
> *Make a practice of speaking to Hashem once a day, telling Him what you need as if you're speaking to your parent or someone else who loves you.*

45

"It Just So Happened..."

Hashem's involvement in our lives is everywhere we look. This knowledge keeps us feeling secure.

A rebbi was getting ready to deliver a shiur one morning when he realized that he had forgotten to bring along a sefer he needed. He knew the shiur would not be complete without quoting a certain thought from that sefer. As much as he didn't want to bother his wife at home to find the material, he felt he had no choice.

When he called her cell phone to tell her what he needed, she was already out of the house. She had just finished an errand and was on the way to the park with the children. However, she wasn't too far from home, so she offered to stop there first and get her husband the information.

Ten minutes later she called back. Her husband noticed that her voice was unusually tense. "Is everything all right?" he asked her.

"Well, no, not really. When I walked into the house, there was a burglar standing in the dining room! He was wearing black gloves and a black hat, and he was holding a bag with our sterling silver menorah in it. When he saw me he dropped the bag and ran out the side door, so Baruch Hashem, no one was hurt and nothing was taken."

Did it just so happen that the rebbi forgot his *sefer* that day? That his wife was close enough to home to run back and find the information for him? That she entered the house just as the burglar was committing his crime, and not five minutes later when he would have already run off with the menorah and perhaps more valuables as well?

For a Jew, there's no such thing as "it just so happened." Hashem's eyes are on us always (*Iyov* 34:21), not only to see where we are going, but to guide us along the path He has chosen for us. Often we don't realize how events coordinate and line up just perfectly to bring about a certain result, but if we look back, we can practically trace Hashem's footsteps:

> *A girl who had distanced herself from her religious family in Eretz Yisrael enrolled in a college in a southern American state, where she thought she'd be far away from anything Jewish. A well-known kiruv lecturer traveled to the college to make a speech, but because the wrong date had been printed on the posters for the event, only four people showed up. The speaker looked at all the empty seats and decided that he would give it his all anyway: Who could know why Hashem brought him to this place? One of the four people in the audience was the Israeli girl.*
>
> *The speaker noticed that she was weeping throughout much of his speech, and so, when he finished, he approached her and asked if there was something he could do for her. She poured out her story, telling him, "You were speaking directly to me!" Soon, she was back in Eretz Yisrael with her family, living a religious life.*

The lecturer had flown many miles to speak at this college. It was in the middle of nowhere, far from any major Jewish community. The Israeli girl had attended the speech only because the organizer was her friend and had begged her to come help fill up the hall. Had the poster provided the correct date, the organizer would not have felt compelled to draft people to attend. This girl, who was on the run from her Jewish roots, would have probably stayed far away. In addition to all this, the speaker overlooked his disappointment. Rather than canceling the event and heading home, he gave the powerful speech he had planned to deliver.

None of this "just so happened" to occur. Hashem did not take His eyes off the ball for one second. Instead, He wove a thousand strands together to create the potential for a profound and lasting *teshuvah* for this girl. Her parents, her family and the family she will one day raise are all part of the plan.

Whether we see miraculous turnarounds as in the above story, or just-in-the-nick-of-time salvations as in the story of the burglary, or something as simple as coming face-to-face with someone just when we need to speak to him, Hashem's involvement in our lives is everywhere we look. This knowledge keeps us feeling secure. Everything in life is under control, planned out to the last detail.

Hashem has written the script and we are here to play our part. We may have no idea what the next scene will bring, but we do know that the script is perfectly written. All the loose ends will be tied up, all the mysteries solved, all the good guys rewarded and all the villains defeated. It cannot be any other way, because it is all from Hashem.

> ## MAKE IT REAL:
> *Think about the events of the past few days or weeks. Are there any "unbelievable coincidences" you've experienced? Try to trace how Hashem brought the situation about; who had to do what, who had to be where, what the timing had to be, in order for the situation to have worked out as it did.*

46

Don't Ruin the Cake

When a person longs to be what he simply cannot be or have what he can never have, he robs himself of the focus and energy he needs to reach the potential he does have.

Sugar is the taste we crave when we eat a piece of cake. No one smacks his lips and says, "Mmmmm, baking soda!" or "Yum! Flour!" But try to bake a cake without all those other ingredients. The flour, baking soda, eggs, oil and a pinch of salt are essential, even if they don't take center stage as does the sugar.

If those other ingredients could complain, they probably would. No one notices them. They just do their job quietly in the background. Why can't they all be sugar?

We know that a recipe that's all sugar would never work. But do we realize that a world in which everyone is brilliant, everyone is rich, everyone is powerful, everyone is attractive and everyone has a turn at center stage would also never work? Often, we don't see why we should take a backseat to others in some areas of our lives. We look at what they have and long to have it too.

Sometimes we are even being idealistic with these thoughts: *I wish I had her energy and outgoing personality so I would be able to do all the chesed she does.* Or, *I wish I had his sharp mind and focus so I could learn like he does.* These are noble goals, but we are mistaken if we believe that we are supposed to have someone else's trait or asset in order to achieve what someone else achieves. The *chesed* Hashem wants from us is based on *our* energy and personality. The learning He wants from us is based on *our* mind and focus.

It's difficult to be content being the flour instead of the sugar. But it's clear that the flour is necessary; without it, there is no cake. Likewise, Hashem created a world in perfect balance, in which each of us has a role to play that cannot be duplicated by someone else. He rewards us for the effort we exert to successfully fulfill our role. The person who seems to be living a charmed life, scoring 100 on every test, winning every award, attracting scores of friends and so forth, may be achieving less, relative to his or her purpose in the world, than someone who seems to lag and struggle.

> *Yaakov's parents were religious, but his father didn't have much time to learn. They kept the mitzvos, but didn't seem very exact about particular halachos. Yaakov felt inferior to the boys in his seventh-grade class whose fathers were learning full-time or working as rebbeim and rabbanim. It seemed that everything in yeshivah came naturally to them, whereas to Yaakov, yeshivah and home were two very different places. "It's not fair," he told himself. "How am I ever supposed to be a talmid chacham when Hashem put me in this family?"*
>
> *Yaakov struggled to grow. He stopped reading the fantasy novels that stocked his bedroom bookshelf and began spending his spare time in the beis medrash. He made sure to daven Minchah and Maariv when he was home, rather than coasting along on his family's more relaxed schedule. By the time he reached high school, he was operating on a whole new level — a full-fledged ben Torah.*
>
> *But what was the impact of his more secular, American upbringing? Ultimately, he became a popular rebbi in Yerushalayim at a yeshivah that catered to American boys who needed a little extra inspiration. He understood them. He knew their challenges. He knew how to reach them, and most of all, he knew what their potential was.*

Looking back, Yaakov understood that he had been born exactly where he was supposed to be born.

Yaakov couldn't become someone he wasn't. No matter how hard he tried, he could not make himself into a Rosh Yeshivah's son. He did not grow up in that pure, spiritually charged atmosphere. But his longing for *kedushah* in his life led him to do the best he could with what he had. Hashem needed a *talmid chacham* who could relate to boys who had grown up with secular influences in their lives. He needed someone who had the sense of humor and tolerance to connect to these boys. Hashem placed Yaakov in the precise family that would prepare him for the job he was here to do.

When Moshe came upon the burning bush, Hashem told him, "The place where you are standing is sacred ground." The place where each of us is standing is sacred ground; it's the place where Hashem has put us, for the purposes we are in this world to fulfill (*Chofetz Chaim Al HaTorah, Shemos 3:5*).

When a person longs to be what he simply cannot be or have what he can never have, he robs himself of the focus and energy he needs to reach the potential he does have. He might give up trying, saying to himself, *If I'm not smart, why am I even studying?* Or, he might plunge himself into a rut of resentment and jealousy, thinking, *Of course she was chosen. Her parents are gazillionaires.* Both of these lines of thought take us away from finding out what we can achieve from the "sacred ground" on which Hashem has placed us. No ingredient is inherently less valuable in Hashem's recipe for creation. Whether we're the sugar, the flour or the quarter teaspoon of salt, the cake will not come out right without us.

> **MAKE IT REAL:**
> *Do you have an "if only..." in your life? Write down some benefits you could potentially discover, now or later in life, from the situation you believe holds you back.*

47

What's My Part?

Our expectations are the measuring stick with which we decide whether or not we will be happy.

A scenario: Shmuelly's little sister Aliza was throwing a fit. It was the most ridiculous thing he had ever heard. Her fourth-grade class was making a Purim play and she got the role of Haman. She was so outraged that a person would have thought she had gotten the role of Haman's horse.

"I won't do it! It's not fair! Why can't I be Queen Esther? Why can't I at least be one of Queen Esther's maids?" she ranted.

Shmuelly, the oldest in the family, slipped into a fatherly role. "Aliza, you got a big part! Your teacher must think you'll be very good at playing Haman. You can make it really fun," he consoled her. "People always like the funny parts best. You'll see, you'll be the one to get all the applause."

"I don't care!" Aliza replied. "It's not the part I want."

The little girl's tantrum surely seems childish in our eyes. No doubt there was a whole class of fourth graders who were hoping to be Queen Esther, but there were plenty of other roles to play with plenty of potential for an enjoyable experience. What plummeted Aliza's spirits was not the role she *did* get, but the one she *didn't* get. Her expectations were disappointed and because of that, she refused to be happy.

As childish as her behavior was, it demonstrates a way of looking at life that can persist long after childhood. Our expectations are the measuring stick with which we decide whether or not we will be happy. In truth, however, we always get the role that Hashem knows is right for us, and we can find happiness by playing it as well as we can.

People are often thrust into roles they didn't plan to play. For instance, an older sibling in a family might be called upon to run the household because of an emergency in which both parents must be away from home. All of a sudden, her day is consumed with getting the little kids dressed and off to school, getting them bathed and ready for bed, serving dinner and helping with homework.

She might feel resentful. *Why can't I just come home and do my homework and have a normal night? Why do I have to do all this?* she might ask herself as she breaks up the 15th squabble of the evening.

There is only one answer to her question: this is the role Hashem has given her to play. If she accepts her role and makes up her mind to play it as well as possible, she can do so much good. She can keep her younger siblings happy and safe, and take a burden off of her parents. Meanwhile, she will discover her own capabilities: the patience, strength and sensitivity to do the job.

The difference between a star-quality performance and a lackluster one comes from her willingness to see the situation that she is in right now as it is "supposed to be." If she wants to hold onto the idea that a high-school girl is "supposed to be" free to focus on her homework and to socialize with her friends, then she will resent her role and play it poorly. If she thinks instead, *This is what is needed right now and I'm the one Hashem chose to do it*, then she will put her best effort into playing her role.

The "supposed to be" mentality can make many of life's situations difficult when instead, they could provide a stage upon which we can stretch ourselves beyond our present capabilities. Let's look at some examples: a single girl who feels, "I should be married by now"; a yeshivah student who feels, "I should be able to get into this *beis medrash*"; a young couple that feels, "We should own a house."

In all of these scenarios, there is much to be accomplished in the present situation. The girl can use her unexpected single years to grow in *middos* and *emunah,* and to acquire *parnassah* skills; the yeshivah student can find his success in the *beis midrash* that accepts him; the couple can concentrate on making their home a *bayis ne'eman,* even if it is only a two-bedroom apartment.

We can be sure that whatever situation we are in at the present moment is the part Hashem has given us in the play, at least for now. If we can step into the role without the nagging "should be" injecting resentment into our minds, then we will play the role with all our energy and heart. We can find our stardom by giving it our all, no matter what we are called upon to do.

> ## MAKE IT REAL:
> *The next time you find yourself in a situation that is not to your liking, imagine that you are playing a role in a play. Then give it your best.*

48

Never Say Never

We can set our sights high in life; we can take on goals that might seem beyond us, knowing that we're not in it alone.

Imagine a beggar praying every day to be a millionaire; a boy who is the shortest one in his class praying to grow tall; a girl who is shy praying to be the most popular girl in class. In all of these instances, the outcome the person is praying for seems very unlikely. In the natural course of events, people's fortunes, appearances and personalities don't change so drastically.

That, however, is only the natural course of events. For Hashem, none of these requests is the least bit difficult to fulfill. Hashem wants us to trust that He can do anything, and therefore we can and should ask Him for anything. Furthermore, we should pray with confidence that Hashem will give us what we want, rather than with the attitude of, "It can't hurt to ask." The only issue is whether what we want is good for us. It is never too late to pray for help and there is no order too large for Hashem to fill.

This is important to remember and believe when we deal with difficult situations. If we lose hope and stop praying to Hashem, we are cutting off our only possible source of rescue. This would be as if we saw that someone was injured badly and instead of calling Hatzolah, we would say, "What's the point of getting an ambulance? He's not going to make it anyway." Of course we would call for help, even if the person's condition seemed hopeless. We would do so because we know that Hashem can always help.

> In 2012, a 2-year-old girl fell into her family's swimming pool at their home in Long Island, New York. When the little girl was pulled out, her face was blue and she had no pulse. It seemed that she was gone. The father immediately began doing CPR and while he did, the mother cried out to Hashem to save her daughter. At that very moment, she made a serious commitment to improve her Torah observance. Miraculously, the girl's pulse came back. Hatzolah was called and the girl was taken to the hospital.
>
> No one knew what her condition would be, because she had been underwater for a little over three minutes. Being without oxygen for that long a period of time would normally cause brain damage. However, to the amazement of the top doctors who took care of the girl, there was no damage at all. The chief doctor called the girl "a walking miracle."

This mother looked at her child, whose face was blue and whose heart had stopped beating, and did not give up on her. Instead of despairing or being overwhelmed with fear, she went directly to Hashem. She looked for a *zechus* that would turn the situation around. In her eyes, all was not lost. And she was right! Her little girl's heart began to beat again, and miraculously, whatever damage might have been done while she wasn't breathing had left no lasting mark.

It didn't make sense, but it happened. This is why the Gemara advises us that "Even if a sharp sword rests upon a person's neck, he should not withhold himself from prayer" (*Berachos* 10a). There are many stories from the Holocaust of people who were headed for certain death, when out of the blue, through some completely unexpected means, they were saved. Even in that most hopeless of situations, people continued to hope and people continued to experience miracles.

But this message is not just for terrible accidents and times of great danger. It is a message for us, for every day. We can set our sights high in life; we can take on goals that might seem beyond us, knowing that we're not in it alone. We can place our trust in Hashem and ask Him to help us do more than we think we can do. We should never say "never" to ourselves, but rather we should turn to Hashem and ask for what we need, even if it seems out of reach.

One way to help the process along is to do as the mother in the story above did, and try to create a *zechus* for ourselves. We can do this by taking on a mitzvah that we have been perhaps avoiding, or by setting a higher standard for ourselves with a mitzvah we already do. When we bring ourselves to a new spiritual level, we can change the way in which Hashem interacts with us. The challenge we needed at our lower level might not be needed any more.

This doesn't mean that we can make deals with Hashem: "I'll do this for You and You do that for me…" It simply means that we should never stop asking for Hashem's help, and never stop believing that He can help us, no matter how unlikely it seems.

MAKE IT REAL:

Are there areas in your life which seem to be hopeless to you? Make it a point to revive your hope and daven for improvement.

49
Until We Are Awakened

We can judge where we stand on the ladder of emunah by recognizing what kind of reactions we have to challenges.

Did you ever have a long, detailed, very realistic bad dream? You're trying to run away from some terrible danger but your feet won't move! Or you're trying to scream for help but nothing comes out of your mouth! Then, as you're tossing and turning, your eyes flash open. You sit up straight in bed, wide awake, but your heart is still pounding. Slowly you look around and see that you're safe in your own room. The terror was an illusion. With tremendous happiness, you realize, *None of that was real. Everything is good.*

It's interesting to notice that when you have a bad dream, your body reacts just as if the situation were real. Your heart pounds. You might begin sweating. You might try to call out. Your hands and feet might start moving as if you are fighting off an attack or running away. But sometimes, a person actually thinks, right there in the middle of the dream, *This is just a dream. None of this is really happening.* When he realizes even in the midst of the drama that it's not real, he stays calm and waits it out.

Why are we talking about dreams? The reason is that this describes the life we are living in this world, and the "awakening" we will have when *Mashiach* comes. The first line of *Shir HaMa'alos* (*Tehillim* 126:1) says, "When Hashem redeems us from this exile, it will all feel like a dream. Then our mouths will be filled with laughter."

We will see that all the challenges and troubles in this world only seemed like troubles. All the time we were tossing and turning, sweating and trying to run, Hashem was creating the best possible life and the best possible world for us. We will wake up into that world one day, and we'll be so filled with relief and happiness that we will burst out laughing.

But what does Hashem want from us in the meantime? He wants us to train ourselves to realize, even in the middle of the drama, that it's a dream. "It seems scary, but Hashem is taking care. I'm safe in Hashem's world." This is the kind of *emunah* that not only gets us through our difficulties with a calm heart, but helps to bring the *Geulah,* the moment when our eyes flash open and the reality finally becomes clear to us (*Yalkut Shimoni, Eichah, Remez* 977).

Remaining calm in difficult situations is not a trait we are born with. It's something we learn from our role models and *sefarim,* and work throughout our lives to build. We build it every time we accept a setback with love for Hashem and confidence that He is in control of everything.

The next obvious question is, "How can the disappointments and pain Hashem sends me inspire my love for Him?" This is a good question, because people do not normally love those who hurt them. The exception to that rule is when we know that the person is hurting us for our own good.

For instance, you have a toothache and you go to the dentist. He jabs your gums with a needle and pushes and pulls and drills. Your mouth bleeds and aches for the rest of the day. But you're grateful to the dentist because he got rid of your decayed tooth and the far worse pain it would have caused.

Imagine what that trip to the dentist would have been like if there were no purpose. It would be just plain torture. You would not pay the dentist; you'd have him arrested. You would not be sitting in the chair trying to stay calm and thinking about how it would all be over soon. Instead, you'd be kicking and screaming and fighting to escape.

This is the difference between the life of someone who accepts his difficulties with love, knowing it's all for his benefit, and one who cannot see past the difficulty itself. The second person lives in a state of agitation, kicking and screaming against the difficult situations of his life. He sees no purpose to his suffering and does everything he can to escape it.

We can judge where we stand on the ladder of *emunah* by recognizing what kind of reactions we have to challenges. Do we kick and scream? Or do we say, "This isn't what I wanted, but it's what Hashem wanted, and I know that it is best for me." When we don't get what we want, or someone slights us or speaks negatively about us, are we filled with anger and resentment or do we look for the growth opportunity in the situation? The more we accept our pain and frustrations with love, knowing that they come from Hashem's love, the greater the power of our *emunah*.

For each of us personally, this is the power to live a life that is calm, focused and happy. For Klal Yisrael, it's much more. It's the power to bring *Mashiach*, when everything will at last become clear and "our mouths will be filled with laughter."

MAKE IT REAL:

Listen to yourself when you complain. Ask yourself where Hashem is in the picture you are painting.

50

Just Because You Asked

When we place our trust in Hashem, we show Him that we completely believe He knows what is best for us, and that His love for us is His only motivation.

How special, how holy and pure do you have to be to have Hashem accept your prayers? This is a question we might ask ourselves when we need something from Hashem. Are we good enough? Do we have sins on our record that might make Hashem's *malachim* block our call? Maybe it's a real chutzpah for us to think we have the right to ask anything from Hashem at all.

But here is an amazing fact: Just asking is enough to merit an answer. By asking Hashem for what we need, we show Him our *bitachon* — our trust in Him as the provider of everything. He won't abandon someone who depends on Him.

A scenario: A young man drives up to a house, gives a quick knock on the door of his parents' home and walks in.

"Eli! What brings you here?" the man's father says.

"Well, Leah and I are trying to figure out which school to send Racheli to and we decided that you would be the best one to ask. You always have a clear way of thinking. So do you have a little time to sit and talk about it?"

The father's heart is filled with happiness. His son

trusts him. His son turns to him for advice whenever a difficult situation arises. The father will make sure to always be there for his son.

What does it mean that this son seeks his father's advice? What does his trust symbolize? It shows the father that the son respects his wisdom and feels that his father will be able to figure out the best move. It shows that the son wants to follows his father's path in life. It also shows that the son trusts in his father's love and knows that he has no other agenda when he offers his advice. The father wouldn't choose a certain option because it's cheaper or easier for the father; he wouldn't pay attention to such things as what people will think or what advantages he might gain for himself. His only agenda will always be, "what will best serve my son and his family."

In the same way, when we place our trust in Hashem, we show Him that we completely believe He knows what is best for us, and that His love for us is His only motivation. *Bitachon* is the moment when we move from a feeling: "I believe Hashem is the Creator and He runs the world," to an action: "I'm going to do what Hashem wants of me." Praying to Hashem for help with our challenges is a powerful way to make that move. Once we do, we are surrounded by Hashem's kindness, even if we have a mile-long list of misdemeanors on our record.

Another amazing fact we need to know is that Hashem's love for us is not based on our merits at all. He doesn't love us because of who we are; rather, He loves us because of Who He is. Everything He does for us is purely out of His kindness. We are no more worthy of Hashem's care than a baby is worthy of his mother's 24/7 devotion. She takes care of her baby because he's her baby. There's nothing he has to do — and there's really nothing he is capable of doing — to earn that care.

Even someone as great as David HaMelech did not rely upon his greatness to appeal to Hashem for help. He wrote, "I have trusted Your kindness" (*Tehillim* 13:6).

But what happens when we trust in Hashem but our help doesn't come? Might we not be justified in thinking that perhaps we didn't deserve His help? Thinking this way is dangerous because it can cause us to separate from Hashem rather than to come closer just when we need Him most. We might feel rejected and left to struggle on our own. Eventually, we begin to feel bitter toward Hashem and bitter with our situation. We lose the ability to accept our situation with love, because we don't feel the love coming toward us from Above. All of this is like a heavy weight piled onto a flimsy, leaking ship of *emunah*. When we feel unworthy of Hashem's help, we sink our own boat.

If instead we hang in there, believing that our help will come, praying with more sincerity and emotion than ever, then we will not only get the help we need, but even more than we need in the merit of our *bitachon* (*Kad HaKemach, Erech Avel*).

In *Ashrei* we say "His compassion is upon all His creatures." This includes the birds and beasts, cows and chickens, and it surely includes each of us. We should never feel unworthy to ask Hashem for what we need, for He is never anything less than perfectly kind, compassionate and loving toward us. We may change, but He never does. He stands there at the door, delighted to see us, happy and honored that whenever we face a challenge in life, He is the One we turn to.

> ## MAKE IT REAL:
> *Whenever you are feeling that Hashem isn't answering you and wondering if it's because you lost His love, tell yourself, "Hashem loves me and takes care of me no matter what."*

51

An Impossible Family Reunion

Wherever we turn, Hashem is there, hearing our prayers, drying our tears and preparing for us an answer, a solution that we cannot even imagine.

One of the most powerful ways to build *emunah* is to hear some of the thousands of true stories people tell about the way Hashem brought about solutions to their seemingly impossible situations. A person with *bitachon* absorbs the message of these stories: Pray when you need Hashem's help, and if you're not answered, rally your energy and pray some more. And if you're still not answered, pray even more. When we realize that there are so many miracles happening every day, we can build up our own confidence that we, too, can have our prayers answered.

Let's look at one story that shows us the roundabout, completely unexpected ways in which Hashem can work miracles:

> *Yaakov and Miriam Kaplan were baalei teshuvah who had settled in Eretz Yisrael. Twelve years had gone by since they were married, and despite every effort, they still had no children. They decided that they would get a divorce so that each of them would have the chance to remarry and perhaps start a family.*
>
> *With broken hearts, they obtained a get from a beis din and tried to go on with their lives. A few weeks after the*

get, Miriam realized that she was expecting a child. This would have been wonderful news if her husband could have remarried her, but he couldn't; he was a Kohen.

Yaakov was devastated. He went from rabbi to rabbi trying to find some loophole that would allow him to remarry his ex-wife, but no one could find an answer. His last stop was Rav Elyashiv, one of the generation's greatest experts in halachah. Yaakov hoped the Rav could find something wrong with the get document that would make it invalid. However, Rav Elyashiv found it to be in perfect order. The divorce still stood. He offered Yaakov one bit of advice: Go to the Kosel and pray. "Only Hashem can help you," he said. "Many people have found their salvation at the Kosel."

Yaakov went straight to the Kosel and cried without end, begging Hashem for some solution. After awhile, a stranger approached him and told him, "You have to go see your father." Yaakov ignored the advice. After all, his father was in Dallas and he was on pretty rocky terms with him. What good would he achieve from going to see him? But the man interrupted his davening once again to repeat his advice.

That night, Yaakov decided that maybe he should listen to the stranger. He had followed Rav Elyashiv's directions to the Kosel, and now perhaps he should follow the directions he had received once he got there. He booked a flight to Dallas. When he walked into his father's home, his father greeted him for the first time ever by his Hebrew name rather than the English name he had always been called. "Where's your wife?" his father asked.

Yaakov poured out his whole sad tale. His father listened quietly, and then said to him, "My son, I have to tell you something. Your mother made me swear to keep it a secret, but now you have to know. You are not really my son. We were childless and your mother wanted a child very badly, so we adopted you. We never told a soul. Everyone thought you were our biological son, and you grew up thinking you were a Kohen. But you're not."

> *Yaakov saw the adoption papers, which verified his father's information. He went home and remarried Miriam, and they were able to raise their child together. The obstacle that had seemed utterly insurmountable had dissolved in mere moments, and the joy for which they had longed during their 12 years of waiting was finally theirs.*

This remarkable story is just a window into the behind-the-scenes activities going on in *Shamayim*. Not one rabbi in all of Eretz Yisrael, including the leading *gadol* of the generation, could find a way that Yaakov would be able to remarry Miriam. However, Yaakov didn't give up. He followed the trail as it opened up in front of him, step-by-step, until he reached his father's house. Then, suddenly, the problem no one could solve was solved in minutes.

The more we hear stories like this one, the greater is our simple faith in Hashem. We don't have to do the figuring — the how and why belong to Hashem. All we need to know is that whatever our problem, Hashem can solve it. Whatever our need, Hashem can fulfill it. And wherever we turn, Hashem is there, hearing our prayers, drying our tears and preparing for us an answer, a solution that we cannot even imagine.

MAKE IT REAL:

Get a book that tells stories of hashgachah pratis and obvious miracles and read a few each week. Keep up a steady diet of emunah stories so that the sense of Hashem's constant kindness sinks into your heart.

52
It's Not What You Think

> By working to remind ourselves that everything happening in our lives is supervised directly by Hashem, we can redirect our energy, using it to go full speed ahead toward our goals in life.

"If only I had left the house when I was supposed to, I wouldn't have gotten injured by the boy riding his bicycle so fast!"

"I wish I didn't agree to go to this wedding. I have so many other things I need to do tonight."

"If I had gone to a better school, I'd have a much better job today."

"I shouldn't have screamed at my brother."

"I should have agreed to sell my stamp collection when it had more value."

What is the common thread in all these statements? On first glance, we might say that the speakers are people who have learned a lesson from their mistakes. They regret things they've done, especially when they find themselves living with the consequences of those decisions. But of all the actions we see mentioned here, only one was really in the speaker's hands to have done differently: "I shouldn't have screamed at my brother."

All the rest of these statements are basically wasted emotion.

That is because even though we may think about the choices we make and believe we are making decisions, in reality, Hashem is directing our steps every inch of the way. The only exception to that rule is in our *yiras Shamayim* — the choices we make about serving Hashem. Allowing ourselves to lash out at another person is one such decision. When choosing right from wrong, we have the responsibility and we get the credit.

"Everything is in Hashem's hands except for the fear of Hashem," the Gemara (*Berachos* 32b) tells us. In every other area of life, we make our choices based on the information we have in front of us, how we're feeling at that moment, where we are and what we think is best. Sometimes those choices work out as we expected and sometimes they do not. But in every case, they work out as Hashem expects, because He is planning our decisions for us. There is nothing to regret. There is no such thing as "I should have" because in reality, you *couldn't* have. You did exactly what Hashem planned for you to do.

Our lives are not a solo performance. There are hundreds, if not thousands, of other actors involved in the events of our lives and only Hashem can coordinate the whole performance, with all its scenes and action, to come out as it should. If a person decides to attend a wedding and then, when the time comes, wishes she had the night to get a head start on her studies, she can be sure that her presence at the wedding has a purpose. Perhaps she will meet someone there who will be helpful to her in the future, or perhaps she will end up being helpful to the other person. Perhaps her friend, the *kallah,* will have greater *simchah* because she's there. Perhaps she'll be able to give an elderly relative a ride home. We have no way of knowing why our lives play out as they do. We only need to know that there is nothing to regret. It is as it should be, as Hashem wants it to be.

This is not to say that we cannot learn from our mistakes. Thinking about how to avoid a negative consequence in the future is a very worthwhile endeavor. It's how we mature and grow. However, part of the growth process is to avoid kicking ourselves over what has transpired in the past. *The thoughts that led us to make the decision in the first place were given to us by Hashem.* His very purpose might have been to motivate us to rethink our habits.

For example, you know that pizza gives you a stomach ache. You eat it anyway, just to be sociable with your friends, and you wake up in the morning feeling awful. If you spend time replaying the pizza party in your mind, silently scolding yourself for being so foolish, you're not only wasting your effort, but you're lowering yourself in your own eyes. Hashem gave you this opportunity to strengthen your self-control next time around, or perhaps to be able to stand up to the pressure of your friends saying, "Come on, one slice isn't going to kill you." This is strength that you will be able to use in many ways in the future. Drawing a lesson from what's gone wrong is different from wallowing in regret.

It's interesting to read the biographies of very successful business people. Almost without exception, they count their failures as their most important experiences. That's where all the learning takes place. They don't spend time regretting the bad investment or the failed idea. They recalculate and move forward. Their minds work like a GPS when the driver has taken a wrong turn. It doesn't say, "How could you be so dense? You should have turned left! Now you're lost!" It simply tells the driver how to go forward from there.

Even when it comes to choices that relate to *yiras Shamayim* — the choices that are in our hands — regret is only appropriate as part of the *teshuvah* process. We have to recognize what we've done wrong, regret it and resolve not repeat our mistake. At that point, we have to let go of our regret.

Regret is an energy drainer and confidence killer. By working to remind ourselves that everything happening in our lives is supervised directly by Hashem, we can redirect our energy, using it to go full speed ahead toward our goals in life.

MAKE IT REAL:

Catch yourself the next time you think, "I should have..." Reroute your thinking to "What can I learn from this?"

53

Believe It Will Be Good

When we live life with the simple awareness that everything is from Hashem, we can remain calm and work through whatever challenge presents itself.

Four drivers, one car. The nightmare of every suburban dweller. Mrs. N.'s two unmarried children were just back from Eretz Yisrael. The son was learning in a local yeshivah. The daughter had a job in a local store. Both of them had to get to their destinations in the morning, come home for lunch, get back to their destinations for the afternoon and then come home again. Along with that, Mrs. N. picked her grandson up from playgroup several afternoons a week.

Really, there were three cars. Her husband used one to commute to his job as a teacher in a city public school. The second car was suffering from some electronic glitch that no mechanic was able to figure out. The third car had been in an accident and waited at the body shop for repairs. The one car the family had available was a rental and only Mrs. N. was allowed to drive it.

She was driving all day, eight trips a day. She was getting no other work done. Her business was on hold. Nevertheless, she stayed calm, telling herself that car problems are "the best kapparah in the world. They're nothing more than money and inconvenience — no pain, heartbreak or illness. We'll get through this. It's just a matter of time," she reminded herself. *But when the day came to return the rental, she had reached the end of her rope. All night she thought about how they would get through the next day.*

When she opened her siddur to daven the next morning, it all came out. "Hashem, I'm not complaining. There are so many troubles worse than car troubles. But I can't figure out what to do now. I don't know how You are going to help me, but I know You will!"

No sooner had she closed her siddur than the phone rang. It was her husband. "You won't believe this, but today is a school holiday. I got here and the place is empty. When I called up another teacher to find out what was going on, she said it's Eid Al-Fitr."

"It's what?" Mrs. N. asked.

"The last day of Ramadan, the Muslim holiday. This year the city made it a day off. I'll be home in about an hour and a half."

Imagine the feeling of Hashem's care and love this woman experienced when her answer came just moments after she asked for help. Who would have imagined that Hashem would send her salvation by way of a citywide recognition of Ramadan? But just as Hashem took her cars out of commission unexpectedly, He arranged for her rescue in an even more surprising manner.

One thing she knew for sure. This was all from Hashem. Throughout a two-week period of constant driving, visits to the mechanic, calls to the insurance company and so forth, she tried to accept the situation. She even found reasons to be grateful. After all, perhaps the car problems were taking the place of some more serious problem. Furthermore, although the expense of fixing the cars was unwanted, *Baruch Hashem* the money was there; they wouldn't have to borrow. Most importantly, if there was money that had to be spent, she was grateful that it was going to car repairs rather than medical treatments. Clearly, The Great Car Shortage of 2017 was an act of Hashem, done for a reason that may never become apparent in this world.

Realizing that Hashem was in control of the situation all the time, Mrs. N. was able to ask, with complete sincerity, for Him to step in when the going seemed to be getting too difficult. What did she expect Him to do? Did she imagine that a brand-new car in perfect working order would drop down into her driveway? She didn't know, but she knew that the answer, whatever it was, rested with Hashem. He had what she needed.

When we live life with the simple awareness that everything is from Hashem, we can remain calm and work through whatever challenge presents itself. We realize that just as Hashem put us into our situation, He can easily take us out of it. The more we train ourselves to think this way, the more we will see Hashem's help in our own life.

> **MAKE IT REAL:**
> *The next time you find yourself getting tense and worried about how a situation will work out, use your imagination to visualize how Hashem is controlling everything like a puppeteer staging a show.*

54

Impossible? For Whom?

For Hashem, anything — absolutely anything — is possible. We can never stop hoping and praying for what we need.

A person has a bad case of strep throat. The doctor prescribes an antibiotic, but it doesn't work. He tries another one, and that one isn't effective either. Eventually, the doctor goes through all the possible medications that are available, but the person is still suffering with a fever and the feeling, whenever he swallows, that he's swallowing fire.

"I have nothing more to offer," the doctor says.

A student can't seem to catch on to math. His teacher gives him some extra help, but he's still lost. His parents hire a tutor for him; he does just fine when he's working with the tutor, but as soon as he's on his own, he's all confused again. "There's nothing more we can do for him," his parents despair.

The captain leads his troops into an attack on the enemy. Despite having scouted out the situation, the troops are surprised by an ambush. The next thing they know, they are surrounded on three sides and enemy planes *are heading in to drop bombs on them.* "There's nothing more we can do," says the captain. "Retreat!"

For human beings, there's such a concept as "impossible." We try everything we know how to try. We use all our efforts and all our intelligence to come up with a solution, but nothing saves us. At that point, we have to admit, we're out of options.

With Hashem, however, the options never run out, "*ki harbeh imo f'dus*" — because with Him there is an abundance of redemption (*Tehillim* 130:7). Hashem's help can come in ways that are completely unexpected — even unexplainable. People have gotten into legal trouble only to have the officials "forget" about the entire case. People have been told that they can never have children and gone on to have large families.

One such amazing story is told by a man named Rabbi Kornreich, who was the only member of his family to survive the Holocaust. He married after the war, hoping to start a new family. When years went by without a child, they went to a doctor to find out what was wrong. The doctor told them that because of the wife's treatment at the hands of the Nazis, her ability to have children had been destroyed. However, the couple didn't take the doctor's word for it. They went to *tzaddikim* for *berachos* and they kept on *davening* with all their hearts. Despite the doctor's "absolutely positively never" verdict, Mrs. Kornreich had a child. And that child had many children, and they too had many children. Rabbi Kornreich became the head of a family of more than 100 souls in just two generations.

Now imagine what Rabbi Kornreich might have been thinking if he had not lived with such strong *emunah*. He had lost his entire family in the war. He was all alone in the world, and then he met his wife and he felt a little hope; he could rebuild the family that had been almost completely wiped out. As the years went by and no children came into his life, he could easily have felt abandoned by Hashem. "Why don't I deserve to have any happiness? Why, after everything I've been through, am I going to die a lonely old man?" Then, when a doctor confirmed that no children could be born to this couple, he might have thrown up his hands and shouted, "Retreat!"

Looking only at the "facts on the ground," the reality in front of him, all of these responses would have been reasonable. In this world, there were no more options, but Rabbi Kornreich knew that no solution — whether simple or miraculous — comes from this world. It all comes from *Shamayim,* and that means that there's always a way out of a situation. Hashem isn't limited by the rules of medicine; He can turn "absolutely positively never" into a *mazal tov.* Believing that with Hashem, everything is possible, gave Rabbi Kornreich the energy to keep praying and seeking *berachos.* He relied on Hashem, and Hashem helped him.

Whether a person is fighting a virus, a learning problem, a war or anything in between, Hashem has the solution in His hand. Knowing this keeps us from becoming depressed about our situation. It fills us with hope and motivates us to do the things that can ultimately cause Hashem to hand our solution over to us. No matter how unlikely a resolution may seem to be, we can never declare it "impossible." For us, yes, some things are impossible. People cannot grow feathers and fly, jump over mountains or lift an elephant. But for Hashem, anything — absolutely anything — is possible. We can never stop hoping and praying for what we need.

MAKE IT REAL:

Do you have a situation that you believe can't be changed? Think of two or three completely incredible ways it might be changed if Hashem wills it to be.

55
Doing Hashem's Advertising

We make a Kiddush Hashem by doing what the Torah instructs us to do no matter what.

We know there's nothing we can actually do for Hashem. He has everything, controls everything and knows everything. So what are we supposed to do when we're in a tough situation and we want to bring Hashem's help down into our world? Is there anything we can offer Him to open up the vault in which our solutions are waiting?

So far, we've learned that our *bitachon* has tremendous power to help us; when Hashem sees that we are truly relying on Him and Him alone, He does not let us down. Our *tefillos,* which express our *bitachon,* are also an essential step. Certainly we can add more mitzvos and learning to our day as a merit for Hashem's help. But there is one more powerful action we can take, and that is to make a *Kiddush Hashem* — to bring honor to Hashem's Name.

The Sages give us this promise (*Toras Kohanim, Parashas Acharei Mos)*: "If you glorify My [Hashem's] Name, then I will cause My Name to be glorified through you." The more we advertise Hashem's greatness to the world, the more Hashem gives us new ways to spread His reputation.

Imagine you were hired to advertise a new brand of soda. You did a great job, and now the soda is selling everywhere. The soda company is making a fortune, but it won't be happy until every man, woman and child in the country is drinking its soda. Therefore, the company keeps increasing your budget so that you can keep increasing the advertising.

In a way, this is what happens when we make a *Kiddush Hashem*. We are getting more and more people to "buy" the most precious "product" there is; the belief that there is a Creator Who runs the world. But our job isn't done until every person on earth recognizes Hashem, and so, He keeps investing in us. He knows that every kindness He performs for us, every miracle He sends our way, is another opportunity for us to do our job: to bring glory to His Name.

> The name Ruby Schron is well known today because of all the tzedakah Mr. Schron gives. When he was just starting out in the real-estate business 40 years ago, he bought a house for his family in Brooklyn. One day, his children were jumping on the bed when suddenly, a crashing sound came from underneath. The Schrons discovered that there was a safe containing jewelry and bonds worth about $40,000. Did they have to give the money back to the previous owner? Mr. Schron asked Rav Moshe Feinstein, who told them that even though the sale contract included everything in the house, a safe filled with valuables was so unusual that it could not have been what the seller had in mind. Mr. Schron immediately called the seller and told him about the exciting find.
>
> "Our parents left us money somewhere in the house," the seller said, "but we could never find it. We knew that religious Jews would return it if they found it."

Mr. Schron's honesty, despite the great temptation a person would naturally have to keep the money, was the best "advertising" for Hashem. In the years to come, Hashem invested much more in him, bringing him great wealth that he has used to continue the ad campaign.

We make a *Kiddush Hashem* by doing what the Torah instructs us to do no matter what. When we do that, we show that we believe Someone is watching. We believe that our behavior matters. Hashem is a reality in our life.

Rabbi Pesach Eliyahu Falk tells about a *talmid chacham*

whose son got very sick on Shabbos. An excellent doctor lived right down the block, so the *talmid chacham* went to ask him to treat his son. The doctor insisted on a check for 500 shekels before he would treat the boy. He claimed to be afraid of being cheated out of his fee. The *halachah* clearly allowed the *talmid chacham* to write the check (in an unusual manner) in order to protect his son's life. But instead of writing the check for 500 shekels, he wrote it for 1,000.

The doctor, looking around at the man's poor surroundings, said, "I only asked for 500. It doesn't look to me like you can afford any more than that." But the *talmid chacham* had an explanation. In Hebrew, "500" would require writing two words, whereas "1,000" only required writing one word. He was willing to pay double, although he could not afford it, just to avoid writing one extra word on Shabbos.

The doctor was deeply touched by this glimpse into the heart of a sincere, believing Jew. He ended up learning with the *talmid chacham* and becoming a *baal teshuvah*.

Of course, the *talmid chacham* did not have the doctor's *teshuvah* in mind when he wrote the check. He simply did what Hashem wanted him to do. There is nothing more powerful to bring Hashem's blessings into our lives.

MAKE IT REAL:

The next time you face a difficult decision, ask yourself, "Which way would be a Kiddush Hashem?"

56

Gam Zu L'Tovah: It's Real!

> When things don't work out as we hope, then this too is for the good — gam zu l'tovah — because at that very moment, Hashem is directing us to the place we need to go.

A non-religious couple had a baby boy. Sadly, the boy's ears were unusually large. The mother felt terrible for her poor child, who attracted stares and snickers everywhere they went. The mother's friend gave her an idea: "Send him to a Chassidish cheder where the boys wear long peyos. That way no one will see his ears."

Although the boy's parents were not religious at all, the mother followed her friend's advice. There didn't seem to be any other way to have her son grow up without constant teasing. She found a cheder that would accept him and he began to learn Torah. Not only did he learn, but he excelled. In fact, he became a true talmid chacham. His mother, who spent many sleepless nights crying about her son's uncertain future, ultimately had the greatest nachas from this child.

Sometimes we think of *gam zu l'tovah* as an empty saying. Does it really make us feel better? Do people really mean it when they say it, or are they just looking for something comforting to say?

If we really believe those words, we are always happy. No matter what happens, we immediately switch from "Oh, no," to "Hashem is taking care of me every step of the way. He loves me and will lead me to the best possible outcome." To be able to switch tracks like this, we have to keep our eyes and ears on the lookout for situations in which the good result becomes apparent to us. The more we pay attention to these situations, the more we realize that *gam zu l'tovah* is real.

> *Toby didn't get the well-paying job she wanted. Instead, she got a poorly paying job. Because it paid poorly, she eventually decided to further her education and change careers. She enrolled in law school, where she met her husband. Today, she is a grandmother of many grandchildren. She says, "I remember how disappointed I was that I didn't get the glamorous job in the glamorous office building. But it had to be that way, in order for me to have all the amazing blessings I have in my life."*

Could Toby have known, while she was struggling along with a job she didn't enjoy and receiving a salary that was barely enough for her to live on, that her predicament would lead to her becoming a happy wife and mother of a large family? There is no way she could have known this. However, if she would have known that her troubles were leading her somewhere good, then they would not have troubled her as much. She would have been able to get over her disappointment quickly, telling herself that if the direction in which she wanted to go was blocked, then it obviously wasn't going to lead her to the destination Hashem chose for her.

> *You're in a maze. It's a great big maze created out of many tall shrubs with a path that turns this way and that. You cannot see any further than the turn that is right ahead of you. The shrubs block your view of all the other paths. You begin at the beginning, at the entrance of the maze, and your goal is to reach the exit.*
>
> *There's only one way to get to your goal. You must move forward. But what happens when you take a turn and run into a dead end? Do you bang against the shrubs that are blocking your path, hoping to knock them out*

of the way? Do you stand there and complain that it's not fair, you're trying so hard to get out of this maze and now you've hit a dead end?

Most likely, you will say to yourself, "Oh, this way is the wrong way. I better try the other way instead." You'll repeat this procedure over and over until you find your way out. There's no question that you'll get to the end; you just have to see what pathways are open and follow them. Every time you hit a dead end, you learn something valuable: that you're going the wrong way. The dead ends are instructive. They push you onto the right path. They are l'tovah.

This is how a person with *emunah* deals with setbacks. If we smack head-first into a dead-end, we know that this is only in order to push us onto the path that will get us where we need to go. Life is not one straight path with visibility clear to the end; it has got twists and turns galore, and we can rarely see beyond where our next few steps will lead us.

Gam zu l'tovah captures the spirit with which we must make our way through the maze. When things work out well, that's clearly good. When things don't work out as we hope, then this too is for the good — *gam zu l'tovah* — because at that very moment, Hashem is directing us to the place we need to go.

> ## MAKE IT REAL:
> *Start a conversation with your family or friends asking each person to tell a story about a disappointment or problem that ended up being clearly l'tovah.*

57

If It's All Good, Why Pray?

Praying for what we want is not complaining. It is unburdening ourselves to Hashem.

If you were going through a difficult time, but you had perfect faith that the troubles were for your own good, why would you pray to Hashem to end your troubles? If they are a gift, why would you try to return the gift? If you are supposed to accept what happens to you and believe that it is positive and necessary, how can you pray to change your situation? Can you hold two different thoughts — *"Gam zu l'tovah"* on one side of your brain, and "Help! Hashem, please get me out of this mess!" — on the other side?

Rabbi Ephraim Wachsman explains that you actually can do both: accept what has happened in your life and pray for relief. The reason, he says, is that we live in two different worlds. There's the world we step into when we pray, and the world we inhabit all the rest of the time.

In the world of *tefillah*, we can open up our hearts and let out all of our worries, fears and longings. That is the time to envision life the way we want it to be, with everything we feel we need to be happy and fulfilled. If we're not learning well, this is the time to ask for greater ability. If we're having trouble making a big decision, we can pray for clarity. If we've had a falling-out with friends, we can pray for forgiveness and *shalom*. We can pray to lose weight, gain weight, sleep better, have more money, get along better with our family — anything our heart desires.

Praying for what we want is not complaining. It is unburdening ourselves to Hashem. Shlomo HaMelech tells us based on the explanation of Chazal that if a person has worries in his heart, he should speak about them (*Mishlei* 12:25). Sometimes we feel free to do that; we have a friend who understands us and a problem we are willing to share. Sometimes, however, we feel alone with our problems. We might be embarrassed to share or feel that no one will really understand our situation. But we never have to be ashamed in front of Hashem; He already knows everything. When we speak to Him with an open heart, we feel closer to Him, and even if nothing changes, we feel better.

Of course we are not aiming for nothing to change when we pray. We are aiming for answers, solutions, resolutions to our problems. Even though Hashem has obviously given us the problem and done so out of love, we still have plenty of reason to pray. One is that by praying, we are showing *bitachon*, recognizing that our help comes from Hashem. As we have mentioned already, relying on Hashem alone causes Him to come to our aid. In addition, our troubles and our acceptance of the troubles raise us to a new spiritual level. Sometimes Hashem sends us challenges in order to get our attention and force us to focus on what is important in life. Once He has our attention and we are focused, we no longer need the challenge. **Therefore, the situation He sees as being the best for us can change as we change.**

We can never lose by praying. Any language, coming from our heart, is acceptable to Hashem. We can and should pray as hard as we can, as long as we must, until we receive our answer. It is impossible for us to imagine how much power our prayers have, as the story below illustrates.

> *The Kesav Sofer, the son of the Chasam Sofer, was the Rabbi of the city of Pressburg. At one time, a Jew in the city was convicted of a crime he didn't commit, and was sentenced to be executed. The Kesav Sofer did everything in his power to get the authorities to review the case, but*

nothing worked. The night before the execution, he cried himself to sleep. As he slept, his father came to him in a dream.

"How can you sleep when a Jew is sentenced to die in the morning?" said his father. The Kesav Sofer answered that he had tried everything. "What else can I do?" he asked.

"You have to pray and pray and pray some more," the Chasam Sofer answered.

The Kesav Sofer gathered the community into the shul and they prayed all night long. In the morning, the judge agreed to review the case. The man was saved.

It is especially at those times when we feel lost and alone in our troubles that our prayers have tremendous power to arouse Hashem's love for us. "Hashem is close to the brokenhearted," *Tehillim* (34:19) tells us. When we drop our resentments, our expectations and pride and turn to Hashem with our pain, we are leaving our hands wide open to receive Hashem's *berachah*.

The world outside of *tefillah* is a world in which we must do our best to smile, accept our situation and move forward. But when it's time to pray — and that can be any time of day we wish to reach out to Hashem — everything in our hearts can flow. As we remind ourselves each day when we recite the prayer of *Ashrei*, "Hashem is close to everyone who calls out to Him, to everyone who calls out to Him sincerely."

MAKE IT REAL:

Set aside some time either in your Shemoneh Esrei or at some other time of day to ask Hashem in your own words to take care of a challenge you are facing.

58

Trust the Driver

It's not what I asked for, but it's what Hashem wanted for me. That means it's what is best for me, and so it's what I want too.

Did you ever ride with a nervous passenger who's convinced that the driver doesn't know what he's doing? The problem isn't that the driver is doing something wrong; he's just not driving at the same speed, at the same distance from the car in front of him, or on the same route as the passenger prefers. The passenger spends the whole time petrified that he's going to crash, pounding the floor with his foot as if he's pressing the brakes and yelling at the driver: Slow down! Take a left! Don't pass that car yet! Pass now!

The passenger is having a heart-thumping experience because he isn't in control; the driver is. Even so, the passenger is trying to exert control because he's convinced that he knows what should be happening at every given moment.

Imagine if that passenger trusted the driver. He could relax, look out the window and enjoy the scenery. He could listen to some good music or drop off into a comfortable sleep as the car cruises along. He could feel confident that the driver will get him where he needs to go.

This is the way life is for a person who lives by the words of the Rosh: "Want what Hashem wants for you" (*Orchos Chaim, Os* 69). When we believe that the road we are on, the stops we make, the detours we run into and all the various parts of our journey through life are exactly as they should be — even when they're not what we expect or prefer — we live an optimistic, satisfied and secure life. "This is what is happening, and it's coming from Hashem, and Hashem knows just what He's doing."

The challenge is to actually be able to feel this way when we're dealing with a situation we don't want. For example, imagine that on the way to shul on Shabbos morning, a boy trips on a crack in the sidewalk, falls down and breaks his ankle. While everyone else is sitting at a Shabbos table enjoying their *cholent,* he's moaning in pain as he waits in the emergency room for a doctor to examine him.

This boy could be thinking like the nervous driver: "This is the wrong way! I was on my way to shul — there shouldn't be a big huge crack in the sidewalk. It should be a smooth path. And what about my Shabbos meal and the learning I was going to do this afternoon? We went right past all those mitzvos and headed to the hospital instead. And how can I enjoy Shabbos like I'm supposed to when my ankle is throbbing and burning? And why does everything have to be ruined for the next six weeks by this cast I'm going to have to wear? I won't be able to dance at my cousin's wedding. Everything is heading in the wrong direction and there's nothing I can do about it! This is so wrong!"

Probably if you asked this boy, a good Jewish boy who *davens* every day, how he managed to trip on his way to shul, he'd answer, "Well, I guess it's what Hashem wanted to happen." However, it's not what *he* wanted, and because of that, he's angry. If he doesn't turn his anger around and use his pain to come closer to Hashem, then the admittedly difficult challenge he's been handed won't give him all the benefits it could give. How can he turn it around? He can do so by forgetting about the path he believes his life should have taken and instead, trust that the detour on which Hashem has taken him is the best possible route.

"It's not what I asked for, but it's what Hashem wanted for me. That means it's what is best for me, and so it's what I want too." This is the thought that, like helium in a balloon, lifts us up to meet our challenges in the best possible way. Hashem always knows what He's doing. He is always taking us where we need to go, on the road we need to travel. Sometimes, we get to see the reason.

Rabbi Avraham Schorr tells of a rabbi in Eretz Yisrael who was suffering from a dangerous disease in his kidney. Shortly after his condition was diagnosed, he was bitten by a poisonous snake. He had to travel to Ramat Gan to see a specialist who could treat him for the bite. Ten days later, he went back to the kidney doctor to check on his condition. The doctor ordered some tests, and when he got the results, he was astounded. The rabbi's kidney was in perfect condition. The snake venom had destroyed the disease.

It's not very likely that the rabbi felt blessed when he was bitten by the snake. It wasn't one of the stops he had planned for his life's journey. However, Hashem drove the rabbi straight to the snake, drove the snake straight to the rabbi and brought about a frightening, life-threatening situation. It turned out to be precisely the right way to go.

Wouldn't it be great to know someone who could always tell you just what to do, just what would work out best for you? When you trust Hashem, you have exactly that. Trust Him and you'll never feel lost.

> **MAKE IT REAL:**
>
> *The next time you find yourself worrying about the consequences of an unexpected turn of events, imagine yourself in the passenger's seat riding safely to a surprise destination.*

59

The Big Question

When our eyes don't see the truth, we have to know that the flaw is in our vision.

Everyone in the Jewish world knows the name of Rabbi Nosson Tzvi Finkel, zt"l, who was the Rosh Yeshivah of the Mir in Yerushalayim for many decades. Under his leadership the Mir became the world's largest center of Torah learning, where students from countries all over the world found a home. Many of the leaders of Torah communities across the globe got their start at the Mir.

If anyone would seem to merit good health and strength, it would be Rabbi Finkel. After all, his every waking moment was devoted to Torah learning, building his yeshivah and providing guidance and support to his students.

Nevertheless, in the late 1980's, he became ill with Parkinson's Disease, a condition that eventually causes the sufferer to lose his ability to walk, speak and use his hands. Rabbi Finkel's words of Torah and encouragement became difficult to speak and difficult to understand. His many trips abroad to raise money for the yeshivah became physically exhausting. When he passed away in 2011, he had endured over 20 years of disability. He had continued guiding his beloved yeshivah throughout the entire time, always with the warmth and simchah for which he was renowned.

Why do the righteous suffer? Why does a devoted servant of Hashem, whose every moment is devoted to spreading Hashem's Torah, find himself afflicted with a disease that interferes with his life of *avodah*? This is the "big question" because it is a question that, if not properly understood, can eat away at a person's *emunah*. Our belief in reward and punishment is challenged when we see the suffering of someone who does only good.

The other side of the question is why good things happen to some people who seem to be outright selfish, arrogant and perhaps dishonest as well. For example, such a person might be enjoying a wonderful retirement, traveling all over the world, sailing, golfing, dining in the fanciest restaurants and staying in luxurious hotels while someone else, who lived a good and honest life, is spending "retirement" in a wheelchair in a nursing home.

If we search for answers to these questions using our own eyes and our own minds, we are bound to head in the wrong direction. All we see and understand about life tells us that these situations should not be. It hurts us to see someone who is good, patient and full of faith suffering blow after blow. It also hurts us to see the bad guy succeed.

That's why Hashem tells us that understanding this fact of life is not possible for us. "My thoughts are not [like] your thoughts" (*Yeshayah* 55:8). However, we can at least come to understand why Hashem would not make His reasoning clearer to us, especially since these questions are so dangerous to our *emunah*.

The bottom line is that Hashem created us in order to do good for us, as we previously learned. The best good He can give us is good that we earn. Good that we do not earn is actually embarrassing rather than pleasant for us. Imagine that your school singled you out as valedictorian and asked you to speak at the graduation on the topic of "How to Be a Successful Student." You would be quite honored if in fact you had been a great student who had worked hard throughout your high-school years. But what if you coasted by on Cs and Ds, doing just the bare basics to enable you to graduate? How would you feel standing up there in front of all your classmates and their parents? How would you be able to look the worthier students in the eyes?

We can imagine the churning stomach and red face of the person who gets what he doesn't deserve. That's not the reward Hashem wants for us, and therefore, he sets up challenges in our lives so that we can earn our reward. *Emunah* is always the challenge. Therefore, reward and punishment cannot be obvious. If it were, we would not need *emunah*. We would also lose sympathy for those who suffer, seeing clearly that their suffering is for their good.

If everything were perfectly clear, we would simply do whatever we had to do to receive blessings and avoid punishment in this world. We would be more like trained puppies than children of Hashem. Our reward would be unearned.

The *tzaddik* who suffers knows that his suffering is earning him the greatest, most glowing reward in the World to Come. He accepts it with love, knowing that it comes from love, and in doing so, he reaches levels beyond our imagination.

In Moshe Rabbeinu's final words to Klal Yisrael in *Parashas Ha'azinu,* he leaves us with the words the Jewish people are to live by (*Devarim* 32:4): "The deeds of the Rock [Hashem] are perfect, for all His ways are just; a faithful G-d without injustice, He is righteous and upright."

This is the truth, told to us directly by Hashem. When our eyes don't see the truth, we have to know that the flaw is in our vision.

MAKE IT REAL:

When you see a situation in which someone seems to suffering unfairly, use your sympathy only to motivate yourself to try to help, rather than to question Hashem's ways.

60

Ask the Manufacturer

When our thoughts begin to lean toward hopelessness, we have to remind ourselves that the One Who made Heaven and Earth knows how to fix any situation.

A scenario: Although it was only a few years old, Danny's Honda was making a terrible racket. Every time he turned on the engine, it rattled and roared like a race car. He took it to his mechanic, who looked under the hood and said, "I don't see anything wrong."

"But what about the noise?" Danny insisted.

"Cars make noise," the mechanic said. "It's fine. It's not going to break down on you."

"But it wasn't making this noise a week ago," Danny replied. "Something must have gone wrong."

"You know what? I think you should take it back to the Honda dealer. They're the ones who know their own cars, and they have all the parts you might need. I'll just have to fiddle around with it until I figure it out, and I might not figure it out. Take it to the people who know the car."

The one who designs and manufactures a product is the one who knows how to fix it when something goes awry. This is all the more true regarding the world we live in. Hashem, Who created the Heaven and the Earth, is the only

One Who can readjust the world's machinery. Everyone else is just fiddling around.

At times, the machinery of our lives seems to be in disrepair. Things aren't working as they should. We look here and there for solutions, yet nothing changes. An older sibling isn't finding a marriage partner despite all his or her efforts. Someone who is ill isn't getting better despite all the doctors' treatments. We begin to wonder if anything will ever change. After all, who says that Hashem intends to repair this particular situation? Perhaps the suffering is what He has decreed and it will not be resolved.

When our thoughts begin to lean toward hopelessness, we have to remind ourselves that the One Who made Heaven and Earth knows how to fix any situation. We cannot lose hope. A simple "turn of the screw" can change everything in a flash.

Let's take as an example a situation related by Rabbi Avraham Schorr:

> There was a religious Jew who was found guilty of a crime and sentenced to New York's Riker's Island prison, a notoriously dangerous place both physically and spiritually. He was innocent of the crime, but no one who tried to help had any success. There was one man, a non-Jew, who had a lot of influence in the justice system, but he didn't want to get involved.
>
> One day, that man was returning from a funeral in North Carolina and was standing outside Penn Station, a train station in Midtown Manhattan. It was a brutally hot day and he was waiting, with two heavy suitcases, for a cab to take him to his apartment. Just at that moment, two yeshivah boys walked by and noticed the man standing there in the heat. They offered to carry his suitcases home for him and he accepted the offer. When they got to his home, they offered to carry the bags up two flights of steps. Then, when they arrived at his door, they refused the man's offer of $20 each for their trouble.
>
> "No thanks," they said. "We just wanted to help."
>
> The man walked into his apartment, picked up the phone and called the lawyer of the man who was to go to

jail. He assured the lawyer that he would do everything he could to bring the evidence of the man's innocence to the judge. "I've never seen such a thing in my life," he said of the two boys. "I never imagined that Orthodox Jews are such beautiful people."

Imagine the thoughts of the man who was facing jail. He was about to be locked behind bars for years, surrounded by the lowest element of New York City's inhabitants. His life would be in danger every day as a Jew, a non-gang member and a human being unskilled at the art of self-defense. His *avodas Hashem* would be reduced to whatever few *sefarim* and few occasions for prayer were allowed to him. His level of *kashrus* would be decided by the prison system. He would be torn away from his family and friends. He was facing the greatest test of his lifetime, and he hadn't even committed the crime of which he was convicted.

Suddenly, everything changed. Hashem directed the feet of these two yeshivah boys to Penn Station on a hot summer day. He placed in their hearts some empathy for the weary traveler standing there with his bags. He placed in their minds the idea to approach the man and offer their help. The Manufacturer knew just what to do to fix the situation. No one else could manipulate Heaven and Earth to accomplish what had, until that moment, seemed impossible.

"I raise my eyes to the mountains. From where will my help come? My help is from Hashem, Who makes the Heaven and the Earth," *Tehillim* (121:1) tells us. There's no repair too complicated or difficult for the One Who made it all.

MAKE IT REAL:

Get into the habit of asking Hashem for help when you are in a difficult situation. It doesn't have to be complicated or eloquent. Accustom yourself to answering your own worries with the words, "Hashem, please help me out of this."

61

Why Get a Berachah?

Each of us has a direct line to Hashem; we just have to keep it clear of static.

How many stories have you heard of people going to a *tzaddik* for a *berachah* when they face a big challenge in life? Sometimes, the *tzaddik* tells the person to make some improvement in his *avodas Hashem* to bring about a solution. Sometimes the *tzaddik* does what seems to be nothing more than uttering a few words of encouragement. Always, the *tzaddik davens* for the welfare of the person.

Not always do a *tzaddik's* efforts result in a solved problem. However, they often do succeed, sometimes in what appears to be a miraculous way. We are so accustomed to the practice of seeking a *tzaddik's berachah* that we may not stop to wonder: Why does this work? If everything is in Hashem's hands except for our *yiras Shamayim*, why are some human beings given the power to move the universe?

The fact that this is true is not in question. The Gemara tells us that "When a *tzaddik* prays for something, Hashem answers him" (*Taanis* 23a). His power comes from his purity. He is so completely attached to Hashem, so attuned to Hashem's will, that he is working hand in hand, so to speak, with Hashem. Therefore, his words have tremendous power.

Knowing that there are people in the world who can help to unclog the channels of *berachah* and bring Hashem's salvation into our life can strengthen our *emunah*. First and most obvious, this gives us another way of alleviating a difficult situation. We're much less likely to give up hope when we know that the advice and *berachah* of a holy person can break through the barriers that have been standing in our way.

Also, knowing that closeness to Hashem can fill a human being with this level of spiritual power helps to affirm our faith. We might have access to the strongest, smartest and most well-connected person in the world, but that person cannot change what Hashem has decreed. Only someone whose *neshamah* is open to receiving Hashem's will, someone who has no other agenda anywhere in his heart or mind, has this ability. The *tzaddik* is "plugged into" Hashem. This doesn't only tell us about the *tzaddik's* power, but also tells us about the strength of his Power-Source.

It's a power that even non-Jews can perceive. The following famous story of Rabbi Aharon Kotler, founder of Lakewood's *Beis Medrash Govoha*, illustrates the point.

> *During World War II, there was a period of time when the rabbis of Italy were being imprisoned by the Nazis. Rabbi Aharon Kotler was one of the greatest forces in America devoted to saving Europe's Jews, and he desperately wanted to save the imprisoned rabbis. But who could influence the Italian government, which was allied with the Germans?*
>
> *Rabbi Kotler joined with Mr. Irving Bunim, who was active in the Vaad Hatzalah, to pay a visit to the renowned Mafia boss, "the godfather" Joe Bonanno. As the men sat down together, Joe Bonanno asked Mr. Bunim, "Who is this old gentleman sitting with you?" Mr. Bunim did not hesitate for a moment. "He is the godfather of all the Jewish people," he answered.*
>
> *Joe Bonanno was impressed. He asked Rabbi Kotler for a berachah. "You will merit a long life and die in your bed," the Rabbi responded. To a Mafia member, dying in bed at an old age was a miracle. The violent lifestyle of these men made it far more likely that they would meet with a violent death. Mr. Bonanno was delighted with the blessing. He promised that the rabbis would be freed*

within two weeks — and they were.

About 25 years later, two well-dressed men emerged from a black stretch limousine parked outside Beis Medrash Govoha. They entered the building and asked to speak to "the dean." Rabbi Shneur Kotler had by then assumed his father's position, and so the two men were brought to him. They introduced themselves as Joe Bonanno's sons. Their father, still alive and well, had retired and turned the "family business" over to them. Now they, too, sought a blessing from the holy rabbi. After all, they could see with their own eyes that it worked!

While stories such as the one above can inspire us to have greater faith in *tzaddikim*, we must remember that they are human beings who achieve their level of holiness through effort and self-discipline. They win many battles against their *yetzer hara* and never let down their guard. Through their example, we learn not only how powerful they are, but also, how powerful our own words can be. If we strive toward holiness and closeness to Hashem, we will have greater power to pray on our own behalf and on behalf of the people in our lives. Each of us has a direct line to Hashem; we just have to keep it clear of static.

> **MAKE IT REAL:**
> Build up your emunah in tzaddikim by reading stories of the miracles their tefillos have effected.

62

It's on the Way

With emunah, we too can wait calmly. Hashem will never fail to respond to sincere prayers.

Think about this typical scenario: There's a baby asleep in his crib. At 2 a.m., he wakes up with his stomach grumbling. In his mind, there's only one interpretation: "I'm starving!" He begins to cry, at first quietly, but then, when no one hears him, he picks up the volume and starts screaming for his life. After all, if no one comes with his bottle, he's doomed!

His cries wake up his mother, who goes downstairs to the kitchen, mixes up a bottle of formula and heats it up a little to perfectly suit her infant's needs. Meanwhile, the baby is becoming downright desperate, screaming at the top of his lungs. Where is his food? Why isn't his mother answering him? What will calm his hunger pangs?

At last his mother arrives with the bottle, gently lifts him out of the crib, sits with him in a rocking chair and puts the bottle in his mouth. His desperation turns to total contentment. The whole sequence of events took exactly five minutes, but in the baby's mind, it was an eternity.

Why are we taking this peek into a baby's mind? The reason is that it accurately illustrates the way we feel when our prayers appear go unanswered. There's something we need. We ask Hashem to send it to us, but it doesn't come. We ask more loudly, with more emotion, and still it doesn't come. We feel that without an answer, we can't go on, and so we cry out and beg Hashem. Where is our answer? What's going on? Why have we been abandoned?

We, like the baby, don't realize that our answer might have been in the making since we first began to ask. The baby doesn't understand that, "Mommy heard me and she's downstairs making me a bottle." If he knew help was on its way, he could wait calmly.

Likewise, with *emunah*, we too can wait calmly. We never have to fear that our prayers are going unanswered because we know that "Hashem is close to all who call out to Him" (*Tehillim*: 145:18). Hashem will never fail to respond to sincere prayers. We might find ourselves waiting for an answer, but that is only because our answer takes time to prepare. Hashem can help us in the blink of an eye, but sometimes, the best help for us requires time for the groundwork to be laid.

> There was a fine, accomplished girl who wanted to go to a seminary in her home city, where all her friends would be going. However, the head of the seminary and this girl's father had a conflict with each other, and the girl wasn't accepted. The father tried everything he could to get the girl in, but nothing worked. The girl was understandably devastated. Why couldn't she go with her friends?
>
> The father brought his daughter to speak to a gadol. He told her, "Forget about seminary. It's not working out, so drop it. Instead, take some courses and further your education. Maybe learn to be a teacher. But keep praying. Pray very hard, because Hashem obviously wants your tefillos."
>
> The girl followed the gadol's advice. She studied hard and prayed hard that her husband would be someone who was already excelling in Torah and would someday be a rabbi. She graduated three years later at the top of her class and began to seek a shidduch. But when people heard she had not been admitted to seminary, they immediately dismissed her, thinking "there must be something wrong."

The father decided that he would have to be the shadchan. He went to a yeshivah he thought highly of and prayed there three times a day, observing the students with an eye to finding the right one for his daughter. After a few days, he noticed one particular boy who seemed very serious about his learning and also seemed to be liked and respected by his fellow students. The Rosh Yeshivah confirmed that this boy was an outstanding student. The girl's father spoke to the boy's father, and the boy's father advised him, "Speak to my son. He's the one who has to decide."

The conversation got off to a rocky start as soon as the boy heard that the girl hadn't gone to seminary. But the father explained that his daughter had nothing to do with the situation, that she had been put through a test and met the challenge beautifully. He told the boy about the advice of the gadol.

"When did all this happen?" the boy asked. The father explained that it was four years ago at the start of the school year.

"I don't believe it!" said the boy. "When I first came here, I wasn't doing well and I was thinking about dropping out. Exactly four years ago, I decided to improve. I asked for a new chavrusa, and ever since then, it's been great. I never understood what happened until now."

The four years the girl spent *davening* for her ideal husband were the four years this student spent becoming that person. The answer was on its way, and the girl's prayers were hard at work for her all along.

MAKE IT REAL:

What is the last thing for which you prayed and got the answer you wanted? How long did it take and what events led up to your prayer being answered?

63
Round-the-Clock Security

It's never wise to dwell on the dangers around us, it's always wise to recognize the loving care that surrounds us.

In our world, very few people have security guards watching them 24 hours a day. The president of the United States and other world leaders are among the few that warrant that kind of protection. It would seem that you'd have to be a very important, indispensible individual to belong to this class of people.

Therefore, it might surprise you to know that you, too, have round-the-clock security. To Hashem, each of us is as indispensible and important as the president. We each have our vital mission in this world to perform, which no one else can perform for us. Therefore, Hashem keeps watch over us at all times, never taking a rest. "He never slumbers and he never sleeps," *Tehillim* (121:4) tells us. He sticks to us like a shadow, going wherever we go (121:5), keeping danger away from us as we go about our lives.

If you want to picture for yourself the great extent of protection He gives us all the time, imagine all the dangers that surround us that never reach us. We only know what *can* happen because of what occasionally *does* happen for reasons only Hashem knows. For example, how do we not become ill from the millions of bacteria that are all around us in the air, on our skin, on everything we touch? How do the cars heading toward each other on the road each keep to their side? How do millions of volts of electricity pass through our homes without setting it on fire? How does our heart keep pumping evenly and unfailingly, 70 times a minute for eight, nine or ten decades?

Thinking about all these potential dangers can thrust a person into a state of anxiety. In fact, there are people who do indeed worry incessantly about the dangers lurking all around us. However, that is the opposite of what we are meant to derive out of an understanding of what *can* go wrong. Instead, we are urged by the words in *Tehillim* to feel as though we are living in a bubble of protection, like astronauts walking around on Mars. It is only with Hashem's constant shadow at our side that we can live at all.

When you think about it, the Earth is just a terrarium spinning through infinite space. Our little bubble of atmosphere contains within it everything we need to live the most beautiful life. Hashem set down the perfect mixture of chemicals to give us earth, water, fire and air. He created a tiny little environment, a speck in the vast universe, which not only sustains our lives, but provides us with beauty and delight as well. It is a perfectly balanced world, placed exactly where it needs to be in the infinite universe so that it gets the right amount of heat and light and the right gravitational pull to make life possible. Were Hashem to "slumber" or "sleep" or leave our side for one split second, life would be over. Our own lives and the life of the universe itself are constantly under His watch.

The Jewish people as a whole are especially under Hashem's special protection. This is the only explanation for the fact that we are still here after thousands of years, still walking to shul on Shabbos, still eating matzah on Pesach, still praying the same words our ancestors prayed and still learning the same Torah. Even in the midst of the most horrendous destruction, Hashem was preparing the ground for our regrowth. We are His eternal people, and although we might sometimes suffer, Hashem will always stand by us and ensure that we rise again.

> *A man sat with his son reviewing Mishnayos. The boy was in fourth grade, and he was with his family visiting his grandmother for Shabbos. The grandmother was a*

Holocaust survivor who had met her husband right after the war, married in a refugee camp and had her first child right there in Germany. The new young family managed to get a visa to America. They eventually settled in Brooklyn and supported themselves through a small manufacturing business the husband set up.

The man who now sat with his son had seen his own father sitting over a Gemara in the middle of the night when he couldn't sleep. When his father passed away, the man inherited his sefarim. Along the margins, he saw that his father had marked off ideas that he particularly found interesting. He would write "tov," meaning "good" alongside ideas he liked, and "tov me'od," meaning "very good" next to the best parts. By learning his father's sefarim, the man came to realize how even after all he had been through, the Torah was the light of his life.

Now, as the grandmother watched father and son sitting at the dining-room table learning together, she spoke up. "This wasn't supposed to be," she said. "The Germans thought this would never be again. There would be no more Jews and no more Torah. But here we are. It's a miracle."

Hashem is always with us, protecting us individuals, as Jews and as a part of His vast creation. While it's never wise to dwell on the dangers around us, it's always wise to recognize the loving care that surrounds us.

MAKE IT REAL:

Think of an "almost" accident or problem from which Hashem saved you. Ask others to relate their own stories, so that you can build up your awareness of Hashem's protection.

64

"Is This the Thanks I Get?"

The only way to avoid falling into the trap of feeling angry or hurt is to remind ourselves, that everything, everything, EVERYTHING Hashem does is for our ultimate good.

At times, a person makes a big effort to improve himself: to really get serious about living the right way, to grow up and use his time wisely. That person might begin thinking more of other people, learning with more concentration, taking on more mitzvos or perhaps making sure to be on time for prayers. He might even make a commitment out loud to himself: *From now on, I'm going to...*

Of course he hopes and expects that his self-improvement will help him "get in good" with Hashem and bring him rewards right here in this world. He might even have made his commitment as a way to earn merit for himself or someone else who needs a special dose of help from Heaven.

But what happens if, instead of things getting better, they seem to get worse? This is a big challenge to our *emunah*. We might feel that Hashem doesn't approve of us, that we're not important or worthy in His eyes. We might feel like a student who tries hard in class but never gets noticed. *The teacher just doesn't like me* is a difficult enough feeling for a person to deal with. *Hashem just doesn't like me* is a thought that is impossible to deal with.

The only way to avoid falling into the trap of feeling angry or hurt is to remind ourselves, exactly when our spirits are sloshing around in a deep mud-puddle, that everything, everything, EVERYTHING Hashem does is for our ultimate good. The story below is the kind of story that might fit right into an angry person's skeptical outlook, and yet, if we look at it from the view of Heaven, we see that it is an uplifting story.

From the first month of David and Shaindy's marriage, there was money trouble. Neither of them had parents who could offer much help. The plan was for Shaindy to get a job while David continued learning and took college courses. But Shaindy couldn't get a job. "Doesn't Hashem want me to learn"? David wondered bitterly. "Why is He making it so hard for me? I went and got married, and now I'm flat broke!"

Things only went from bad to worse. David and Shaindy had to move in with Shaindy's parents. During the course of those years, they had two children, who were of course loved and welcomed, but made money even tighter. "I'm doing what I'm supposed to do," David thought sadly. "Hashem is against me. Everyone else's life is working out just fine and I have to beg and borrow."

By then, he had stopped learning, quit college and taken on a low-level job just to keep some money coming in. After a long two years, David and Shaindy were able to move into their own apartment again; money was tighter than ever. Shaindy was studying for a new career, but it would take time until she would graduate. Meanwhile, every week was a challenge. Their parents helped out as much as possible, and they, too, were being stretched to the limit.

The couple often thought about moving to a less expensive out-of-town community, but they were too overwhelmed to take action. Then the biggest problem of all came up. Their daughter was entering kindergarten and they could not afford the tuition. Now what? Weren't they even entitled to give their child a Torah education? What did Hashem want from them, anyway?

One day, Shaindy overheard a woman talking about

a school in another town — a school that was just exactly the type she was looking for. She looked into it and discovered that it had a very reasonable tuition and was located in a small, friendly community where she and David thought they would be happy.

For their daughter's sake, they got mobilized. The moment they decided to enroll their daughter into this school, things began changing. Shaindy got a good job in the new location. They found an apartment that was far nicer than the one into which they had been crammed. They found a shul where they felt they really belonged. A year after their move, David looked back and saw that all the troubles that had driven them out of their old community had one purpose: to bring them to a place where they and their children could really grow and thrive.

It took years, and no one would blame David for feeling abandoned by Hashem as he scrimped and scraped and borrowed to pay his bills. But bitterness didn't solve his problem; Hashem solved it by literally forcing him, in ways that felt very unpleasant, to go where he needed to be. When we know that this is the case, we can drive away our negativity and grasp Hashem's hand harder, even as we follow a difficult path.

MAKE IT REAL:

Drive away thoughts of resentment, anger or disappointment at Hashem's dealings with you by assuring yourself that "He's taking me where I need to go."

65

One Hundred Times Over

Troubles are a great gift from Hashem, Who is giving us a chance to earn much-needed merit.

Imagine you need to travel 100 miles. It's a cold, rainy day and the streets are wet and slippery. You really don't want to make this trip, but it's important. You're going to visit your grandfather, who is really looking forward to your visit. You gear up for the trip — a tall cup of coffee, some good music on your MP3 player and a full tank of gas. Then, when you've traveled five minutes — covering what should have been just one mile — you find yourself at your destination. You've covered 100 miles with the effort of one mile's trip!

This is the "magic" that happens when we do a mitzvah that comes with difficulty. "One good deed performed with difficulty is worth more than 100 mitzvos performed easily" (*Avos DeRabbi Nassan, Perek* 6). We get 100 times the mileage out of our mitzvah because of the struggle we went through to do it.

That means that when you're in a bad mood, but you force yourself to smile and act pleasant to your family, you've done the mitzvah of *v'ahavta l'rei'acha k'mocha* — loving others as you love yourself — not once, but 100 times. When you open up a *sefer* and focus on your learning despite the fact that you're tired and your mind is somewhere else, you've done the mitzvah of *limud Torah* not once, but 100 times. When you choose to stay home and help out your mother rather than going out with friends, you've done 100 acts of *chesed*.

Thinking about our struggles in this light, we would wonder why everyone doesn't cheer when they hit a roadblock. These troubles are a great gift from Hashem, who is giving us a chance to earn much-needed merit by overcoming one test instead of 100. It's His way of giving us a fast-track to a higher spiritual level.

When we face a challenge in our effort to serve Hashem, we might look at our friends to whom the same thing comes easy and wonder, *Why him/her and not me?* There is an answer to that question; in reality, we are getting the better end of the deal. If Hashem were paying us by the hour for our service to Him, we, with all our troubles and challenges, would be making 100 times more per hour than the person of whom we are so jealous.

If you had a choice of working as a counselor in a camp with air-conditioned bunkhouses, or one with nothing more than a fan and some windows, which would you choose? Most people would choose the camp with the air-conditioning. But what if the fan-and-window camp was paying $3,000 for the summer while the air-conditioned camp was paying $30? A person would have to be extremely devoted to his personal comfort to choose the $30 job.

This is the thought that we must grab onto when we find that there are obstacles in the way of our goal to improve in our service to Hashem. He isn't stopping us; He is trying to ensure us of the maximum reward for our effort.

> *One year following Yom Kippur services, the Chozeh of Lublin announced that he could tell each congregant what he had prayed for. One man took him up on the offer. The Chozeh told him, "You had a very hard time learning this year. You came home late every night from work and had to rush through dinner and run off to learn. You could only fit in an hour a night. So you asked Hashem to lighten your load so that you could learn for a longer time and do so in peace."*
>
> *The man was amazed. That was exactly what he*

had prayed for. "Can you tell me what Hashem has answered?" the man asked.

"He said, 'No,'" the Chozeh responded.

The man was upset. All he wanted was to do a better job learning Hashem's Torah, but Hashem had refused to help him! Why?

The Chozeh explained that the man was not losing anything at all by Hashem's refusal to lighten his load. In fact, the man would gain, because the learning he managed to do under pressure with such great difficulty was so precious to Hashem.

When we look around us at the advantages other people have in their service to Hashem, we might feel that they have been given an unfair head start in the race to the finish line. By remembering that Hashem rewards us according to our effort, not according to our results, we can banish this sense of injustice from our minds. Every single one of us has the opportunity to get to the finish line — to the destination Hashem has chosen for us — as long as we keep our eyes on the road in front of us.

MAKE IT REAL:

Do you have trouble concentrating on praying or learning, or feeling enthusiastic about some of the mitzvos? Think about the great value in your continued effort to do that mitzvah to the best of your ability.

66
Don't Let Your Arms Go Numb

The person who believes in Hashem and His kindness overcomes the pitfalls along the path of life, but people who are blinded by their anger and resentment keep tripping and falling.

A psychologist was talking to an audience about stress. He held up a glass of water and asked for volunteers to guess how much it weighed. After getting a few answers, he commented, "It doesn't really matter what it weighs. What matters is how long I hold it up. If I pick it up for a minute, I can handle it easily. If I hold it longer, my arm will begin to ache. If I try to hold onto it all day, my arm will go numb and I won't be able to do anything."

This, he said, is the way stress operates. If we think about a problem for a minute, we can handle it. Even if we give it some consistent thought, we can usually manage to still function. But if we hold onto our problems all day, we become paralyzed. We can't function. The key, said the psychologist, is to learn how to let go of stress.

Good advice, right? But he left out an important follow-up question. *How* does a person let go of stress? The answer is not in the psychology books; it's in the Torah. First, we have to remind ourselves that Hashem controls our lives. No one else can affect us. Secondly, we have to remember that Hashem wants only the very best for us. No matter how a situation might look to us, these are the facts. We have to repeat them to ourselves and remember them when we need them most. Eventually, this outlook will become second nature. Our reaction to setbacks and challenges will become calm and accepting.

When we do this, we are not only making our lives more peaceful and secure, but we are also fulfilling the mitzvah to see the hardships in our life as a child sees his father's occasional strictness (*Devarim* 8:5). If we believe that our Father loves us and that He knows what is best for us, we can accept even what we don't like.

If we did not have our *emunah* to rely on, we might see this as a cruel world and be constantly filled with fear that something terrible could happen to us. Two people can live through the exact same experience, but depending on their *emunah*, they might see the experience in very different ways.

For example, a car carrying a driver and a passenger is in an accident. The car is totaled but both people are unharmed. The person with weaker *emunah* will think, *What a disaster! We were almost killed! What did I ever do to deserve this?* The person with stronger *emunah* will think, *What a miracle! We could have been killed! Hashem was right there protecting me!* One will retell the story from the point of view of a victim of tragedy, while the other will retell it as the lucky recipient of a miracle.

Even when we can't see the good in what happens, a person with *emunah* trusts his faith more than he trusts his eyes. The Torah answers all our doubts and questions, and if we depend on it, we won't be steered in the wrong direction. Often, our eyes deceive us.

For example, Rabbi Pesach Eliyahu Falk comments on the theory of Charles Darwin that human beings were descended from monkeys. Darwin's Theory of Evolution, which directly contradicts the Torah's account of Creation, has become the "religion" of atheists and drawn millions of people away from faith in Hashem. Darwin based his theory on the many similarities between monkeys and people, which he observed with his eyes. However, if Darwin had instead taken a peek into the Gemara (*Sanhedrin* 109a) he could have been saved from leading the world astray. There, we learn that when Hashem punished the builders of the Tower of Babel, he divided them into three groups, one of which was turned into monkeys. So Darwin was right that people and monkeys are related, but in a very destructive way he was wrong about what the relationship is.

When our beliefs are straight, our vision is clear as well. The person who believes in Hashem and His kindness overcomes the pitfalls along the path of life, but people who are blinded by their anger and resentment keep tripping and falling. "Hashem's ways are straight. Righteous people walk in them and rebellious people stumble in them" (*Hoshea* 14:10). We see this over and over in life.

With these thoughts firmly planted in our minds, we have no need to keep holding up our glass of worries hour after hour, day after day. We can hand the glass over to Hashem, Who was holding it all along.

> **MAKE IT REAL:**
> *To really live with emunah, so that it becomes the way you react to the events — positive or challenging — in your life, remind yourself as often as you can that Hashem runs the world and that Hashem loves you. Choose a few times in your daily schedule to review those thoughts.*

67

Not So Fast!

Our job is to keep going as long as possible, fueled by the knowledge that our efforts will bring us tremendous rewards, even if we don't get to our goal.

A scenario: Aaron had a great inspiration; he would volunteer to learn with his neighbor's son. The boy, only 8, had lost his father and Aaron was sure that having an older friend/chavrusa would be a big help to the boy and his mother as well. He marched right over to the neighbor's house to offer his services, but no one was home. The next day, he saw the little boy playing with a friend in the park. "Ask your mother if I can come and learn with you," he told the boy. The mother called later in the evening to say that it might work out in another week or two, but right now wasn't convenient.

Two weeks later, Aaron saw the mother parking her car in her driveway. He approached her as she got out of the car and repeated his offer. "I'm sure he would love it," the mother said, "but I think he's got enough on his plate at the moment."

If you were Aaron, what would you think? Some people would look at the situation and say, "I tried. Obviously, Hashem doesn't want me to do this particular mitzvah. If

He did, He wouldn't throw so many obstacles in my way."

Other people would say, "The harder I try, the greater the merit. I'm not giving up until there's absolutely no hope left!"

Many people suddenly become *neviim* when they run into obstacles in doing a mitzvah. They believe they are seeing signs from Above telling them that their mitzvah is not meant to be. But the fact is that we have no way of knowing that this is the case. In fact, we can assume the opposite; because Hashem has commanded us to do mitzvos, we can assume that this is what He wants us to do. The obstacles might just be Hashem's way of arranging for us to earn greater reward for the mitzvah, as we discussed in a previous lesson. Obstacles are never a clear sign to stop trying.

We see this played out in the stories of two famous *shidduchim*. One was between Yitzchak and Rivkah. In that case, Avraham sent his servant Eliezer to his homeland to find a wife for his son. He gave Eliezer almost no direction at all, but Eliezer landed in just the right place and met just the right girl. He got her father's permission to bring her to Yitzchak and the *shidduch* was done. It could have been very complicated, but Hashem eased the way.

The opposite happened with Yaakov and Rachel. Yaakov ran to his uncle Lavan's home with very specific instructions from his mother, Rivkah. Nevertheless, it took him seven years to earn Leah's hand in marriage, and that was not even the wife for whom he had been working. He then married Rachel but had to work for another seven years to pay up his debt. Yaakov might have thrown up his hands and said, "Leah is the one Hashem wanted me to marry. Rachel was obviously not meant to be my wife." However, he persisted. The strain and stress he and Rachel went through became the merit that enabled Rachel to bear children.

This idea that "It's not meant to be" can come up in many situations. *Tzedakah* organizations, for example, often hit many dead ends and roadblocks as they get off the ground. Yet the people who start these organizations don't see the obstacles as a sign to give up. Instead, they see it as a sign to try harder.

There are, of course, times when our best efforts won't bring about the result we're aiming for. Sometimes Hashem is causing us to hit a roadblock because this particular mitzvah is not ours to perform.

> *Chana's friend's daughter, a young married woman, was in the hospital 40 miles from Chana's home. The friend, who lived hours away, called Chana and asked her to check in on her daughter. "She's probably lonely and a little scared," the friend said.*
>
> *Chana was glad to oblige. With a couple of free hours before her children got home from yeshivah, she got in her car on that sunny Sunday afternoon and headed to the highway. Once she paid the toll and traveled a few miles, the traffic began to slow down. Then it came to a standstill. Since the highway was near a beach area, it was clogged with beachgoers. Chana crept along with the traffic as the clock ticked on. A half-hour later, she had progressed only two miles. There would be no way to reach the hospital and get home again before her children arrived. When she got to the next exit, she turned around and headed home.*

As it turned out, Chana's mission was impossible. She could not physically get to the hospital and get home in the time it would take. She tried her best, but in the end, she had to quit. However, there's a long, rocky road between "difficult" and "impossible." Our job is to keep going as long as possible, fueled by the knowledge that our efforts will bring us tremendous rewards, even if we don't get to our goal.

MAKE IT REAL:

The next time you tell yourself that a mitzvah is just "not meant to be," think again. Is there another avenue to try? Are you really being stopped, or just challenged?

68

How Do You Keep Going?

We may have to endure difficulties, but we should never give up.

What's the biggest obstacle people have to *emunah*? Perhaps it's the sense that sometimes, nothing seems to help our situation. We turn to Hashem with our prayers, we do the mitzvos, we keep believing that what is happening is for the best, that Hashem loves us and that He will help us, but there we are, stuck with the same old troubles. Maybe we even see our troubles growing worse. In situations like that, we can hardly blame a person who gives up and says, "What are my *davening* and mitzvos and *chesed* doing for me? Forget it!"

Let's take a moment to examine this person's thinking. Imagine you desperately need a computer but you can't afford to buy one. One day, a store in your area has an incredible sale; everything is marked down by 75 percent. It's your chance! It's also the chance for the other 75,000 people who live in your area. But you don't care; you get to the store three hours before opening and wait on a long, long line of people. Finally, at 9 a.m., the doors open. The store staff allows in the first 200 people. You have to wait some more. In another half-hour, they let in another 50 people. After another half-hour, they let in another 50. You wonder if you'll ever get in, and if you do, whether there will be any computers left.

You've been waiting already for four hours. Your feet are tired.

You're cold. You begin thinking that maybe you don't need a computer after all. Maybe you can borrow one. You've got lots of other things to do today. You give up and go home. Little do you know that in another hour, you'd be inside the store. The longer you waited, the more you dealt with the discomforts of your mini-ordeal, the closer you were coming to the payoff. While you were getting more and more discouraged, you were in reality getting closer and closer to your "redemption."

What we see from the scenario above is that there is no benefit to quitting on Hashem. The only place this person could get the computer he needed at a price he could pay was in this store. Quitting after all the time he had already spent and all the discomfort he had already endured didn't solve his problem. It didn't fulfill his need. Instead, it left him with the same need and no way to fill it. The same is true for someone who throws up his hands and says he's had enough with Hashem. He might be walking away an hour before his salvation, or it might be 12 years until his salvation. The fact remains that his salvation can only come from one place.

There are many people who spend long years dealing with major challenges and unfortunately, they don't see an improvement. Not every sick person recovers. Not every poor person finds his fortune. Not every single person gets married. People suffer great, painful voids in their lives. But if they lose their connection with Hashem, they suffer the greatest void of all. There is no comfort for them, and they lose the tremendous merit they can earn by serving Hashem even in the midst of their struggles.

When people struggle, they do not always understand why. They do not see ahead to the rewards they will have in This World or the Next World, or both, as a result of holding tightly onto Hashem during their rough ride through life. But Hashem gives us one piece of information that we can hang onto in such times. We aren't alone. "In all their distress, He is distressed," says *Yeshayah* (63:9).

Rabbi Ephraim Wachsman illustrates the value of persevering with the story of Yosef HaTzaddik. Imagine having your own brothers — *talmidei chachamim* — sell you into slavery and send you off to a foreign land. How could you keep your faith when you see respected Jews do such a thing? Imagine that after that traumatic event, you keep your faith and do your best to serve Hashem even in slavery, and instead of being rewarded, you end up being trapped by your master's wife! But you don't fall for the trap; you hold onto your values and instead of being rewarded for that, you are led straight into a dungeon. Who had a better reason to give up on Hashem than Yosef?

Yet he clung to Hashem with all his might. When the going got tough, his *emunah* got even tougher. In the end, he became the second in command to Pharaoh, the most powerful monarch in the ancient world. He saved the world from starvation. He set in motion the beginnings of the Jewish people's history as a nation. He didn't know how it would all end, but he knew that he could only triumph over his challenges by holding onto Hashem.

It's not easy. Not at all. When people have serious troubles that don't go away, they deserve our help and compassion. Even when it is we, ourselves, who are suffering through a situation that seems to have no solution, we have to be compassionate to ourselves and give ourselves time to think, rethink and deal with each twist and turn. But a person can only help himself by "staying in the line" and waiting for the door to open for him. We may have to endure difficulties, but we should never give up and go home empty-handed.

MAKE IT REAL:

Do you know of someone who has been facing a difficult situation for a long time? If that person came to you for advice, what would you tell him or her? Can you apply that advice to a predicament in your own life?

69

What's My Job?

When you've done everything you can, it's time for emunah to take over.

If Hashem is taking care of everything, what's our job? If He gives us all the money we need, what does it matter whether or not we work? If He keeps our heart beating for as long as He has decided we should live, what does it matter whether our diet consists of sour sticks and potato chips or vegetables and tofu? If He has our *bashert* all picked out for us, why bother with a *shadchan*? Don't all these proactive measures show a lack of *emunah*?

As we know, we are supposed to live our lives in a natural way, doing whatever the norm is to accomplish our goals. This is called *hishtadlus* — effort. We are not supposed to go off on crazy, dangerous adventures with the idea that if it's not our time to leave the world, we'll be perfectly safe. We're not supposed to sit home waiting to win the lottery with the idea that if Hashem wants us to have *parnassah,* He can send it this way just as well as through a job or a business. We're not supposed to take it easy in school on the theory that if we are meant to do well, Hashem will put the right answers in our head. While it's true that every person has certain things designated for him, it's not true that we can abandon ourselves to fate. We have to care for ourselves and our lives.

Emunah is a mitzvah, but *hishtadlus,* when it's in the right balance, is also a mitzvah. Finding the balance is the hard part. How do you know when you've found it?

You know when you've done everything you can, everything that makes sense. Once you've done that, then your *hishtadlus* is done; it's time for *emunah* to take over. The result, whatever it is, is what Hashem wants it to be; we accept it, whether it's something to celebrate or it's a disappointment to us.

> There was a girl who had a hard time in high school. She struggled through ninth and tenth grades with the help of tutors and heaps of encouragement and prodding from her parents. At the end of 10th grade, she told her mother, "I can't do this anymore. It's so depressing. I feel so dumb every single day. Can't I just drop out and get a job? Maybe I'll go to a night seminary."
>
> Her mother didn't want her to leave high school. "It's important to finish, even if you don't pass everything," she insisted. So 11th grade began. The girl kept trying, but her grades never improved. She felt that the other girls in her class saw her as inferior. Her teachers never called on her, and while she was glad not to be put on the spot, she also felt as if she were invisible. It was another year of tutors and modified tests, another year of sore throats, headaches and stomach aches that kept her home in bed for far too many days.
>
> At the end of 11th grade, the girl knew she had tried as hard as she could to succeed in school. Her parents, too, knew she had given it her all. The girl was clearly running out of steam. No one — not the mother, the father nor the girl — felt they could make it through another year like the one that had just passed. "I think we've done everything we can to make this work out," the mother said. "It's time to try something else."
>
> The girl signed up for a night seminary, got a full-time job and began feeling success for the first time in years. She was a great salesgirl! She learned everything she needed to know about the merchandise and the store procedures. It was complicated and it took focus, but she did it. Her classes at night were inspiring, too. By the

next summer, she was feeling confident and happy, and eager to take on more learning. In the fall, she went to a seminary in Eretz Yisrael, and her life was back on track.

How much do we keep trying? When do we say, "Here's where it stops"? These are complicated questions and we can easily fool ourselves into thinking we're doing the right thing when we are actually out of balance. We might say, "I tried everything and now the rest is up to Hashem," when in fact we've quit far too early. We might say, "I can't give up!" when in fact, we're attempting to gain something Hashem doesn't want us to have. We might think, *How could Hashem not want a girl to be happy and successful in school?* But the truth is that many very successful people built the foundations of their success by dealing with such struggles. Even some great teachers were unsuccessful students.

To avoid falling into these traps, we have to examine our thoughts. When we're working our heads off and nothing is succeeding, are we trusting in Hashem enough? When we're throwing up our hands in defeat, are we doing enough *hishtadlus*?

We are given just one life. We have opportunities in front of us that Hashem wants us to grab and run with. These are the efforts that will bring us where He wants us to go, to fulfill the jobs in this world that He has designated for us. All He asks is that we try our best while always trusting Him to decide where our success will lie.

MAKE IT REAL:

What is one of your major goals in life right now? Write down the steps you must take to reach that goal and take the first step.

70

If It's Good, Why Pray?

> *There's no contradiction between believing that whatever Hashem does is good and asking Hashem to change our situation.*

A person gets sick. Because he has *emunah*, he says to himself, *This is from Hashem and Hashem only does what is the very best for me. So, being sick must be what I need most right now.*

What sense would it make in this case for him to pray to get better? If it's all good, why ask Hashem to change it? This was addressed earlier in the book but now we will elaborate on it more.

Here is one way to understand the answer: When everything is going well, we tend to overlook the Source of it all. Everything becomes part of the scenery, like the house we wake up in each day and the sky that is always above us. Instead of giving us motivation to recognize Hashem and come closer to Him, all our comfort and ease makes us forget Him. Only when we are lacking something do we suddenly realize how much we need Hashem's constant help. Sometimes, the very reason we lack something is because Hashem wants to encourage us to turn to Him. He wants us to pray to Him.

In that case, praying is absolutely the right response to a challenge. It's the whole purpose of it. Once we open up our connection with Hashem and ask Him for what we need, we've fulfilled the purpose and we are primed to receive what we're asking for.

At other times, we don't have what we need because it really isn't the best for us as we are at the present moment. But prayer can change that too, as this story told by the Chofetz Chaim shows us:

> A man died and his soul went to Shamayim. The Heavenly Court heard his case and told him that he would have to experience some suffering because of sins he had done in his lifetime, but after that, he would be welcomed into Gan Eden.
>
> But wait! They noticed that one of the sins on his record was that he had insulted someone and he had never asked for forgiveness. The only way to erase that sin was to go back to earth and treat people properly. No soul, even one facing suffering, wants to return to earth, but it was the man's only choice. Worse yet, he was told that he would go back to the world as a rich, handsome businessman.
>
> "How will I ever be able to do my job like that?" the man asked. "How will I avoid becoming arrogant and making even more mistakes?" After much arguing, he was granted his wish to come back as a poor beggar. He was thrilled. But when he arrived back in the world of the living, he had no recollection that his situation was a gift which he had begged for. He wondered, "Why can't I earn a parnassah? Why is Hashem doing this to me?"

In this case, wealth and success were truly not to the man's benefit. They would have interfered with his ability to fulfill the mission he had come back to the world to accomplish. We might think, then, that if he prayed for wealth and was answered, he would be doing himself great harm for eternity. If Hashem was really helping this man, He would ignore his prayers and keep him just where he was, on the bottom rung of the social ladder. Only in that way could he climb to the top of the spiritual ladder.

Now let's imagine being this man. We would surely not just resign ourselves to a life of misery. We might visit a *gadol* and ask for a *berachah* and some advice. The answer we would get, no doubt, would be, "Pray very hard every day for Hashem to help you."

So we would pray. And how would we approach Hashem in those prayers? We would approach Him like a beggar, with both hands open. We would say, "Hashem, I have nothing. There is nothing I can do to help myself. I only have You, Hashem. Please help me!"

Those are the words of a humble heart, a heart that has no illusions that he is running his own life. He reaches up to Hashem like a small child reaches up to his mother with both arms held high, asking to be held and carried. Now this man is a very different man from the one who originally went up to *Shamayim*. When his prayers are answered and he merits to finally live in dignity, his wealth will not make him arrogant. Poverty used to be the best situation for him, but now, he can accept Hashem's gifts without endangering his soul.

When we pray sincerely, we change who we are. The challenge that was good for the old us might not be necessary for the new us — the one who feels strongly connected to Hashem and treasures the gifts He gives us. There's no contradiction between believing that whatever Hashem does is good and asking Hashem to change our situation. Prayer always helps.

MAKE IT REAL:

Is there anything you have given up praying for, believing it's just not going to come to you? Try praying for it again, focusing on how much you are depending on Hashem for help.

71

There's Always an Option

In any situation, we are never out of options. He is our first, last and only resort.

A scenario: *Baruch needed a new pair of shoes for yeshivah. He went to his usual shoe store but couldn't find a style he liked. He went to a different store across town and found something nice, but when he tried them on, they pinched his feet. At another store, they didn't have the pair he liked in his size. He tried a big department store, where he found a good pair, but at about double the price he was prepared to spend.*

Baruch was exhausted and discouraged. When he got back into his car for the fifth time, he paused before turning the ignition key. "Hashem, I've tried just about everything. Please help me find a pair of shoes that fit, that I like and that are a good price."

Why did Baruch wait until he had tried every store he could think of before he asked Hashem to help him? The answer is that in his mind, he was the one who would make this a successful shopping trip. He knew the right stores, knew the style he liked and had enough money in his pocket to buy what he needed. He didn't think he needed Hashem.

Often, we don't turn to Hashem until we've run out of options. That is sometimes the reason we may suffer failure after failure. At some point, we finally say, "Only Hashem can help me now." This is often the phrase used in some frightening situations, when people are very ill or stranded in a dangerous situation and there appears to be no source of help. Rabbi Fischel Schachter tells a story of just such a situation.

> *A man who lived in Yerushalayim had a daughter who became very sick. None of the doctors in Eretz Yisrael had any help to offer her. There was one doctor in America, however, who had successfully treated cases like this girl's, and her father tried desperately to reach him.*
>
> *One day, someone called and told the father that this American doctor would be in Tel Aviv for a short while, and if he came right away, he could get his daughter in to see him. "He's leaving in a half-hour," the man said, "so be here by then."*
>
> *The father knew that it was almost impossible to travel from Yerushalayim to Tel Aviv in a half-hour, but what wouldn't he do to save his daughter? He took all the money he had in the house, ran outside to hail a cab and offered the driver a huge sum to get him to the doctor on time. The driver took up the challenge, racing through the roads and taking shortcuts through fields and back-roads. They arrived at the office building. The father and daughter jumped out and ran to the door.*
>
> *"Sorry, the doctor just left a minute ago," the father was told. From all the emotion and exertion, the father felt faint. He sat down and someone got him a cup of water. As he took the cup to his lips, he started the berachah "Shehakol," which tells us that Hashem's word creates everything. "Baruch atah Hashem," the father began. Suddenly he realized that Hashem was there with him, listening to him. He didn't need to pay a huge taxi fee, race through the streets or beg for a few moments of time from Hashem. "I did what I could. Now let's forget the doctors and the cabdrivers," the father said to Hashem. "This is between me and You."*
>
> *As he finished the berachah, he reminded himself that Hashem created everything, including him and his*

daughter. "You help me, Hashem…" he thought, and he sipped his water. His strength returned and he took his daughter home. Inside, he had the feeling that something had changed.

That feeling was confirmed a few weeks later when he brought his daughter back to the doctor. "It's a one-in-a-million situation," the doctor said. "The medicine seems to be working. She should be just fine."

Why couldn't the man have found this deep, live, electrical connection to Hashem before he had his very last hope pulled out from under him? Why couldn't he have saved himself the hair-raising and very expensive trip to Tel Aviv and the devastating news that the doctor had just departed?

Sometimes we have to give up hope in the natural answers to our problems before we can rise up to the level of *emunah* that will really make a difference in our situation. In every situation, whether it's as simple as shoe shopping or as crucial as medical care, as long as we have Hashem, we are never out of options. He is our first, last and only resort.

MAKE IT REAL:

Practice bringing Hashem into the picture even when you're about to do something routine. For instance, ask Him for success as you go out shopping or for an enjoyable time when you go to a simchah.

72

Perfectly Under Control

It takes time to reach greatness, but we can get on the road right now.

Dressed in his clean, pressed Shabbos clothes, hat upon his head, a rabbi walked through the streets of Yerushalayim on Friday evening heading to shul. His routine was to arrive at shul well before Kabbalas Shabbos, so that he could sit and learn, and then usher in Shabbos in a calm and peaceful way. Suddenly, as he walked along, a bucket of dirty laundry water spilled down on his head from a balcony above. He didn't look up. His expression didn't change. He simply turned around, went home, changed his clothes and started out again.

This story might seem impossible. Yet it isn't. It is the result of living with complete *bitachon*. Whether he's walking through a minefield or a garden, the person with *bitachon* stays calm. He knows that worry won't prevent something from happening if Hashem decrees it. Once trouble has appeared, he knows there's no one to blame. In the story above, the rabbi didn't even look up and catch the eye of the person who had dumped the water; that would have been casting blame.

This calmness, which we call *menuchas hanefesh*, is the sign of a great person. We understand this fact even without learning it. We can feel it. For example, imagine you walk into a pizza shop and order a pie, and the worker who is helping you accidentally drops your order on the floor. The boss is standing right there. Let's consider two different reactions the boss might have:

1. He shrugs and says to the worker, "No big deal. Give him a new pie."
2. He turns angrily at the worker and screams, "Why don't you watch what you're doing? Now that pie has to go into the garbage! You better not let that happen again or you're finished here! I can't afford to be feeding my garbage pail!"

Without knowing anything else about the boss — whether he gives *tzedakah* or learns Torah, whether he's smart or slow, whether he's healthy or sickly — you would have an instant impression of him based on these reactions. The first reaction would make you think, *Wow! What a great guy. He didn't even get upset.* This boss has *menuchas hanefesh,* and it comes from his ability to accept whatever Hashem sends his way. He knows that the profits lost from that one pie were profits he was not meant to have. The worker's hand might have slipped, but the loss was from Hashem. There was no need to berate and embarrass the worker.

By the same logic, we can see that the second reaction shows a small-minded way of thinking. This boss is counting every penny of profit from every pie, believing that it all comes from his ability to produce a good pizza, attract customers and run an efficient operation. He has no patience for a mistake because to him, that mistake is costing him money. He's got his eye on nickels and dimes, while the boss with *bitachon* has his eyes on *Shamayim.* It is clear which man is great and which is petty.

The Chofetz Chaim tells us that a person with *bitachon* "has his *middos* in his pocket." That means that the person is in charge of his *middos.* He takes them out and uses them as they are needed. They don't control him; he controls them. Therefore, if a person has need for anger — say, for instance, he wants to stop someone from bullying another student —

he can pull out just the right amount of anger to do the job. His heart isn't bubbling over with indignation. His arms aren't itching to punch the aggressor in the nose. He uses just enough anger to motivate him to step forward to defend the student and to sound firm and confident to the bully.

Menuchas hanefesh is not the trait of a pushover. Rather, it's the trait of a truly strong person who commands respect. Many students have had the experience of being in a classroom where there is a substitute teacher. Unfortunately, some students see "driving the sub crazy" as a sport. If the substitute holds his ground with dignity, the students usually back down. If they can drive the substitute to screaming and threatening, the students know they've won. No amount of screaming and threatening will get the class back in order. The less self-control the teacher has, the more ridiculous he looks in the eyes of the students.

We've learned throughout our lessons in *bitachon* that we cannot be in command of the events of our lives. Hashem has all of that in hand. However, with *bitachon,* we are in command of our emotions. Of course, we cannot expect to get an instant, long-lasting dose of *menuchas hanefesh* the moment we begin to work on our *bitachon*. This, like every positive *middah,* takes time, practice and experience to build. But we will find that the more we turn *bitachon* into our "default mode" for reacting to challenges, the greater our *menuchas hanefesh* will become. It takes time to reach greatness, but we can get on the road right now.

> ## MAKE IT REAL:
> *The next time you feel yourself getting angry, think to yourself, "I can be great!" and try to inject bitachon into the situation.*

73
No Appointment Necessary

Emunah is the fuel that makes our prayers real and powerful. But at the same time, prayers are the fuel that strengthens our emunah.

A scenario: The baby had been sick for days. The mother took the baby to the doctor and he said it was a virus. "It will go away on its own in a few days. If it doesn't, come back." A few days passed, and then a few more, and the baby was still sick. The mother was worried. She called the doctor's office and was put on hold. After a half-hour on hold, the receptionist came on the line. The mother told her what the doctor had said. "We need to see the doctor today," the mother insisted. "The baby's fever is going up."

"Sorry," the receptionist said. "It's flu season. We have no appointments until tomorrow afternoon."

"You want my baby to just keep getting sicker for another 24 hours?" the mother complained.

"Sorry," the receptionist repeated. "Maybe take her to the emergency room."

When we need help from a human being, we can't always get it. People have their limits. They might not have time for us. They might not feel they are the right one to help us. We might have to wait while our problem gets worse. People are, after all, only human.

This is true when we're seeking regular help that we need in regular circumstances. If for some reason we want to see the top person in a particular profession, the chances of getting an appointment are even less. Imagine that you wanted to become a successful businessperson and you wanted to get advice from Tim Cook, the head of Apple, the famous computer company. How long do you think it would take for Tim Cook to even find out that you wanted to see him? It was reported that in May 2013, there was an auction, and one of the prizes was a cup of coffee with Tim Cook. The winning bidder paid $610,000 for his prize.

To see a top doctor, a person might have to make an appointment months in advance, even though he may be quite sick. To meet with anyone of high position — the president, a senator, a Supreme Court judge — is nearly impossible for the average person.

That's why it's all the more amazing that we can speak to G-d Himself, the Master of the Universe, any time we want. We can bypass all those people who are too busy for us and go straight to the top. They are all His puppets anyway.

Not only don't we need an appointment, not only is our conversation with Hashem not an inconvenience for him, but it is just the opposite. Calling on Hashem when we are facing a problem is an actual mitzvah that He commands us to do. We are earning merit just for opening our mouths and telling Hashem what's on our minds. That alone is a tremendous help to us, even if our specific request doesn't get answered as we wish or when we wish.

One pitfall of praying for Hashem to solve our problems is that the *yetzer hara* sometimes makes us feel as if we're wasting our time. There are situations in which Hashem wants to hear not just one heartfelt prayer from us, but many, because He wants us to have the benefit of all those prayers (*Midrash Rabbah, Parashas Devarim*). So we pray once, twice, a hundred times. We pray for days, months and years. We don't realize that as we are getting closer and closer to the moment that Hashem will answer us, the *yetzer hara* works harder to put despair into our hearts.

I'm asking and asking, and nothing is happening, we begin

to think. *Why should I keep praying? What good does it do?*

We should realize that the harder it gets for us to keep praying, the closer we are getting to our answer. Every *tefillah* we say brings us rewards and benefits. We might not see it today, but we'll see it tomorrow. If not tomorrow, then we'll see it a year from now, or even 10 years from now. There's no such thing as a prayer that doesn't help us somehow.

Best of all, Hashem is always right there, waiting with a listening ear to hear His children's words. Even though He knows exactly what each of us needs, He set up the world so that our prayers are what open the door and let the blessings come down from *Shamayim*. When we pray to Hashem, we show Him that He is real to us. We are not talking to the wall in front of us; we are talking to our Father in Heaven.

Emunah is the fuel that makes our prayers real and powerful. But at the same time, prayers are the fuel that strengthens our *emunah*, keeping us awake and aware that Hashem is controlling every part of our lives. Instead of complaining, pray! Instead of worrying, pray! Instead of crying to a friend, cry to Hashem! Never stop praying. Hashem will never stop listening.

> **MAKE IT REAL:**
> *Try to ramp up the power of your tefillos by taking a moment to become aware that it's a two-way conversation. You are speaking and Hashem is listening.*

74
What Do You Expect?

Unhappiness comes from thinking that we deserve a smooth, easy, stress-free life.

One morning, Chaim, a 12th-grade yeshivah student in Lakewood, woke up, looked in the mirror and nearly fainted. What was that lump on his forehead? Chaim, a born worrier, could only think the worst. It was some terrible disease — the worst terrible disease. He quickly found his mother in the kitchen and pointed to the lump. "Look!" he said. "What is this? What can it be?"

"Looks like maybe a little skin infection or something," his mother said.

"It could be serious!" Chaim insisted. "I don't want to ignore it and then find out that —"

"I'll call the doctor and we'll have him take a look at it," the mother said. She knew he would not be able to calm down until a professional gave him a clean bill of health. She made an appointment for that afternoon and arranged to pick Chaim up from yeshivah.

The hours dragged on with Chaim constantly thinking about the fact that perhaps his whole life was about to change. Instead of being a happy-go-lucky 12th grader looking forward to Beis Medrash and a year in Eretz Yisrael, he might be, chas v'shalom, spending his time fighting a horrific illness. Maybe it was too late for him to "get serious" as he had always promised himself he would do. Maybe he would no longer be able to learn with the concentration he knew he could muster if he tried, or arrive at shul right on time, as he always meant to do.

"I had it all and I wasted it!" he thought to himself "Well, if this turns out to be a nothing, like my mother says it is, then I am changing. Hashem, please listen to me. Let this be nothing and you'll see how much I'm going to grow. I'll be a whole new Chaim."

That afternoon, the doctor took a look at the lump on Chaim's forehead. Noticing his patient's tense expression, his first words were, "You're not dying. It's a cyst that will go away in a week or so."

Chaim felt the most incredible wave of gratitude wash over him. The terrifying images that he had conjured disappeared. He had a new lease on life. And yet, it could have gone the other way. For some people, it does go the other way. "Why am I so lucky, Hashem?" he asked out loud. "What can I do to thank You?"

We might look at Chaim as unusually anxious about his health. Most people would not jump to the worst conclusion as he did. However, the end of the story is worth our taking seriously because even though his challenge was mostly in his imagination, his awakening was very real. It was based on a deep and sudden understanding of how fortunate we are to just have our lives.

Unhappiness comes from thinking that we deserve a smooth, easy, stress-free life. Just being alive and well, with a home to live in and food to eat, a school in which to learn and a family to love and guide us, are so often not enough for us. We expect to have the latest styles in our closet. We expect to get good grades, even if we're not trying our hardest. We expect to be able to do whatever our friends are able to do. If they all go to camp, we must go. If they all go to Eretz Yisrael, we must go. If they get their drivers' license, we must get ours. We use the word "normal" to describe the things we feel we should have, even when perhaps they pose a spiritual danger or a financial hardship.

The idea of the *tefillah* "*Modim*" in *Shemoneh Esrei* is to awaken us to the fact that everything we have is more than we could possibly deserve. The word *hoda'ah,* thanks, means to acknowledge a debt of gratitude to Hashem. Why do we say "debt"? We use that word because when Hashem does something for us, we are not earning it. We are not entitled to it. We're on the receiving end of something He wants us to have. When we see all the gifts in our life through that perspective, every little thing we have makes us happy.

That doesn't mean that we should not have goals. Goals are expectations of ourselves. They keep us focused and motivate us to move forward in life. For instance, if you have a goal of getting in shape, that will keep you from eating unwisely and push you to be physically active. If you have a goal of getting into a top school, you'll prioritize your time to make sure you study and review enough to earn good grades.

We can and should expect ourselves to live up to our obligations, treat people kindly, work on our *emunah* and our *middos* and our connection to Hashem. Those are the expectations that will bring us happiness no matter what happens in our lives. But the other type of expectation robs us of happiness, causing us to see great gifts as nothing more than our due. To fight that very human tendency, we can learn from Chaim and ask ourselves the question that is on a grateful person's mind: *Why am I so lucky?*

> ### MAKE IT REAL:
> *On a Post-it note, write down seven gifts for which you are grateful. Each day when you say Modim, focus on one of those gifts. You can add to or change your list occasionally so your feelings of gratitude stay fresh.*

75

Hashem's Treasure

Knowing we're loved, treasured and never forgotten gives us the strength and confidence to keep hanging on.

Imagine that for some reason, you have to set out on a dangerous trip far from home. Your parents give you a parting letter. In it are all their words of encouragement and advice. Some of the information is essential and practical: how to get where you're going, what to do and who to see when you get there. Some of it is from their heart to yours, telling you how much they love you and trust you to accomplish your mission. They also write words that will keep you connected to Hashem and Torah — quotes from Tehillim, reminders of the importance of davening and keeping the mitzvos and assurances that Hashem is with you every step of the way.

You put the letter in your pocket and set out on your trip. Imagine how much you would treasure this letter. You would constantly be checking to make sure it didn't fall out of your pocket. You would always be aware of where it was. When you went to bed at night, you would put it in a special place for safekeeping. When you got dressed in the morning, you would make sure to put it back in your pocket. You would treasure this letter and never forget about it.

We, the Jewish people, and each of us as individuals, are the "treasure" in Hashem's "pocket." He is constantly aware of where we are and what we're doing. He never forgets about us (*Malbim, Tehillim* 135:4). That is true no matter what we do. To the person in the above *mashal,* it doesn't matter if the letter is written on plain paper or expensive parchment. It doesn't matter if the handwriting is elegant calligraphy or barely readable penmanship. The letter is precious because of what it is. In the same way, we — whether we're brilliant and accomplished or struggling, whether we're filled with energy and enthusiasm or feeling uninspired, whether our peers admire us or think, *What's up with him?* — are Hashem's treasured possession.

Hashem's love is unconditional. That means that it doesn't depend on anything we do. It only depends on our connection to Him. In the same way that parents love their children just because they belong to them, Hashem loves us because we belong to Him. The destruction of the Beis HaMikdash illustrates this point. Chazal tell us (*Yoma* 54b) that when the enemy broke into the *Kodesh HaKodashim,* they saw the *keruvim* on top of the Ark holding each other in an embrace. When the *keruvim* were in that position, this was a sign of Hashem's love for the Jewish people. Why, just as the Beis HaMikdash was being set afire, was this symbol of love on display? It was Hashem's message to the Jews that even as they were being conquered and sent into exile, it was all out of love. It was all for our benefit. Hashem's love never decreased, even in the midst of the destruction.

One of the best ways for us, as human beings, to understand Hashem's love is by thinking about our parents' love for us. Hashem tells us, "You are children to Hashem, your G-d" (*Devarim* 14:1). With these words, He helps us to understand something that is really beyond our understanding. However, we can use this idea to at least get a hint of the powerful love Hashem has for us.

The parent-child *mashal* makes us think about what it means to be loved; to have people in our lives whose main concern is our health, growth and happiness. Our parents' love is so great and selfless that they invest everything in us only to send us off into our own lives. Sometimes children settle and raise their families far away from their parents, and while the parents will miss their children, their real happiness comes from knowing that their children are living a good life and accomplishing what they need to accomplish. This is a love we can rely on, as this story shows us:

> *In 1988, a massive earthquake struck Armenia, killing more than 25,000 people in less than four minutes. The father of a young boy ran to his son's school to see if he could find his child. Onlookers, police and rescue people tried to pull him away, fearing that the loose beams and rocks could shift at any moment and fall on him. The father, however, refused to budge. He dug with his hands. He dug with anything he could find. He recruited anyone who would help him. He had once told his son that he would always be there for him, no matter what happened, and now was the moment to make good on his promise.*
>
> *The father dug for 38 hours, barely taking a rest. At that point, he pulled back a large boulder and heard his son's voice. He yelled his son's name and heard, "Dad! It's me! I knew you were coming. I told all the other kids not to worry — my father promised that he would always be there for me."*
>
> *It turned out that when the building collapsed, a triangular air pocket was formed and 14 children, including this man's son, were saved.*

Knowing we're loved, treasured and never forgotten gives us the strength and confidence to keep hanging on, just as this boy did. As powerful as a parent's love can be, we must keep in mind that it's only a drop in the ocean. Hashem's love is the ocean.

MAKE IT REAL:

When something good happens to you, say to yourself or out loud, "Hashem loves me!" Eventually, as you remind yourself of how beloved you are, you'll be able to tap into that feeling even when a challenge arises.

76

Can You Pray to Be Good?

Once we are clear on what is right and what is wrong, the rest depends upon us.

A scenario: *Devorah and Dina were out for a walk. They were moving at a quick pace along a track around the lake, doing their best to get their hearts beating and muscles working. Dina wanted to lose a few pounds that she had put on during Pesach.*

"If im yirtzah Hashem I just stop noshing, I should be able to get rid of this weight in a month or so," she said to Devorah.

"Im yirtzah Hashem?" Devorah countered. "Hashem doesn't control what you put in your mouth. You do!"

Dina knows that she needs more self-control. She knows that she lets her attraction to sweets overpower her better instincts. It's a situation that involves her health and her self-esteem, but it involves her spiritual self too. It's wrong to keep feeding her momentary urges and ignoring the voice of self-control that keeps trying to get itself heard. But is it Hashem Who determines her success in this area or is it Dina, herself?

When it comes to our spiritual growth, Hashem turns the reins over to us. We have it in our power to be a *tzaddik* or the lowest of the low. Every time we choose between right and wrong, we take a step in one direction or the other. A person may not be able to choose to be a great *baal tzedakah* because Hashem hasn't given him enough money to do that. But he *can* choose what to do with the small amount of money he has. If he gives his dollar or two whenever he has the chance, he's moving in the direction of a *tzaddik*. He's doing Hashem's will with whatever resources Hashem puts in his hand.

On the other hand, what if he never gives *tzedakah* because he always thinks to himself, *I'm not that rich. I better hold on to every penny just in case I need it.* Then he's taking a step away from Hashem. He's making a choice not to do a mitzvah. That choice is entirely his. If he were to say, "*Im yirtzeh Hashem,* I'm going to give more *tzedakah* one day," he would be trying to hand off his own job to Hashem. In this case, it's not Hashem's will that's at work; it's this person's own will.

Does Hashem's will enter into our spiritual growth at all? The *Chovos HaLevavos* says that it does, but in only one way (*Shaar HaBitachon,* Chapter 4). He explains that there are three parts of any decision that involves *yiras Shamayim.* These are 1) the decision to do it; 2) making the preparations needed to carry out the decision and, 3) actually doing it. The first two elements are in our court. We make the decision to do the mitzvah and we make preparations needed to succeed.

For instance, a boy decides to get to shul on time. That's his decision; Hashem didn't plant that idea in his head. Then he buys an alarm clock and sets it for the right time; that's his preparation, which is also completely to his credit. He also makes sure to go to bed at a reasonable hour so that he will be able to wake up more easily. With all that in place, his plan may or may not work out as he foresees. What if there's a blizzard the next morning? What if his alarm clock malfunctions and doesn't wake him up? What if he wakes up with a fever and a sore throat? All of those "what ifs" are Hashem's doing. Therefore, we need Hashem to take our decision and our preparations and turn them into success.

That's where prayers can help. We can pray that Hashem will enable us to execute our plan. It's up to us to want to do the right thing and to prepare to do the right thing in every way we can. Because this is what is in our hands, it is what earns us all our merit in This World and the World to Come. We don't get credit for Hashem's work; we only get credit for our own. However, we want our efforts to bring us to a better place in our lives. We want our plan to work, and only Hashem can ensure that.

One more area in which prayer helps is in being able to see right from wrong. You might think that this comes naturally after all the years your parents and teachers have spent teaching you. Nevertheless, we can easily be fooled by the *yetzer hara*. It makes us believe that what we desire is right, and that whatever opposes our will is wrong. That's why people can fight bitter battles, and each one is positive that Hashem is on his side. We can stumble into many mistakes and *aveiros* all in the name of "doing what's right." Therefore, says the *Ben Yehoyada,* we should pray for clarity.

Once we are clear on what is right and what is wrong, the rest depends upon us. *Yiras Shamayim* is our one and only job in life. While we can ask Hashem to smooth the road for us, remove the obstacles and bring us success, we are the only ones who can put ourselves on the road and follow it step-by-step.

> **MAKE IT REAL:**
> *Do you have goals for personal growth that you are having trouble achieving? What is blocking you? Is it something in your control, or in Hashem's?*

77

Someone Else's Problem

When people see that others care about them, it's easier for them to feel that Hashem cares about them, too.

That classmate who's always complaining that he never gets a break — is his problem your problem? That elderly aunt whose only topic of conversation is how much she misses her husband — is it up to you to cheer her up? What about that younger sister who comes home from school crying that "no one likes me?" Is it up to you to listen to her stories about who sat next to whom at lunch?

In all of these cases, comforting the other person is, in a certain sense, saving his or her life. When people are down in the dumps, when they cry themselves to sleep and don't want to face the next day, they're not really living. If there are practical ways to ease their burden, then, as we learned in an earlier lesson, that is what you should do. But what if there is nothing you can do to fix their situation? Just by listening to them and helping them build the *emunah* they need to deal with their situations, you can give them priceless help.

People who are hurting need someone to really hear them and sympathize with the pain they are feeling, even if you don't think their situation is worth so much distress. You might even think their situation is their own fault, but that doesn't matter. If someone is careless and breaks his leg, you would still visit him in the hospital and sympathize with the pain of his ordeal.

In the same way, when people cause their own emotional pain, they still deserve our care and compassion.

Often, when you first start listening to someone's complaints, he doesn't want to hear anything spiritual or encouraging. If you tell him, "I know it seems difficult, but Hashem loves you," he is bound to react with a negative answer: "This doesn't feel like love to me." You tell him that what is happening is actually good and he responds, "Oh, yeah? Would you want it to happen to you if it's so good?" When this is the situation, your best way to help is to just listen and tell the person that you're sorry to see him in such pain and you hope things will get better.

After awhile, the heat inside the person cools down. He has a chance to blow it all out by talking, complaining, perhaps even crying. At that point, he might be able to look at the possible benefits of his situation, to think about the gifts that he *does* have and to see Hashem's kindness in his life. He might be able to regain his hope for the future.

When we do this for someone, we are living up to the mitzvah of *"V'ahavta l'rei'acha kamocha"* (*Vayikra* 19:18) — love your fellow as you love yourself. We can't always take care of another person's physical needs the way we take care of our own. For instance, we learn in the Gemara (*Bava Metzia* 62a) that if two people are lost in the desert and one of them has only enough water to save himself, he is allowed to drink it. On a modern-day level, if you have just enough money to buy yourself an airplane ticket and your friend can't afford a ticket, you can use your money for your own ticket.

But there is one area in which we have to give the other person our all and consider his needs to be just as important as our own; that is in the spiritual realm (*Chasam Sofer*). Since we all, on a deep level, share a common *neshamah,* taking care of someone else's soul is the same as taking care of our own. If we can lift another person out of depression, give the person hope and help him feel Hashem's love in his life, we are doing exactly what we're in the world to do (*Yeshayah* 41:6). We might not have the right words for someone, in which case we could certainly recommend a book or CD, or ask a rabbi or teacher to help.

In this story about the Chofetz Chaim, we see that comforting an unhappy person is top priority, even for a *talmid chacham* and *gadol* who surely has many deeper and more pressing concerns.

> There was an older, unmarried man living in the Chofetz Chaim's town of Radin. On Yom Kippur night, with no family to go home to, the man sat in shul after the davening was over. Someone came along and sat down next to him, and to his surprise, he saw that it was the Chofetz Chaim. The great sage began talking to the man about his own life and the challenges he met early on.
>
> He recalled that his father died when he was only 10 and he lived in terrible poverty. He left home for yeshivah and was separated from his family for many years. When it came time to get married, he was among an elite group of boys being sought by the wealthiest men for their daughters. However, the Chofetz Chaim's stepfather, who was very poor, wanted him to marry his daughter. To keep the peace in his mother's marriage, he agreed. He wasn't bitter, but he wondered why he did not have the opportunity to learn Torah in ease and comfort.
>
> As years went by, however, he saw that the men who had married the wealthy girls had been drawn away from learning. Meanwhile, the Chofetz Chaim's wife supported his learning in every way possible, which allowed him to reach the heights he had achieved. "Throughout everything, I stayed strong," the Chofetz Chaim told the man. "I knew that Hashem was holding my hand and taking me precisely where I needed to go."
>
> The Chofetz Chaim sat with the man all night giving him encouragement. On the holiest night of the year, he didn't speak words of Torah or teshuvah. He simply made it his business to uplift a downtrodden soul.

When people see that others care about them, it's easier for them to feel that Hashem cares about them, too.

> **MAKE IT REAL:**
> *Is there someone whose complaints make you want to roll your eyes and say, "This again?" Make it a point to really hear that person out the next time you speak to him, and then, if he seems receptive, offer some encouragement.*

78
Hashem Chooses the Winners

When we rely only on Hashem then He, in turn, lets His light shine through us into the world.

In 1975, an advertising executive named Gary Dahl came up with an idea after overhearing his friends discussing how difficult it was to take care of their pets. Jokingly, he said that a rock would be a perfect pet. Everyone laughed, but Gary Dahl got the best laugh of all. He created a product called a Pet Rock, which came in its own box with breathing holes and a straw stuck into it, as well as a funny instruction manual explaining to the owners how to care for their pet. In the course of about one year, he sold 1.4 million Pet Rocks at $4 each and became a multimillionaire. Then the trend was petered out (*Wikipedia*).

This story teaches two lessons. The most obvious might be that people spend money on foolish things. But the real lesson is that Hashem runs the world. He chooses who will succeed and who will fail. An idea as patently absurd as a Pet Rock can change a person into a millionaire while many other, far more useful products never turn a profit.

You've surely seen this yourself. For instance, two pizza shops open in a town. Both make good pizza, both are priced reasonably, both have good locations but one is always packed and the other is so quiet that you can hear the hum of the refrigerator. Another example: Two people graduate the same medical school with the same grades; one becomes the most popular pediatrician in town and the other ends up giving up his private practice to work for a clinic.

Why does the same *hishtadlus* sometimes bring about vastly different results? Why do some people manage to succeed on dumb luck while others do everything right and fail? The answer in one word is *chein* — charm. *Chein* is a gift Hashem grants at will. Rabbi Moshe Malka said it's like a spray from Hashem that makes someone or something appealing to others. People with *chein* are so likeable that it's hard to even be jealous of them. They're succeeding, but they're not competing. They have a natural grace to which people are magnetically drawn.

The same is true for the endeavors of people with *chein*. They seem to have the golden touch. Things work out for them. Their stories get published, their plans get realized, their businesses succeed and even when they experience failure, they quickly turn it into a triumph.

It would seem, then, that *chein* is something everyone should try to acquire. The question is, how? How does someone radiate natural grace and charm? Isn't it an inborn trait, like blond hair or nice teeth?

The answer is to realize that Hashem is the only One Who counts. People with true *chein* are not busy trying to gain favor in other people's eyes. They don't flatter or grovel or behave in a false, people-pleasing manner. They know that no one has anything to give them and no one has the power to take anything away from them. They don't need people for their own self-aggrandizement, and therefore, they relate to people in an open, honest, accepting way. They appreciate other people's talents and strengths because they don't worry about being considered inferior. Someone else's success is not a threat to them because they know they will get whatever is coming to them.

It's very easy to fool ourselves into thinking that other people control our fate. *If the teacher doesn't like me, I won't get a good grade. If I don't get friendly with him, I won't be in the inner circle in yeshivah. I asked to borrow her notes and she said no. Now I won't be prepared for the test.* And so forth.

These kinds of thoughts are *chein* repellents. They cause us to act in ways that are untrue to ourselves. We have to always remind ourselves that none of these thoughts are valid. We will achieve exactly what Hashem wants us to achieve and own what He wants us to own. If one person doesn't help us arrive at the goal Hashem has for us, then He will send us someone else to do the job. If we meet up with impossible obstacles, then it's not a goal Hashem has in mind for us.

Absorbing this idea right down to our bones is the key to earning our *"shpritz"* of *chein*. When we rely only on Hashem then He, in turn, lets His light shine through us into the world.

> **MAKE IT REAL:**
> *Think of someone you know who has chein. What makes him/her so appealing and likeable? What can you learn from this person?*

79

When Your Father Is Rich

We are all children of the richest Father in the world. There is literally no limit to what He can do for us.

A scenario: Yitzy and Yaakov were roommates in yeshivah in Eretz Yisrael. They shared a drafty old room in a run-down dormitory building. Yitzy thought the dorm situation was "going to make a great story for my kids." Yaakov felt abused. "The yeshivah cleaning lady probably lives better than we do."

Once in a while, to escape from the cholent-four-nights-a-week menu, they would head out for some falafel or pizza. For Yitzy, it was a nice break from the routine. He climbed on the bus, swiped his "Rav Kav" bus card and found a seat, a big smile on his face. Yaakov was right behind him. He felt a little uneasy as his card was swiped. How much money was left on it, he wondered? He sat down next to Yitzy and was soon in a better mood.

When they got to the pizza shop, Yitzy put down the money on the counter and happily looked forward to biting into the hot, cheesy slice. It was his last shekel, but it was worth it! Yaakov counted out each shekel with a vague sense of dread. He wondered if he should be treating himself.

What was the difference between Yitzy's and Yaakov's experiences in Eretz Yisrael? Yitzy was from a wealthy family. He saw his living conditions as temporary and was able to make light of it. He could spend his last shekel, knowing that his parents had more to give him. Yaakov, on the other hand, came from a poor family. He had to be very careful not to overspend the budget his parents had given him. He knew they didn't have any more in reserve. Therefore, every shekel he spent took a bite out of his sense of security.

Yitzy's knowledge that his parents were always there backing him up gave him resilience to deal with challenges of dorm life. Yaakov's feeling that he was basically on his own left him feeling a little fearful and troubled even when things were going well.

We are all children of the richest Father in the world. There is literally no limit to what He can do for us. When we teach ourselves to believe this, we can live each moment with happiness and confidence, although we must still eat responsibly. Our Father is backing us up. If we seem to be lacking, we know that He has more to give us, and if giving it is to our benefit, He can and will do so.

The fearful, troubled feeling people like Yaakov carry around with them, known as anxiety, is one our generation's biggest afflictions. It gives people the sense that something bad is going to happen, even when at that very moment they are healthy, well fed, safe and cared for. It makes people afraid to take chances and try new things because they focus only on the worst possible outcome. It robs people of energy to accomplish their goals and keeps them awake at night. Some people require medication to keep their anxiety under control.

There is another treatment, however, that often works, and it is called *Shaar HaBitachon,* a portion of the *sefer Chovos HaLevavos.* This *sefer* was the spark that ignited the career of Dr. David Rosmarin, who founded and runs the Center for Anxiety, which has four offices and a large staff of therapists who help people overcome their anxiety. Dr. Rosmarin got started on this path in college in 1999, when the pressures of trying to excel academically began keeping him awake at night.

He thought of visiting the psychologist on campus, but he first discussed his situation with his rabbi. The rabbi photocopied *Shaar HaBitachon* for him and "prescribed" 10 or 15 minutes of reading each night before bedtime. Dr. Rosmarin followed the advice: "To my surprise, within eight weeks, not only was I able to fall asleep without difficulty, but my anxiety almost completely vanished." Even more surprising, he said, was that the issues that were making him anxious had gotten more intense. Nothing had improved, but "I had increased my level of trust in Hashem and I realized that the events in my life were ultimately controlled by Hashem. Therefore, I had little to worry about."

Even now, in his practice, the wisdom of *Shaar HaBitachon* plays a major role in the help he offers his patients. It is the greatest medication. You don't need a prescription, it isn't expensive and there are no side effects.

Rabbeinu Bachya, the author of *Chovos HaLevavos,* tells us that the first benefit of *bitachon* is peace of mind and freedom from stress. Reading this *sefer* regularly and thinking about what it says has given generations of Jews a shield against anxiety and all the troubles it brings. If we keep these ideas fresh in our minds, they will be there for us when we need them, helping us to calm down and look straight into the eye of any challenge that comes our way.

> **MAKE IT REAL:**
> Get a copy of Shaar HaBitachon and do as Dr. Rosmarin did; read and think about it for a few minutes each day.

80

When the Difficulty Persists

Anyone who has lived in the world knows that not all troubles go away, even with the deepest prayers and greatest trust in Hashem.

Many of our lessons in *bitachon* are miracle stories. People who thought nothing could help them relied on Hashem with a full heart, prayed with complete sincerity and suddenly, the problem that seemed unsolvable disappeared. When we read or hear such stories, we see clearly that Hashem only wants to bring us close to Him and then, when we have reached the goal He has set for us, our troubles are resolved.

But anyone who has lived in the world knows that not all troubles go away, even with the deepest prayers and greatest trust in Hashem. For some reason, He gives some people a very difficult assignment in life. Their job is to face challenges that do not go away, and to do so without losing faith. How can we understand this as the work of a G-d Who loves us?

A hint can be found in the *Midrash* (*Bereishis Rabbah* 9:5). There, we learn a surprising interpretation of the verse, "Hashem saw all that He did and behold, it was very good." The verse refers to the moment when Hashem completed Creation. The Midrash explains that when the Torah tells us that Hashem called his creations "good," it is talking about all the beautiful, wonderful gifts he created for us to enjoy. "Very good," however, refers to *yissurim* — life's troubles.

How are troubles "very good"? The answer is that they give us the means to earn our share in the Next World. Just as you can't win a ball game without hitting the ball, you can't earn *Olam Haba* without overcoming challenges (*Mishlei* 6:23). This is the "game" we're in the world to play. Our troubles are our turn at bat. Hashem pitches us the ball and waits to see what we'll do with it. Will we sit down on the ground and refuse to put in the effort to swing? Will we run the other way? Will we try to get someone else to take our turn? Will we scream at the Pitcher, "You threw me a curve ball! It's not fair!"

People who realize that their suffering is helping them for all eternity don't question Hashem even when they continue to suffer. They would of course prefer to serve Him in a state of good health, happiness and prosperity, but they understand that if that's not their situation, despite all their prayers and *hishtadlus,* then they haven't lost anything at all. Rather, they are gaining rewards they cannot even imagine. They can count each difficulty that they endure without complaining as if they are counting money in the bank.

There is a saying of Rabbi Nachman of Breslov that has become very popular: "All of the world is a narrow bridge, and the main thing is to have no fear." We aren't offered a life on a big, smooth highway. We are set down in the world on a narrow bridge, a place from which the view to the left and to the right is frightening. The only way to avoid living in fear is to look straight ahead and follow the path Hashem has set out for us. Sometimes the bridge shakes in the wind. Sometimes it creaks ominously. Our job is to understand that this is what life is like on a bridge and just keep moving forward.

This is the strength of the *baal bitachon* who steps up to the plate with courage and confidence time after time. He knows that each time he gives it his best, he is earning far more than he could ever earn by just sitting in the bleachers watching the game.

> In Yerushalayim in the 1700's, a man who lived a very difficult life went to see Rav Shalom Sharabi, a great scholar in Kabbalah. The Rav's wife had the guest take

a seat while she went to get her husband. While the man waited, he fell asleep and had a dream.

He saw himself in heaven, standing before the heavenly court. A voice called out for all his sins to come forward, and thousands of dark angels emerged and stood on one side of the scale of judgment. The voice then called for the man's mitzvos, and thousands of white angels came to occupy the other side of the scale. However, the scale was still tipped toward the dark angels. Then the voice called for the troubles the man endured in his life. Many more angels came and stood on the side of the mitzvos. But still, the balance tipped in the wrong direction. In the man's sleep he called out, "More troubles! More troubles!"

The Rav's wife heard him yell and came to find out if he was all right.

"Everything is fine," he said. "I don't need to meet the Rav. I already have my answer."

Most of us won't have vivid dreams that explain to us exactly what is good about our troubles. However, we can capture that strength and hold onto it by reminding ourselves in every situation that Hashem is all good and does only good. In our human view, good equals pleasant. We can't conceive of suffering as pleasant. Yet we can conceive of a hard workout, in which we sweat and ache, as good. We endure it and even enjoy it because we believe we will benefit. That's what we must remember when we begin to think despairing thoughts. Our situation might not feel good, but it most certainly can only be good.

> **MAKE IT REAL:**
> What is the most difficult challenge you have in your life? Try to think of it as your turn at bat, your chance to pass a test and earn a great reward.

81

Beyond Our Grasp

It's a matter of admitting how limited our minds are and relying instead on our trust that Hashem always does what is best.

Sometimes, the news makes us want to run and hide. The sadness seems to be too great for anyone to survive. This is surely the case when terrorists strike families in Eretz Yisrael, ending happy, innocent, promising lives. Closer to home, it's surely the case when an illness or accident takes someone from the world at what seems to be the wrong time. No doubt, the parents of any of these victims prayed for a long life and good health for their children. No doubt, they each tried to serve Hashem to the best of their ability.

Situations like these are difficult for human beings to process. In fact, Chazal tell us that even the angels in heaven have questioned Hashem's actions (*Berachos* 61b). We learn that while Rabbi Akiva was being put to a cruel death by the Romans, an outcry broke out in heaven. The angels turned to Hashem and demanded an explanation: "Is this the reward for Torah?" they asked. How could it be possible that someone of Rabbi Akiva's greatness could deserve such an ending?

The answer Hashem gave them seems like an angry one. He told them that if they didn't keep quiet, He would return the world to *tohu v'vohu* — the emptiness that existed before the world was created. Was Hashem telling the angels that if they continued to question His wisdom, He would punish them by destroying Creation?

Rabbi Shlomo Kluger answered that question with a *mashal* that we can use to help us understand how little we are capable of understanding.

> *A king wanted a magnificent robe. To make sure that it was the rarest and most expensive garment in the world, he decided to have it made out of gold and silver threads. The tailor got right to work, measuring and stitching with great care and weaving the precious threads throughout the robe. When the robe was finished, the king tried it on and beamed with pleasure. The tailor, in his view, was a true genius! Nothing was too good for him.*
>
> *Meanwhile, some of the king's other servants became jealous. Who was this tailor that the king should hold him in such high esteem?*
>
> *They decided to turn the king against the tailor. They did it by telling the king that the tailor had pocketed some of the gold and silver thread. Immediately, the king called for the tailor and confronted him with the charges. The tailor firmly denied any wrongdoing, but the king wasn't satisfied. "Prove you're innocent!" he demanded.*
>
> *"The only way I can do that," said the tailor, "is to take apart the whole robe and pull out each gold and silver thread. Then they can then be weighed and Your Highness will see that it is all accounted for."*

Each event in our lives is woven into everything that came before and everything that will come after. That is why Hashem told the angels that to explain Rabbi Akiva's fate, he would have to unravel the entire Creation.

If you've ever tried to figure out how a certain event came to be, you find that you keep going back in time and branching out in a myriad of directions. Where did it all start? You are here because your mother and father married and had a family. They are here because four other people — your grandparents — did the same. Many people's grandparents or great-grandparents are only here because, by a miracle, they survived the Holocaust. The small twists and turns that enabled them to survive are each, on their own, linked to hundreds of other twists and turns. That's only going back three or four generations, and only including the facts we know. The complexity of every simple fact before our eyes is mind boggling.

Then there are the facts that are not before our eyes. There's the spiritual world, where *neshamos* come and go, sometimes living through many lifetimes as *gilgulim*. The inexplicable things that happen to people may be the most wonderful gift their soul could receive, enabling it to claim its place in *Olam Haba*. A soul's unfinished business on earth may take only a year or two to accomplish. From our earthly perspective, there is a tragedy; a small child has gone back to *Shamayim,* his life cut short. But from the soul's perspective, the news is all good. The job is finished and the reward is at hand.

In light of all this, do we honestly think we have any way of understanding Hashem's workings? It's a picture so vast, so endless and intricate that there's no way we can see it fully.

Even if these ideas are difficult to believe, we can only gain by working on ourselves to believe them. It's a matter of admitting how limited our minds are and relying instead on our trust that Hashem always does what is best. Rabbi Akiva had his moment of greatest joy in the middle of his suffering, when he recited the *Shema* and felt his connection to Hashem become complete. The situation looked terrible to the angels, but to Rabbi Akiva's soul, it was the greatest moment. To us from our vantage point on earth, Hashem's reality is even more hidden, and yet the truth is there. Hashem is good.

MAKE IT REAL:

Think of one remarkable event in your life, whether it was pleasant or unpleasant, and trace it backward, taking into account all the people and events that led up to it.

82

Helping Helps

People who are compassionate receive Hashem's compassion. Our kindness never goes unrewarded.

Your friend is not as good a student as you are. In fact, she is often spaced out in class and her notes are useless. Before every test, you see that look in her eye as she approaches you, a little shy, a little apologetic, and says, "Could I borrow your notes?"

There are two ways to react to this scenario: You could think to yourself, *What am I getting out of this? Let her ask someone else once in awhile.* Or, you could think, *She needs my help. Here's a chance to do something for a friend,* and hand your notes over graciously.

Your next-door neighbor is a 90-year-old man. He has children and grandchildren who live fairly close by, but somehow, you're the one who always ends up shoveling his sidewalk. You could tell yourself, *This isn't really my job. He has a whole family that can help him.* Or you could think, *This man needs someone to help him and for some reason, I'm it! Here's a chance to do a chesed.*

Your old friend from high school moved away. Even though

you both promised to stay in touch, she never contacts you. You are always the one to call her. When you do speak to each other, it's always warm and friendly but you're beginning to think, *Why should I always be the one to call?* You could sit and wait for your friendly gestures to be returned, or you could think, *Some people aren't good at keeping in touch but I know she's happy to hear from me.*

Your brother's job is to take out the garbage. He ran out to a wedding and forgot all about it. Do you leave it there for him to take care of when he gets home late at night, or do you take a few minutes and do the job for him?"

Opportunities to do a little *chesed* for someone are in our lives all the time. They might seem to tax our time and energy, or put unfair burdens on us. However, if we realized what these opportunities do *for* us and our connection to Hashem, we would be searching for more to do.

By helping other people, we are doing one of the most powerful things we can do to earn Hashem's help and answers to our prayers. People who are compassionate receive Hashem's compassion. This, says the *Mesillas Yesharim,* is obvious. When Hashem sees the boy who has his own driveway to shovel taking time to shovel his elderly neighbor's driveway, He says, "This person who has his own needs still goes out of his way to help others. Certainly, I Who have everything should help him" (*Maalos HaMiddos*).

We can imagine a father who sees his 5-year-old son give away his lollipop to his crying 2-year-old brother. The father would instantly want to give the older child a new lollipop. This is a very simplified version of what happens in *Shamayim* when we take from our own time or belongings and help someone who is lacking.

Our kindness never goes unrewarded. If we don't see the reward in our lives, it might arrive at the doorstep of our children or grandchildren, just when they need it most. Here is a story from World War II that illustrates this point:

> *Many years before the war, there was a rebbi who*

taught the boys in a small town. The children's parents couldn't pay him with money, so instead, each day a family would bring him and his family a meal. After many years, the rebbi's wife died and his children moved away. He was alone in his apartment up a long flight of stairs. Eventually, he no longer was able to teach and a new rebbi was hired. Most of the families forgot about the old rebbi.

However, one woman felt obligated to continue feeding the man who had taught her children. Every day she would climb the long staircase to his apartment, carrying a hot, filling meal in her hands. She did this for five years, until the rebbi passed on.

The woman herself died shortly before World War II broke out. Most of the people of the town were taken away by the Germans, but this woman's grandchildren found a place to hide with a non-Jewish woman, who kept them safe behind a false wall in her small apartment. Each day, the woman would spend hours gathering up food for them. She could only buy a little at a time from each store because otherwise, people would suspect that she was hiding Jews.

When the grandchildren finally left the apartment at the end of the war, they discovered that it had once belonged to a different tenant — the rebbi their grandmother had cared for (Loving Kindness, p. 52).

When we know that everything comes from Hashem, we lose our greed; we know we will always have what we need. This frees us to give, which in turn draws an even greater flow of *berachah* into our lives.

MAKE IT REAL:
Get into the habit of doing one "random act of kindness" for someone each day.

83

Wait Until You Find Out

Until we see where life takes us, we have no idea which events will turn out to be just what we needed to survive and thrive.

We think we know good news from bad. But very often, events that start out looking like a disaster end up being the best possible news. Not only does the situation work out, but we find that the good could never have come about without the "disaster."

For example, as often happens when people are seeking to get married, one person is interested in continuing to go out while the other is ready to look elsewhere. The person who is rejected feels hurt, but it's only by going through this process that he or she will arrive at the right person with whom to build a life. Once that happens, he or she will wonder, *What was I thinking? I can't imagine being married to anyone else in the world!*

Many successful business people tell a similar story. It's the failures and bankruptcies that pave the way to success. We can't judge the quality of anything that happens to us without knowing where it is leading. Only Hashem sees the past, present and future as one entity. It's as if He has the entire book, beginning to end, and we are just reading it page by page.

In the stories below, we see clear examples of this idea in action:

A Jewish boy was about to be drafted into the Polish Army during World War I. At the time, because of the anti-Semitism and spiritual dangers of the army, parents would do everything they could to get their sons exempted. This boy's parents went to the Chofetz Chaim to ask him for a berachah that their son would be saved.

"What would be so bad if he learned how to shoot a gun?" the Chofetz Chaim asked. The parents were shocked. Was the great sage uttering a curse on their son?

They decided to try to get a doctor to declare him physically unfit to serve. There were doctors willing to be bribed to write such a report, and they found one. Unfortunately, an army general found him too, just as he was meeting with the boy. The general said that the boy would not only be drafted, but that he would serve in the general's own division, where he would be in charge of assembling machine guns out in the battlefield under fire.

The boy learned his new trade and survived the war. Decades later, he found himself trapped in the Warsaw Ghetto as World War II ran rampant through Europe. He managed to escape into the woods with a group of friends, where they came upon a unit of Polish partisans.

The partisans were no lovers of the Jews. Not only did they refuse to let the Jews join them, but they threatened to kill them. Just at that moment, the man who had served in the Polish Army spotted a dissembled machine gun lying on the ground.

"I can fix that for you and I can hit any target with it." The partisans were eager to see what he could do. With quick, skilled hands, the man put the gun together and then shot an apple hanging from a distant tree. With that, he earned acceptance for himself and his friends into the partisan unit. In this way, they were saved.

For the rest of this man's life, he remembered the Chofetz Chaim's words: What would be so bad if he learned how to shoot a gun? It sounded like a death sentence when in fact it was his key to survival.

A little girl fell into a pool and was underwater for several minutes. Usually, after just a few minutes without oxygen, brain cells begin to die quickly and even if a person is saved, there will be some damage. In this girl, however, tests showed that there was no brain damage at all.

How had Hashem produced this miracle? He did it by giving the child sleep apnea. This is a condition in which people stop breathing in their sleep. Children who have this condition have to sleep with a monitor that rings when they stop breathing. Either the alarm wakes them up or it wakes up their parents, who then wake them up. It can happen many times during the night, which puts a great deal of stress on the parents. They are worried about their child's survival and are also being deprived of a night's sleep.

No one would welcome sleep apnea into their lives. However these parents discovered that sleep apnea had saved their daughter's brain. The little girl's body had gotten used to fluctuations of the volume of oxygen she inhaled and therefore, her brain was "trained" to withstand the minutes she spent underwater. The health problem that looked like a disaster turned out to be a blessing.

Until we see where life takes us, we have no idea which events will turn out to be just what we needed to survive and thrive. We can never look at a downturn in our own lives and think, *Oh, no, I'm doomed!"* We don't even know what's on the next page.

> **MAKE IT REAL:**
> *Think of a disappointment or even a "disaster" in your life that cleared the path for something good. If you can't think of any such instance of your own, ask parents or older relatives to tell you one such story from their life.*

84

"I Knew You'd Need This"

We have to know that He has lovingly prepared everything we need, and it is all waiting behind the scenes for the right time to be given.

A scenario: While Zev was fast asleep, suffering from the effects of the flu, his mother was in the kitchen slicing vegetables and putting them into a large pot of boiling water. Two hours later, when Zev woke up, his mother heard him stir and came to ask him how he was feeling.

"Better. But I'm kind of hungry. Can I have something to eat?"

Moments later, his mother arrived at the door to his bedroom carrying a bowl of steaming vegetable soup.

"Ma, that's just exactly what I need right now! Thanks!" said the grateful boy. It was perfect — soothing on his throat and filling, but not too heavy for his queasy stomach.

"Good. I knew this would be just right," his mother answered.

There's nothing like getting exactly what we need, just when we need it. Better still is when we realize that the answer to our wishes was already in progress before we even asked for it. At times like that, we feel so well cared for. Our needs are being anticipated and lovingly fulfilled before we say a word.

Hashem is always "cooking up" the answers to our prayers. Even before we know what to ask for, He knows what we need. But we need to take one action to bring our answer into our lives. We have to pray for it. The soup was ready and waiting for Zev, but his mother didn't bring it until he asked for something to eat.

We might wonder, if Hashem knows what we need and He's already got it waiting for us, why does He insist that we pray? What are we accomplishing by telling Him what He already knows?

The answer is that He loves us and wants us to speak to Him. Our relationship with Hashem is more important for us than any of the specific gifts we request. When the boy asks his mother for something to eat and she brings him exactly what he needs, he feels his mother's love and care. If he ordered the same soup from a take-out place and it was delivered by a deliveryman, his stomach might be filled but the mother-child relationship would be poorer.

The fact that Hashem wants us to stay in touch can be a very great source of encouragement for us. We're that important to Him. He loves us and wants to answer us. We have to know that He has lovingly prepared everything we need, and it is all waiting behind the scenes for the right time to be given. A business may be starting today that will hire you five years from now. A boy or girl was born perhaps 18 or 20 years ago with whom you will stand under the *chuppah*. Research is underway today for the cure to an illness that may afflict someone 60 years from now in his old age. A *sefer* is being written now that will inspire someone just at the moment he needs it. Sometimes Hashem makes this very clear, as in the story below:

> *A rabbi who lived in Eretz Yisrael would leave money every Thursday night for his wife to buy food for Shabbos. One Thursday, he had no money at all to give her. Not wanting to admit this to his wife or frighten her and their children, he said nothing to them. Instead, he went into his room and turned to Hashem. "I know You run the world and give food to every living thing. I know You*

can take care of my family at any moment," he said. For 20 minutes, he spoke his heart to Hashem, asking for help and voicing his trust that Hashem could change the situation in a moment.

When he came out of the room, he found an entire prepared Shabbos meal on the kitchen table. His wife explained that their neighbor's daughter had just had a baby and they were traveling to her home in a different city for the shalom zachor. Since they had already prepared their Shabbos food and didn't want it to go to waste, they offered it to their neighbor.

The food was cooked before the rabbi said one word of prayer. But what if he hadn't prayed? Wouldn't they have gotten the food anyway? Perhaps not; it could have gone to a different neighbor. It could have gone into the freezer. Hashem prepared the answer, but the rabbi had to reach out to Hashem to acquire what He had prepared.

Knowing that the answer is already there can give our prayers much greater power. If you know there's a treasure buried in your yard, you'll dig and dig and not give up until you find it. If you think that maybe, perhaps, there's a treasure in your yard, you'll give up when you feel like you're not getting anywhere. Hashem wants us to dig deeper into our hearts, to keep speaking to Him and asking him for what we need. Only by knowing that our answer is with Hashem — that He's there cooking up the perfect answer to our every need — do we have the inspiration to sincerely pray.

MAKE IT REAL:

When you pray for something you need, picture the answer to your prayer waiting in a vault in Shamayim and strive, with your prayers, to open the vault.

85

A Hug From Dvir

She had her hug from Dvir, and a warm embrace from her Creator as well.

In 2005, Dvir Emanuelof, an Israeli soldier, was killed during the Gaza war. His mother, Dalia, had lost her husband two years earlier in a car accident. The added tragedy of losing her son was almost too much for her to bear. She missed her son dearly and couldn't seem to rise up out of her sadness. One night, about six months after he was killed, she spoke to Hashem before going to sleep.

"Please, this is so hard. Please give me a sign, a hug from Dvir, so that I can know that his death had some meaning."

That week, her daughter wanted to attend a crafts festival in Yerushalayim. Dalia didn't really want to be out among people in a festival atmosphere, but she didn't want to disappoint her daughter. She agreed to go.

While they were seated at the festival, a 2-year-old boy wandered over to Dalia and tapped her on the shoulder. Since Dalia was a pre-school teacher, she found little children sweet and charming, and they loved her too. She asked the little boy his name and he answered, "Eshel."

"That's a very nice name," Dalia replied. "Do you want to be my friend?"

The boy nodded and sat down next to her.

Eshel's parents were seated two rows behind Dalia and her daughter. The child's father called out to his little boy, "Eshel, come on back here and sit with me and Dvir."

On hearing the name "Dvir," Dalia's heart skipped a beat. She went over to speak to Eshel's parents and saw a baby in a carriage.

"If you don't mind my asking, how old is your baby?" she asked.

"He was born six months ago," said the mother. "Right after the war in Gaza."

"Why did you choose the name 'Dvir'?" she asked.

The baby's mother explained that shortly before the war, her doctor told her that there was a chance that her baby would have a serious birth defect and there was nothing to be done about it. "When I came home that night, I heard that a soldier had been killed in the war. The news made me so sad that I told Hashem, 'Please, if You give me a healthy baby, I will name him "Dvir" in memory of the fallen soldier.'"

Dalia could not say a word. She stood silently absorbing what she had just heard. Finally, she said, "I am Dvir's mother, Dalia Emanuelof."

At first, the baby's parents didn't believe her. But when they looked at Dalia's expression, they realized that it was true. Emotions flooded the heart of little Dvir's mother and on a sudden impulse, she held the baby out to Dalia. "Here, hold him," she said. "Dvir wants to give you a hug."

Dalia held the boy in her arms and looked at his angelic face. He was a living, breathing gift of nechamah — comfort for her loss — delivered directly by Hashem into her arms. She had her hug from Dvir, and a warm embrace from her Creator as well.

Some stories require no explanation. They happen to us or to others, and all we can do is stop, take notice and let our hearts and minds fill up for a moment with the certainty that our loving G-d is by our side. The clarity, the beautiful absence of doubt may only last a minute or two, but if we keep filling up with these moments, they will add up to a life of *emunah*.

> **MAKE IT REAL:**
>
> *Make an effort to fill up your reserves of emunah whenever possible. Think about stories you hear or read. Pay attention especially to Hashem's "hugs" as they happen in your own life.*

86

Building Our Strength

Growing in our emunah is the greatest gift we can give ourselves and pass onto our children.

If you're planning on participating in a long-distance bicycle race, you don't start training the week before the event. You start months in advance. You start on flat roads with easy, gentle hills. You build up your strength, going longer distances and taking on higher hills as you progress. You train in the heat and in the rain, when you're tired and even when you're wondering why you ever thought you could do this.

When you arrive at the starting point of the race, you know you're as ready as you're ever going to be. And still, as you hit the first big hill — higher than anything you've seen in your training — you panic. "Can I make it? It's only the first mile and already I'm working so hard." But if you've trained well, you know how to power through. You know how to shed your doubts and focus on the task at hand, drawing from strength that is somewhere inside you.

Living a life of *emunah* works exactly the same way. We can't expect to have the strength we need to deal with life's challenges if we don't build up our strength on the flat roads and gentle hills. We hope that our lives will be a long-distance ride, and we need to do all we can to be ready for whatever lies ahead. Growing in our *emunah* is the greatest gift we can give ourselves and pass onto our children. It is the key to happiness, fulfillment and meaning, no matter how smooth or bumpy the road.

First and foremost, we have to know that Hashem loves us with an infinite, immeasurable love. When we know that, we trust His *hashgachah*. We know that he has put the strength inside us to "power through" the high hills, the rain and the heat, and arrive at a wonderful destination.

Rav Yechezkel Levenstein, the renowned Mashgiach of the Mir in Jerusalem and later, the Ponevezh Yeshivah in B'nei Brak, believed that the best training for living a lifetime of strong *emunah* was to feel the reality of Hashem's love. His daughter, Rebbetzin Zlata Ginsburg, once described how her father imprinted this lesson in her heart.

She recalled that her father, a person with a serious demeanor, was not free with gifts or lavish praise. There was one way, however, in which she was able to earn constant rewards. That was by keeping a *hashgachah pratis* journal. Her father gave her a notebook and instructed her that whenever she saw Hashem's *hashgachah* in her life, she should record the incident in her notebook. Each time she wrote something down, she would get a reward.

At first, she doubted that she'd have much to write. However, as she began paying more attention to the events she experienced, the people she happened to meet and the words she happened to hear, she became more and more aware of the way in which Hashem engineered every twist and turn of her life.

This was Rav Yechezkel's goal. He wanted to save his daughter from a certain kind of blindness — the kind in which a person sees natural forces at work in his or her life, but doesn't see Who is behind it all, pulling the strings and directing every little detail. He didn't want her to ever believe for a second that things just happened to her. Rather, she should know down to her bones that she was loved, guarded and directed by a Father Who wanted only the very best for her.

This is the training that gets us to the finish line. The more we fill our hearts and minds with real awareness of Hashem's love — not just belief, but facts that we can see with our own eyes — the more strength we will have to call upon when we're sitting at the bottom of a high hill, wondering how we'll make it. We'll still have our doubts and fears. We'll still sweat and ache as we work through our challenges. But with *emunah* strong in our hearts, we will never despair. We will never give up. We will reach the top of the hill and then glide joyously downward, knowing that, with Hashem at our side, we can do anything.

> ## MAKE IT REAL:
> *Start noticing the thousands of ways in which Hashem directs your life! Rav Moshe Feinstein zt"l and Rav Yaakov Kamenetsky zt"l wrote a letter recommending that every person keep a "hashgachah pratis journal" to record any situation in which he could see Hashem's Hand at work. You can wake up your emunah and keep it strong by keeping your own journal. To get one, email <u>info@dailyemunah.com</u>.*

This volume is part of
THE ARTSCROLL® SERIES
an ongoing project of
translations, commentaries and expositions on
Scripture, Mishnah, Talmud, Midrash, Halachah,
liturgy, history, the classic Rabbinic writings,
biographies and thought.

For a brochure of current publications
visit your local Hebrew bookseller
or contact the publisher:

Mesorah Publications, ltd

313 Regina Avenue
Rahway, New Jersey 07065
(718) 921-9000
www.artscroll.com